Additional Praise for *The Lemon Apron Cookbook*

"Jennifer's passion for fabulous food leaps off the page and right into your kitchen. Her debut cookbook will become a classic on your shelf and in your heart. I want to make every recipe in this stunningly beautiful cookbook."
—**MAIRLYN SMITH P.H.EC.**, award-winning cookbook author and media personality

"*The Lemon Apron Cookbook* is a glorious celebration of thoughtful, seasonal recipes everyone wants to eat! Jennifer's warm, witty stories and personal style will make you feel welcome in her very own kitchen. Five stars all around!"
—**EMILIE RAFFA,** bestselling author of *Artisan Sourdough Made Simple* and creator of theclevercarrot.com

# THE LEMON APRON COOKBOOK

# The Lemon Apron Cookbook

Seasonal Recipes for the Curious Home Cook

Jennifer Emilson

appetite
by RANDOM HOUSE

Appetite by Random House® and colophon are registered trademarks of Penguin Random House LLC.

Library and Archives Canada Cataloguing in Publication is available upon request.
ISBN: 978-0-525-61121-9
eBook ISBN: 978-0-525-61120-2

Cover and interior design: Lisa Jager
Cover and interior photography: Johann Headley

Printed in China

Raw eggs may contain bacteria. For recipes calling for raw egg, it is recommended that certified salmonella-free eggs purchased from a reliable source be used. Infants, small children, pregnant women, older persons, and those with a compromised immune system should not eat raw eggs.

Published in Canada by Appetite by Random House®, a division of Penguin Random House Canada Limited.

www.penguinrandomhouse.ca

10 9 8 7 6 5 4 3 2 1

appetite
by RANDOM HOUSE

Penguin
Random House
Canada

*For my parents, who taught me the love of cooking and how to laugh.*
*For my sister, who taught me the art of cooking and how to laugh at myself.*
*For Jim, who taught me how to feed others and who laughs with me daily.*

# CONTENTS

◀ *Clockwise from top left:*
*Mumbai Fog Oatmeal (page 172),*
*Winter White Turkey and Vegetable Soup (page 179),*
*Frozen Horchata Margarita (page 28),*
*Tarte Flambée Flatbread (page 231)*

# introduction

"Mum, what's for supper?" Without fail, my sister, Anita, and I would ask this question before we left for school each morning. The answer had the ability to make or break our day. If the answer was a tasty one, like chicken and rice (page 46), it would get me through the school day. But if she said, "It's a surprise," we eventually learned we would be very disappointed with the result (hello, liver and onions). It took a while for our naive little minds to understand what "It's a surprise" meant!

We were raised by foodie parents, way before "foodie" was a word—or even a concept. Our parents were born and raised in Germany, and food played a central role in their daily lives. Back then, it was common in Germany for everything to be made from scratch. In my parents' case, it was a family effort. Everyone, from the kids all the way to the grandparents, had their individual harvesting, preparing, and cooking assignments. As a young boy, my dad would pick mushrooms in the forest—I'd imagine his walks in the woods back then turned into a true Germanic fairy tale with talking animals and all—and clean the casings for sausage-making days.

My parents continued this approach to cooking even after immigrating to Kitchener, Ontario, where I was born. It was normal to find half a pig spread out on the kitchen table of our apartment, ready to be sausage-ified. I still don't know how they managed to get that carcass into the elevator. I was that girl sitting next to you in the school lunchroom with a liverwurst or garlicky salami and mustard on rye sandwich, at a time when bologna on white bread was the norm.

We later moved out of the apartment to Amherstburg, in Southwestern Ontario. A mini farm and orchard were squeezed into our suburban backyard, with row upon row of fruits and vegetables. This delicious bounty brought hard work, some surprises, and delicious results. When green beans were in season, so were grasshoppers. And filling a bowl meant getting pinged and attacked as those nasty bugs flew out of the branches and leaves. Picking the raspberries out back meant scratches and juice-stained fingers as we checked for worms before popping those luscious berries into our mouths. Beside the raspberry patch was the chicken coop. Yes, we had a chicken coop! We would also smoke fish in an outdoor smokehouse and make wine in oak barrels in the basement (which we raided regularly in our late teens when the house was parent-free!). After we moved out, they (my parents, not the chickens) went on to run a successful bed and breakfast in a small east coast fishing village. Their guests were welcomed with cozy, comforting meals and genial company.

My parents taught us not only an appreciation for where our food comes from but also about our German heritage—though we may have gently teased their teachings growing up (didn't every immigrant kid go through this phase at some point?). My mum made me wear a dirndl (traditional German folk dress) to school, which was mortifying for an eight-year-old living in a Canadian city. In the kitchen, we helped her make cabbage rolls, preserve peaches for the winter, and glaze fruit-covered German cheesecake *Käsekuchen*. We inherited the sausage case–cleaning task from my dad. As adults, we developed an even deeper respect for the cuisines, lifestyle, and heritage our parents taught us about. What we made suddenly took on special meaning when we moved away from home.

My personal cooking journey really began in Toronto, where I have lived for over 25 years. Before then, I never really had to cook on my own much. My mum could take the most meager ingredients and turn them into a meal fit for royalty. My sister became a pastry chef. Why would I take up space in such a talented kitchen?! But when I was thrust into the big, cruel world all on my lonesome (it wasn't quite as traumatic as all that!), there was no one to share the kitchen with. There were my roommates, but it's not like they were going to make my mum's Sauerbraten (German pot roast)—they were Jamaican, after all (but I was served up the best goat curry with dumplings). If I was nostalgic for my mum's potato pancakes or Marmorkuchen (marble cake), I had to learn how to actually make them. I can't tell you how often I was on the phone with her, trying to nail down a recipe. I was also a server at restaurants, where I picked up tricks while watching the chefs and cooks work their stations. And when my sister and I were living apart, even during the days of snail mail, we would devote pages and pages of letters to planning recipes, meals, and celebrations inspired by our work and travels (we also inherited the traveling gene from our parents). It was all worth it. The more I cooked at home with this new knowledge, the more my confidence grew.

While I wasn't trained by the Cordon Bleu or a pastry school, my tenacity (the fancy word for "stubbornness"!) got me to where I am today. Even when a recipe got the better of me, I would try and try again. Like my first pie crust. It sucked. So I experimented with different recipes and adapted my method until I figured it out, which made me a much better baker. I will happily admit to seeking help from cookbooks and websites (and even recipes on the sides of cereal boxes!) through the years. Those recipes influenced my cooking, and eventually my own recipes. I fell in love with everything related to cooking and baking, and I soon ventured into cooking recipes from cuisines that were new to me.

This is where Toronto stepped up. Almost every street is home to a different culture and restaurant scene, and there are many specialty grocers. And my neighbors were a great source of cooking knowledge. I'd walk down the hallway to my apartment, enjoying the intoxicating aroma of curry or other spice blends, knowing it was only a matter of time before I'd be knocking on doors and asking for a cooking lesson! What a great way to explore rich and flavorful cuisines that warm the heart. Much of my cooking style is influenced by living in this bustling and energetic city.

Then I met Jim. You know the saying "some people live to eat, and others eat to live"? This quickly became a reality for us. Jim is a prairie boy who grew up on simple pot roasts and mashed potatoes (which are great, of course!), and his idea of foreign cuisine was Canadian Chinese takeout, so eating alongside my foodie family was a startling experience for him. Through the years, though, he embraced it all. These days it's Jim who will suggest going out for Ethiopian, Persian, Pakistani, Moroccan, or Palestinian food.

However, he has never been one to hold back his frank opinions. Once, when we were first dating, he came over late and asked if I had any dinner leftovers. I gladly warmed up a plate of potato pancakes with sautéed bacon and onions, with sour cream on the side. The onions, bacon, and sour cream were vacuumed up, but most of the pancakes remained. He said it was because he'd never had potato pancakes before. I suggested they might be an acquired taste. He proclaimed, "You mean I have to eat these again?!" He figured that if he didn't say anything, he'd be stuck eating something he didn't like for the next 20 years. But I appreciated his frankness (and still do!). Now he is willing to try, and hopefully enjoy, almost everything, but at the same time he keeps me grounded, not letting me get overly fussy with trying to fuse all the cuisines into new dishes. If it gets two thumbs up from Jim, I know for sure it will be a hit with all of you!

And that's where *The Lemon Apron* blog, which partially started thanks to our cats, Phineas and Zelda, comes in. They have their own Instagram account (Jim is still jealous that they have more followers than he does!). Through the years, I'd post the odd dinner dish or pie, amidst a sea of cats sleeping, wrestling, or grooming themselves. Eventually followers around the world started asking for the recipes, which I'd happily email to them. Then they requested a cooking blog. Around the same time, my mum's health started failing. My sister and I realized that if we wanted her incredible soul-soothing recipes to live on, we would need to follow her around the kitchen and write them down—all of my mum's recipes were in her head. Asking how much paprika was needed turned into her filling a spoon, handing it to me, and saying, "Till it tastes like this." I shadowed her, taking note of every move she made. I soon had a respectable collection of recipes, and starting a blog was a way for me to preserve them.

In a major way, the blog—named after my first apron, which had lemons on it—is a tribute to my mother, her skills, and the recipes and dishes of her homeland. I'm also grateful to my dad, and the many grandmas, nonnas, neighbors, and other guardians of cultural cuisines who have been my teachers along the way. The blog has flourished as I continue to experiment and share recipes inspired by mum, my German heritage, my travels, and my efforts to find fresh ways to use ingredients found in local markets.

Then came the cookbook. When I set out on this journey, I wanted to create a cookbook you would use all the time. A cookbook that becomes dog-eared, its binding cracking and its grease-stained pages coming loose from overuse. The recipes here are ones that Jim and I actually eat on a regular basis. Ones that got Jim's seal of approval. In fact, he regularly voiced his opinion on what should be in the book, like the Spiced Savoy Cabbage Rolls (page 194). I tried to listen, but I insisted on

sneaking in some others, such as my mum's steak tartare recipe (page 94). There are some family favorites (like on page 43), and you might recognize some beloved recipes from the blog, such as the French Onion Soup (page 177). I've updated all the blog recipes to make them fresh and worth exploring again!

These recipes also embrace the unique beauty each season brings. While we can obtain just about anything we want at any time of the year, I'd rather have Cocoa and Red Wine–Braised Short Ribs with Herbed Polenta (page 197) in the middle of winter than the middle of summer, wouldn't you? Also, eating what is local and in season means we get to taste fresh ingredients the way they're meant to taste. So I've divided this book by season, but if you're craving a dish and you have all the ingredients to make it, do it! Enjoy that bright summer salad (page 83) with the cozy winter tourtière (page 199)! I included a Year-Round chapter (pages 215 to 261) too, since Jim and I also enjoy recipes that aren't really dependent on a specific fruit or vegetable being available. And bonus, they will satisfy any cravings you have—like pizza (page 241), which should be enjoyed all year round!

These recipes aren't difficult. Truly. I've divided them into easy steps so you can enjoy the process of making them. They have also been made and tested in our condo-sized kitchen—so yes, they are all doable in any kitchen, no matter how small (see page 13)! The ingredients are easy to source too (see page 7). All too often we as a society tend to purchase all our cooking ingredients from only one grocery store. If it isn't there, we just do without. But there is a whole world of flavor just waiting to be explored. And it may be just around the corner from where you live. I hope you will explore your own city, big or small. There are sure to be gems waiting to be discovered.

Ultimately, I hope this book will keep you company and get you cooking if you are new to the kitchen or give you some fresh ideas if you're an experienced cook. So the next time a loved one asks, "What's for supper?" you'll have an answer they'll daydream about.

*love Jennifer*

# ingredients and tools

## Key Ingredients

When a recipe calls for Aleppo pepper, don't be quick to dismiss it because your local grocery store doesn't carry it. I'm sure there is a shop nearby that carries not one but two or more versions of it! This is where farmers' markets, neighborhood produce shops, and specialty food boutiques come in handy. They will have a treasure trove of quality ingredients, and the owners will take into account the desires of their regular customers and stock up accordingly. If you just can't source a dried item from your local spice emporium or well-stocked grocery store, you'll probably find it online! Here are some key ingredients that are used in the recipes in this book.

## Spices and Seasonings

*Kosher salt* | Unless otherwise stated in a recipe, I always use kosher salt, Diamond Crystal to be exact. It isn't as strong as sea or iodized salt. If you use iodized salt, start with a smaller amount and work your way up, to avoid an overly salty dish.

*Flakey salt* | I use flakey finishing salt, mainly Maldon, for finishing savory or sweet dishes. Its crystals are large, but it's not an overpowering salt.

*Sea salt* | This is great for salting pasta water. Don't be shy with it: add enough and your pasta will have extra flavor, as will your sauces if you add pasta water to thin them out!

*Peppercorns* | I love coarsely ground and freshly cracked pepper, as they have a totally different flavor from purchased ground black pepper. A good peppermill is your friend here. Of course, the difference in taste is most evident when finishing a dish.

*Aleppo pepper* | A burgundy-hued ground chili pepper, from the Halaby or Turkish pepper, with subtle notes of raisin, pomegranate, and sun-dried tomato. It adds a flavorful mild heat perfect for chili, sauces, pizza, eggs, etc.

*Espelette pepper* | A bright red chili powder, popular in the Basque region, which straddles France and Spain. It has a fruity and fresh presence, with just enough heat! Smoky sweet paprika would be an acceptable substitute.

*White pepper* | This is peppery, but it's a bit hotter than black pepper. It's common in European cuisines. My mum always had it on hand.

*Harissa, rose harissa* | Warm spice and pepper blends are common in North African cuisines and are wonderful with vegetables, meats, and even some fruit. You can find harissa in both paste and dried forms. I use dried most often, as it doesn't add extra moisture, but the paste is great for marinades and sauces.

*Sumac* | The most amazing dark-purple-brown-colored flakes ground from the dried berries of the sumac bush. Sumac is used in many Middle Eastern dishes. I also use it with fruit-based desserts for a touch of drama because of its color. Its citrus vibe brings out the lemony side of dishes really well.

*Urfa biber* | These dark, smoky pepper flakes with an almost raisin-like flavor hail from Turkey. Urfa biber has a fruity presence as opposed to just a peppery one. Great for both savory and sweet dishes.

## Oils, Sauces, and Condiments

*Olive oil* | Use regular or extra virgin olive oil for cooking—but don't break the bank on it. Save your dollars for the next oil.

*Finishing olive oil* | A highly flavored grassy or peppery olive oil perfect for salad dressing, for drizzling over soup, as a dip for bread, or as a finishing touch over ice cream. Your local specialty grocer will carry a vast array of them. Choose the flavor profile that suits your palate. If you feel overwhelmed, just ask the owner—that's what I do! Don't waste on cooking or marinating—they're far too expensive for that!

*Neutral oil* | For high-temperature cooking and frying, you're best off with avocado, canola, or vegetable oils thanks to their high smoke point.

*Preserved lemons* | Deep-flavored, brined lemon rinds that add so much depth to sauces, vinaigrettes, dips, etc. Having a jar—like Mina Preserved Lemons from your local Middle Eastern or Mediterranean grocer—at the back of your fridge will make you happy. You can also make your own.

*Hot sauce* | Almost all cuisines have their own hot sauces. Mexican chipotle or habanero, Thai or Indonesian sambal oelek, Jamaican hot pepper sauce, American Louisiana hot sauce, African harissa, Portuguese piri-piri, and Korean gochujang are common in my kitchen at any given time! Each has its own level of heat and complexity, bringing something different to the party. Add a little to yogurt for a great dip, use it in a base for a marinade for meat or veggies, or even drizzle some on eggs or potatoes for instant flavor.

*La Bomba* | An antipasto spread with the thick, jammy goodness of hot peppers, tomatoes, eggplant, mushrooms (don't tell Jim), herbs, and spices. There are many variations with varying degrees of heat available, and they all do the job. Great in Italian dishes and sandwiches.

## Dairy

*Butter* | Salted butter has gotten a bad rap over the years. I have no issue with it at all. I use it all the time in baking and cooking. If I'm at all concerned about it, I will just adjust the amount of extra salt I add to a recipe.

*Yogurt* | Fermented milk products, like skyr, Greek yogurt, and labneh, are useful in cooking and baking. Great for topping desserts or oatmeal and creating the most tender and moist cakes. Turning yogurt into labneh is quite easy (just strain the yogurt through a cheesecloth), but feel free to use store-bought.

## Finally, Unless Otherwise Indicated:

Eggs are large

Flour is all-purpose

Heavy cream can be substituted with whipping cream—just look for between 30% and 38% fat

Herbs are fresh

Hot sauce is your choice: Frank's RedHot, Cholula, and sriracha are all good

Milk is whole

Olive oil is regular

Parsley is flat-leaf

Pepper is black and coarsely ground

Salt is kosher

Sugar is granulated

## Tools of the Trade

Once you've brushed aside some flour and are sitting on a stool in my kitchen, you will notice that there is no microwave, bread maker, slow cooker, pressure cooker, or other big gadget of any description. I like cooking the way my mum and her mum cooked. It forces me to be in the moment, which is exactly where I want to be when it comes to preparing a meal. Of course, I do love kitchen tools that take much of the effort out of cooking. And I contend that many of the following tools will save you just as much time as the big guys do. While I won't list everything in my kitchen, here's a list of the tools that make cooking easy breezy for me. Depending on how you cook and how much space you have, you may end up relying on all or only some of them.

*Baking sheets with cooling racks* | If you have a full-sized oven, a full-sized (15- × 21-inch) baking sheet is really the way to go. If you don't have the storage for large baking sheets, two smaller ones will do just fine. A large one just makes things go faster. Grab ones with fitted cooling racks.

*Bar zester* | Yes, a Microplane works great for grating (pun intended), but nothing beats a bar zester for getting those perfect thin ribbons of lemon or orange zest for finishing a recipe. Get one!

*Bench scraper* | This little tool will be such a help when you are trying to move pie pastry, loosen up dough from the counter (without smooshing it), or even transport a large amount of cut-up veggies. And it cleans all the bits of dough or pastry off the counter after you're done!

*Blender and immersion blender* | A large stand blender, small (NutriBullet-type) blender, and an immersion blender all do the same thing: blend stuff. Sometimes it sure is easier to bring the immersion blender over to the pot of soup rather than having to transfer the soup to the large blender.

*Crank-style citrus juicer* | A crank-style juicer with the lever extracts way more juice than a reamer. I juice a lot of citrus, so this helps—and it just looks so cool sitting on the counter!

*Dutch oven* | A classic cooking pot, often cast-iron and coated with enamel, which braises meat, makes chili or soup, and even fries onion rings. A good one may be an investment, but you will have it forever. Select the size based on how many you typically feed—I use one with a 10-cup capacity.

*Food processor, spice grinder, mortar and pestle* | All variations of a theme: making things smaller! I use all three, but in a pinch the mortar and pestle will do what the spice grinder does. The food processor does what the mortar and pestle can't!

*Mandoline* | No matter how good the knife, you will just never get the precise thin slices that you can get from a mandoline. A good one with adjustable blades and thicknesses does not have to be expensive these days. If you have space for one, your salads, chips, and scalloped potatoes will thank you.

*Scale* | Scales don't lie. If you like to bake at all, please get a scale. There is no way of guaranteeing that how you filled your measuring cup is the way the recipe creator did. A scale is more accurate. This is why most of my baking recipes offer weight measurements.

*Serrated knife (a very sharp one)* | Yes, a set of sharp knives is non-negotiable. A serrated knife, in particular, is the workhorse I rely on. You will get the cleanest cuts through bread, tomatoes, or pie crusts from this knife. Get one.

*Small offset spatula* | Even though I have a large offset spatula, it's the small one I turn to almost daily. It's not just for icing cakes. It can get under waffles in a waffle iron, a pie crust, a slice of cake, or tinned muffins without any damage. And it's cute.

*Spider* | A shallow wire basket attached to a wooden handle. Because of the open design, it easily scoops out fried foods from their cooking oil, leaving the oil behind. Great for pulling out steamed eggs from a hot pot and, of course, for transferring fried chicken and fish from oil to paper towel–lined plates.

*Stand mixer, handheld mixer* | A stand mixer just makes baking a breeze—you can walk away while the egg whites are whipping. If you don't have room, a handheld mixer, or even a whisk, bowl, and plenty of elbow grease, will work!

*Temperature probe* | I use a ThermoPop. It looks like a lollipop or pen with the thermometer sitting on top. This little guy takes up no room and measures the internal temperatures of meats, baked goods, liquids, and even bread.

*Tongs* | Having two sets is always a good thing. Great for turning items that are being seared or grilled. They also work really well to help you reach up and retrieve something on the top shelf of your cupboard!

*Your senses* | Yes, your hands, eyes, nose, and taste buds are the best tools you own. And you didn't have to pay for them. I eyeball measurements when I season to taste. I rub dried herbs between my fingers to activate any residual oils before adding them. I toss a salad with my hands, as it gives me a better feel for if the oil has spread out evenly. And of course, your taste is your taste—you know your palate! If you want more vanilla or whatever, go for it.

# kitchen tips and tricks

If you ask me to describe my future, it includes an old stone farmhouse in a glen in the Scottish Highlands. With sheep and goats grazing in the pasture, a milk cow by the barn, and chicken gossiping out by the kitchen door. Jim will have his horses. There will be a barn, orchards, and time to spin yarn and bake bread. And why not have a rare vine and fig tree to sit under—even in the Highlands. It will happen one day. But until then, I'm taking full advantage of living in a condo in a vibrant city like Toronto. And yes, it's possible to do your everyday cooking or cook for guests successfully in a condo-sized kitchen without the chaos! Here are some organizational and cooking tips and tricks I have learned along the way.

## Organizational Pointers

Not a huge surprise, but organizing your menus, ingredients, and kitchen before you dive into a recipe can go a long way toward making life easier!

### Keep Your Grocery Lists and Menus in One Place

Hang up a blackboard—or if you are lucky enough to have someone like Jim who is open to it, paint an entire kitchen wall with blackboard paint!—to plan menus or write out your grocery list. You can easily scribble out what you are working on or what you need. At the end of the week, take a picture with your phone before heading out grocery shopping.

### Optimize Your Kitchen Space (Think Outside the Box!)

If you don't have a spacious pantry, larder, cantina, or extra prep room and counter space, no problem! It just means the space you do have available will have to do double duty. Here's how I find and use hidden or extra spaces:

*Use those cupboard doors*  |  The insides of them, to be exact. Fasten go-to measurement lists, conversion charts, and favorite recipes (I type them out for this) to the inside. This way, when you can't remember that exact measurement conversion or how many tablespoons of coffee are needed for the French press, you can just open the door to find the answer.

*Use the dishwasher—and not just for washing* | I'm one of those weirdos who doesn't mind hand-washing dishes (even for a dinner for eight!). But don't get me wrong, I will use it for a huge load of dishes. When I know I won't immediately need it, my dishwasher can temporarily store large platters and out-of-season storage containers.

*Turn an unused corner or area in your kitchen into a dedicated space* | For example, I like to have a baking corner so my sugars, nuts, chocolates, dried fruit, etc. are together in baskets for easy access. For even less running around, you can place your stand mixer and baking tins and tart pans all against the same wall, with your baking ingredients on a shelf or in a cupboard right above them.

## Organize Your Ingredients Based on How You Cook

Some say to organize the ingredients in your cabinet alphabetically, but that may not reflect how you cook. Do you know your flavor palate? Do you gravitate toward certain cuisines and spice blends? Are you a baker first and foremost? You may want to organize your spice cupboards by region and style of cooking. I have all my Italian spices near each other, my vast array of peppers grouped together, and my baking spices grouped together on one shelf. You could even group spices in their own little labeled baskets or containers. Then you can just reach for the Indian basket when you want to make mulligatawny soup (page 127).

## Reuse Glass Jars and Label Everything

Disclaimer: The organizing geek in me loves uniform, perfectly labeled jars filled with ingredients looking like soldiers ready for battle. But this look can get expensive. Instead, reuse that empty pickle or jam jar. With a bit of elbow grease (and a good scrubbie and degreaser) these jars will work just fine for storing pantry items like dried nuts. Instead of permanently labeling the jar with fancy labels, just use some painter's tape. Many restaurant kitchens do this for easy switching. If you are storing something that has the packager's cooking instructions (such as dried lentils or a specialty rice), cut the instructions out and stuff them inside the jar so they're accessible.

## Use Your Freezer (and Not Just for Leftovers)

The amount of freezer space you have, your style of cooking, and how many people you cook for will all affect what you store in the freezer. Make it earn its keep. If you are cooking or baking in stages, you can often store parts of a dish in the freezer and thaw them in the fridge overnight so they're ready to use (my recipes indicate where this is an option). Many ingredients can be stored in the freezer—not just the standard frozen peas. Of course, the tips on the next page reflect the way I cook, but you can adapt them according to which ingredients you use the most. Your wallet will thank you!

*Butter* | After buying it on sale, I slice up butter into four lengths, just like the butter sticks that cost even more than regular butter. I cut some of these ½ cup (8 tablespoons/110 g) lengths in half again. I then wrap the butter sticks in wax paper, and store them in a large freezer bag in the freezer. So, when a recipe calls for ¼ cup of butter, I can just pull out one of the smaller sticks.

*Lemons* | I'm a lemon geek. Each week I pick up a bag or two of organic lemons, wash them well, then zest them. I store the zest in a container that I keep in the freezer for 4 to 5 months. I figure out how much lemon juice I need for the week—for salad dressings, baking, cooking, etc.—and then squeeze the desired amount and store it in the fridge. The rest of the lemons get sliced up, are frozen on wax paper–lined baking sheets, and once frozen, put into a freezer bag. This way I can access them for drinks, the water jug, etc. Now no lemon will go to waste!

*Nuts, seeds, and flours* | Nuts, seeds, and flours that aren't going to be used quickly—in my case, nut-based flours—are much better off in the freezer. This way you don't have to worry about opening the container and being assailed by that rancid odor of past-their-prime nuts or poppy seeds.

*Bread* | Set aside the amount of bread you will use in the next week, then slice up the rest, lay the slices flat on a baking sheet, freeze for 30 minutes, and put them into a freezer bag, all lined up like a loaf. Then, when you have a craving for brioche French toast, you only need to reach into the freezer for a couple of slices.

## Cooking Pointers

Or, final musings on how to make a recipe without the stress and still get the best results—and even enjoy yourself too!

*First things first, get the tunes going* | I can't imagine cooking without some great 80s, Big Band, or funky jazz keeping me company. How do you feel about Level 42? Or Benny Goodman? Hope you all like some Nina Simone! Listen to the tunes that get you grooving in the kitchen. To listen to some of my favorite playlists, visit my Spotify profile, @JenniferEmilson.

*Read the recipe—twice* | And I don't mean skim it. There is nothing worse than starting a recipe and then finding out that it's prepared over 2 days. Suddenly dinner will mean mac 'n' cheese, because the marinade will not have the meat ready in time. Is the butter soft? If not, those cookies may not happen on your timeline. Take it out the evening before.

*Don't rush a recipe* | Many recipes need some resting or cooling time, so allow for that. If you want to serve that fruit pie for dessert, you can't start it 2 hours beforehand and expect to be slicing it into lovely slices for your guests. If I want to serve a pie on Sunday, I bake it on Saturday.

*Meal prep is your friend* | You'll see throughout the book that I try as often as possible to give you the option to prep components of a meal ahead of time. This way the actual time spent on the recipe assembly or cooking doesn't seem as daunting. For example, you can prep and cut veggies or nuts the night before and store them in the fridge until needed. Or combine the dressing or marinade ingredients in advance.

*Mise en place can help* | Mise en place—that is, having all your ingredients prepped and measured in small bowls by the stove, with the proper tools right next to them—may sound all chichi. But it's integral to the success of a recipe. You don't want to scramble to find the paprika that isn't where you thought it was, leaving the onions and garlic in the skillet to scorch while you look for it.

*Don't just go by the suggested cooking or resting times* | There are many other variables, such as the weather, the thickness of an ingredient, or your oven (see below), that can affect the times suggested. So start checking before the time stated or be prepared to cook or wait a bit longer. If a recipe says it will take 50 minutes for the chicken to be done, start checking earlier based on the visual cues provided in the recipe. This is where your senses come into play. Is the chicken properly golden brown? Are the juices running clear? Does the bone move easily? Of course, also use an instant-read thermometer to check meat for doneness. (And if your ingredients look like they're on the verge of scorching while you sauté or fry them, adjust the heat of your burner accordingly. Do the same if something seems to be taking too long to cook.)

*Oven temperatures can vary* | The digital display on the outside may say 375°F, but that does not mean the ambient temperature throughout the entire oven is there yet. Oven temperatures can fluctuate wildly, even with newer models. So, in addition to using a thermometer to confirm doneness (see page 11), use a thermometer that hangs off the rung of a rack to confirm that the oven is ready.

*Season to taste* | You know your taste, and the taste of those you are feeding. Most recipes have the amount of seasonings specified as needed, but please use this as a guideline. (If I don't specify, you can assume I want you to season to your taste.) I usually err on the side of caution, especially when it comes to salt, but I go the opposite way when it comes to a bit of heat. Feel free to add more of what you like as desired. Just taste before serving.

## A Note on Salads

I love eating salads. I just never like preparing salads. Sounds like an episode from *Seinfeld* ("You know how to *take* the reservation, you just don't know how to *hold* the reservation."). One of my pet peeves when it comes to traditional salad recipes is precisely measuring the ingredients. If you want to serve the salad as a meal, why stop at a specific amount of lettuce or cucumbers? If you really like tomatoes but aren't a green pepper fan, why can't you just do more of one than the other? Sure, I have given measurements for the salads in this book, but to me, eyeballing ingredients is the best way to make salads—this isn't baking, for goodness' sake! You should be able to figure out how much your family will eat and purposely cut up extra of what you like.

Many recipes say to toss the salad with the dressing and serve. But this doesn't have to mean the whole salad. Just pull out what you want to serve, and the rest will be ready to go (and not soggy) for tomorrow's salad. In fact, if you are making the salad for a dinner party, place the various veggies, heaviest to lightest, in a serving bowl, finishing with the tender greens on top, then cover with a lightly dampened sheet of paper towel, and store in the fridge. This will keep everything crisp until it's time to serve. Then you can dress the salad just before serving.

Speaking of dressings, my other salad pet peeve is that salad recipes come with their own dressings when a handful of go-tos will suffice, and so many of those dressings call for a long list of ingredients. Yes, I do recommend a few dressing recipes here in the book, but use them as a guideline. If you want to simply use oil, salt, lemon juice (or vinegar), and cracked pepper, or another favorite family dressing of yours, I won't be offended! In the end, salads should be all about enjoying the freshness of the season. You do you!

## Breakfast
Ploughman's Breakfast
Milk Toast with Stewed Orange-Cardamom Prunes

## Appetizers
Frozen Horchata Margarita
Grilled Halloumi with Pomegranate, Lemon, and Mint
Avocado, Feta, and Herb Dip

## Soups and Sammies
Shrimp and Lobster Bisque
Niçoise Tuna Melt

## Sides
Cinnamon and Sumac Sautéed Brussels Sprouts
Minty, Creamy Peas and Shallots

## Mains
Olive and Spring Herb Linguini with Lemon Pistachio Pangrattato
Spinach and Ricotta Crespelle
Mustard-Infused Pot Roast
Mum's Chicken and Rice
Ginger and Miso Sticky Roast Chicken
(Queen) Margherita Chicken and Spaghetti

## Desserts
Rhubarb Bumbleberry Crumble
Lemon Mascarpone Chiffon Pie
Cardamom-Scented Carrot Cake

SPRING

After the winter monotony of gray skies and cabin fever, spring is the season that I anticipate most. It may be bashful, taking its time, but when it finally arrives, it's as if a huge weight has been lifted. Suddenly I feel lighter, even if I am carrying a couple of extra winter pounds! The early-spring sun shines differently, creating more optimistic shadows than the winter sun's dreary, dramatic shadows. And red-breasted robins poking about the thawing grass, with their optimistic chirp as if they know something we don't, have always been the first harbinger of spring for me. Even as a kid, on my walks to school, I'd diligently look for them.

I'd also keep an eye out for the other early signs of spring: buds on naked tree branches, daffodils and tulips starting to push through the dirt, ducks swimming on the lake where the ice had thawed. I loved going for my first bike ride of the season down the country concession roads and seeing bright-yellow forsythia bushes in bloom. Knowing that my mum's irises, lilies of the valley, and spring poppies would be close behind. And when the lilacs arrived, well, I couldn't think of a better moment of the year!

Spring, in our family, also meant spring-cleaning. It became a tradition that on March 21st, whether it was warm or not, all the windows and screen doors were opened, the flannel sheets were replaced with crisp cotton sets, and the cupboards and closets were emptied and scrubbed. A general feeling of brightness and lightness then settled into every nook and cranny of our home. To this day, I relish making room for the clothes and foods of the new season. All the grays, browns, and blacks of winter get replaced with the pinks, greens, yellows, and pastels of spring, in both my clothing and our table linens.

Spring for me also means taking advantage of what the local farmers are growing and bringing to market. Eating fresh, wild local asparagus in May is just so much more satisfying than eating imported asparagus in December. This fresh bounty changes our menus. Heavy chilis, stews, and braises with rich cream sauces step aside to make room for fresh peas and asparagus, fava beans, and artichokes. And even if we are still making stews or comfort meals, they have a different feel to them. There are more fresh vegetables and fruits to pick from and add to these dishes. The transition from winter to spring may be pronounced, but we can create an incredible bridge between the two seasons just by replacing one or two items. Maybe the yams and sweet potatoes are set aside for roasted fennel and green beans. Sweet peas and radishes can make up our salads. Our mains and desserts start reflecting what is popping up from the ground and covering the bushes.

*◄ Clockwise from top left: Niçoise Tuna Melt (page 35), Rhubarb Bumbleberry Crumble (page 53), Minty, Creamy Peas and Shallots (page 37), Grilled Halloumi with Pomegranate, Lemon, and Mint (page 29)*

# ploughman's breakfast

SERVES 6

MAKES 12 to 14 crumpets

PREP TIME 20 minutes + resting

COOK TIME 20 minutes

When I was traveling across England in my twenties, one of my favorite discoveries was the ploughman's lunch: a wooden board with bread, cheese, and ham, often served with a beer. It's what farm workers would eat for their lunch break. This recipe, though, is for a ploughman's *breakfast*, with jammy soft steamed eggs and craggy but charming English crumpets. Crumpets' yeasty batter creates holes on the surface as they cook, just begging for butter to melt into them. Best of all, they're even better the next day! So make them ahead and toast before serving. The rest of the accoutrements are up to you, but the marmalade, pickles, veggies, and cheeses will give tasty options for a scrumptious brunch with friends.

## Crumpets

2¾ cups (420 g) flour

1½ tsp salt

1 tsp baking powder

1½ cups water

1 cup milk

4 Tbsp butter, melted, divided

1 Tbsp runny honey

2½ tsp instant yeast

2–3 Tbsp neutral oil, for frying

## Soft Steamed Eggs

6–12 large eggs, at room temperature

## For the Crumpets

In a large bowl, or the bowl of a stand mixer fitted with the paddle attachment, sift together the flour, salt, and baking powder. Use a handheld whisk to combine.

Combine the water and milk in a pot, and place over medium heat. Cook until it reaches 110°F (lukewarm). Add 2 tablespoons of the butter and the honey and stir to combine. When the mixture is warmed through, add the yeast. Add the milk and honey mixture to the dry ingredients. Using your whisk, or the stand mixer on medium speed, beat the mixture until it turns into a thick, smooth batter, about 2 to 3 minutes. Use a rubber spatula to push the batter down the sides of the bowl.

Cover the bowl with plastic wrap and let the batter rest at room temperature until it expands and gets bubbly and has risen and starts to fall back down, about 30 to 50 minutes, depending on the room temperature. Toward the end of the proofing time, pull out a large nonstick skillet and heat it over medium-high heat.

In a small bowl or cup, combine the remaining 2 tablespoons of the butter with 2 tablespoons of the oil. Using a brush, lightly grease the surface of the pan. Grease three or four metal English muffin or egg rings, about 3½ inches in diameter (see Note, page 24). Place one ring on the skillet.

*recipe continues*

## To Serve

6 oz (170 g) assortment of sliced
  or cubed cheese (old Cheddar,
  Red Leicester, Stilton, etc.)

6 oz (170 g) sliced cold cuts
  (ham, salami, cold roast
  beef, etc.)

6–8 radishes, sliced if large

4–5 dill pickles, sliced, or
  handful of cornichons

1–2 heirloom tomatoes, sliced

Condiments (mustards, chutney,
  or both)

Spiced Seville Orange
  Marmalade (page 269)

### NOTES

If your rings are new or haven't been used in a while, the crumpet will probably stick to the sides as it cooks. Just use a sharp knife to cut around the outside of the crumpet to release it. Rings will get seasoned and will release the crumpet more easily after each use. If you don't use rings, the crumpets won't turn out perfectly round—but they will still taste amazing.

Crumpets are best made a day ahead, as it gives them a chance to cool down and establish the chewy, spongy texture. Toast them, and the butter will melt joyously into the airy tops. They can be popped in a resealable plastic bag and stored at room temperature for a few days, or individually wrapped in plastic wrap and stored in the freezer.

Using a ¼-cup measure, scoop the batter from the bowl and pour it into the ring. Using a small offset spatula or the back of a spoon, gently and evenly spread the batter to fill the ring to about the halfway mark. Do not overfill.

Cook over medium-high heat for about 1½ minutes. Small holes will start to appear, but they won't open. Drop the heat to medium and cook for another minute. Some bubbles will start to appear on the outer edges. If not, slightly increase the temperature until they do, then drop the heat to medium-low. Bubbles should start to appear all over. After 5 minutes, the top should be covered with holes that stay open and the surface should appear totally dry and have no loose batter. If need be, use a knife to gently poke any bubbles that need opening.

Cook the crumpet until it's golden brown underneath, checking the underside frequently, about 1 to 2 minutes. Using tongs, remove the ring from the skillet. Flip the crumpet over and bake for another 30 to 45 seconds to gently add some color to the top. Place on a cooling rack to cool. It may look weird, which is fine. Snack on it while you make the rest. This first crumpet will help you determine if you need to adjust the final temperature drop.

Repeat with the rest of the batter, using as many greased rings as will fit comfortably in the skillet at one time. Once cooked, transfer the crumpets to a cooling rack.

### For the Soft Steamed Eggs

Place a steamer basket in a pot filled with 1 inch of water. (If you don't have a steamer basket, just steam the eggs directly in ½ inch of water.) Cover and bring the water to a boil over high heat. Add the eggs in a single layer (you may need to do this in two batches), cover with the lid, and steam for 6½ minutes. While the eggs are steaming, prepare an ice-water bath. When the eggs are ready, immediately transfer them to the bath to stop any residual cooking.

### To Serve

Lay out the cheeses, cold cuts, veggies, and condiments, on a serving board and place the eggs in a basket. Add the toasted crumpets to a bread basket and cover loosely with a towel. Add salt and pepper for the eggs, and butter on the side for anyone who likes their crumpets buttered. Have a pot of coffee ready and let everyone help themselves.

# milk toast with stewed orange-cardamom prunes

SERVES 2
MAKES 1½ cups stewed prunes
PREP TIME 10 minutes + cooling
COOK TIME 15 minutes

One of my favorite childhood breakfasts was Zwieback (twice-baked toasts, similar to rusks or biscotti, but shaped like little slices of bread) soaked in milk sweetened with cinnamon and sugar. These days I get the same comforting sensation and satisfaction from toasting brioche slices, sprinkling them with cinnamon-sugar, then soaking them in steaming milk. It's the adult version! I often serve it with something Europeans gobble up regularly at breakfast buffet tables, but North Americans still need to discover: stewed prunes. Yes, I love them (and not for their medicinal properties, if you know what I mean!). They are not overly sweet, and they get perfectly plump from simmering in the orange juice and spices—and the flavors complement each other.

## Orange-Cardamom Prunes

8¾ oz (250 g) dried prunes

Juice of 2 navel oranges

Zest of 1 navel orange

1 Tbsp sugar

½ tsp ground cardamom

¼ tsp orange blossom water

⅛ tsp ground cloves

## Milk Toast

1 cup milk

Salt

2 (1-inch-thick) slices brioche (keep in the fridge until needed)

2 tsp sugar

1 tsp ground cinnamon

1 Tbsp butter

### For the Orange-Cardamom Prunes

Separate any prunes that are stuck together and place them in a pot. Add the orange juice to a 1-cup measure. Top up with water. Add the orange-water mixture and remaining ingredients to the pot.

Bring to a boil over medium-high heat. Partially cover and drop the heat to a simmer. Cook until the prunes are plumped up, but not mushy, and the liquid has reduced to a lovely light syrup, about 8 to 10 minutes. Let cool in the pan and then store in an airtight container in the fridge until ready to serve. The syrup will thicken as it cools.

### For the Milk Toast

In a small pot over medium heat, bring the milk to a steam (or you can use an espresso machine attachment, if you have it), about 2 to 3 minutes. Add a pinch of salt. Remove from the heat and cover to keep warm while you prepare the toast.

*recipe continues*

In a small bowl or cup, combine the sugar and cinnamon. Butter both sides of the brioche slices. Heat a large skillet over medium-high heat. Add the brioche to the skillet and toast until the bottom is golden brown, about 2 minutes. Flip and toast the other side until golden brown, about 2 minutes. Immediately transfer the slices to a cutting board, sprinkle with the cinnamon-sugar mixture, and use a knife or the back of a spoon to gently press the coating into the bread. Cut each toast into eight or nine pieces and divide the toasted pieces between two cereal bowls. Gently pour the steamed milk over the toast. Serve with the orange-cardamom prunes on the side.

NOTES
The prunes will keep in an airtight container in the fridge for up to 5 days. You can also serve them with oatmeal or yogurt. Depending on the size of the bread slices, you may want to prepare 2 slices per person and cook them in batches.

# frozen horchata margarita

SERVES 4
PREP TIME 15 minutes

Jim and I went to Cancún for our honeymoon. Along with swimming with dolphins, exploring the Chichén Itzá ruins, and a wild Jeep trip on Cozumel (where Jim set the Jeep on fire, but that's another story!), we tried horchata for the first time. Not only is it fun to drink, even in coffee, it also works great in pancake and waffle batter and over oatmeal. Or add a little extra oomph and turn it into a frozen margarita! Oh yeah, baby! For best results, start the homemade horchata 2 days in advance. *Recipe pictured on page vi*

### Homemade Horchata

1¼ cups blanched almonds

⅔ cup long-grain brown or medium-grain white rice

1 (3-inch) piece cinnamon

½–¾ cup sugar

2 cups milk

### Margarita

4 Tbsp turbinado sugar

2 Tbsp ground cinnamon

½ cup Salted Bourbon Caramel Sauce (page 270)

8 oz Homemade Horchata (see above)

8 oz tequila

4 oz amaretto

1 Tbsp agave nectar or other sweetener

4 cups ice

4 cinnamon sticks, for garnish

## For the Homemade Horchata

Bring a kettle of water to a boil. Let the water cool a bit.

In a large heat-safe container, combine the almonds, rice, and cinnamon. Add 2½ cups of the cooled water. Cover and refrigerate for 12 hours to 24 hours (I prefer the latter).

Pour the mixture into a blender and add ½ cup of the sugar. Remove the cinnamon stick if still hard. Blend on high speed for several minutes, until the mixture is as smooth as it will get (it will still have a hint of grittiness). Gradually strain through a fine-mesh sieve set over a bowl, pressing down on the solids until a dryish pulp remains. Pour into a pitcher and add the milk. Stir well. Taste and add more sugar, if desired.

Cover and store in the fridge for up to 1 week. Some sediment may settle to the bottom—just give it a good shake before using.

## For the Margarita

Use rocks, margarita, or martini glasses. To rim the glasses, combine the turbinado sugar and cinnamon in a small bowl and pour onto a small plate. Pour the caramel sauce onto a separate plate that the glasses will just fit into. One glass at a time, dip no more than ⅛-inch of the rim into the caramel, then immediately press the rim into the cinnamon-sugar mixture, moving the glass until the caramel is covered. Set aside. Continue with the remaining glasses.

In a large blender, combine the horchata, tequila, amaretto, agave, and ice. Blend until the mixture is completely slushy. Pour into the prepared glasses. Serve each with a cinnamon stick.

# grilled halloumi with pomegranate, lemon, and mint

SERVES 4 to 6
PREP TIME 15 minutes
COOK TIME 15 minutes

Halloumi cheese (or squeaky cheese, as I like to call it) is a wonderful brined cheese that hails from Cyprus. It can be grilled or broiled without fear of it melting. In a dish like this, where it gets to hang out with the Middle Eastern–inspired dressing and the crunch of the pomegranate arils, the Mediterranean cheese is fit for a king or queen. Perfect on a mezes table or beside a lamb burger or roast, it just needs some prosecco or arak to wash it down. In fact, it was Mezes, a local Toronto restaurant, that introduced me to halloumi about 25 years ago! *Recipe pictured on page 20*

4 Tbsp olive oil, divided + extra for frying

2 shallots, finely sliced

2 Tbsp chopped preserved lemon, rinsed

Salt and pepper

2 (each 8¾ oz/250 g) packages halloumi

¼ cup chopped mint

2 Tbsp pomegranate arils

2 tsp lemon juice

In a small bowl, combine 2 tablespoons of the oil with the shallots and lemons. Season with pepper. The preserved lemon will have a saltiness already, so taste before you season with salt. Set aside.

Preheat a grill pan over medium heat. Spray or brush the pan lightly with oil. Slice the halloumi into ½-inch-wide slices and place them in a bowl. Drizzle with the remaining 2 tablespoons of oil, season lightly with salt and pepper, and toss to coat.

Place a cheese slice on the grill pan and grill on both sides until lovely grill marks have appeared, about 2 minutes per side. You don't want to char the outside before the cheese has warmed through, so you may need to adjust the heat under the pan. Use the first slice to guide you. Repeat with the rest of the cheese slices.

Place the grilled cheese on a serving platter. Finish the dressing by adding the mint to the oil in the bowl. Drizzle the dressing over the cheese and toss to coat lightly. Sprinkle the pomegranate arils all over. Drizzle with a final touch of lemon juice, season with more pepper, and serve.

# avocado, feta, and herb dip

MAKES 2 cups

PREP TIME 5 minutes

We all need a quick dip—beyond hummus—that we can whip up when company is coming. This dip has a bit more life than hummus, in my opinion. The creaminess of the avocado, tang of the feta and yogurt, kick and heat from the garlic and chili pepper, and grassy goodness of all the herbs make this a great dip for all occasions. You can serve it with grissini, warmed focaccia or flatbread, or crudités, or as part of a mezes spread. You can even spread it on crusty bread, top it with a poached egg, and call it breakfast!

1 ripe avocado, chopped

2 Tbsp olive oil

7 oz (200 g) feta

2 handfuls cilantro, roughly chopped

1 handful dill, roughly chopped

1 clove garlic, crushed

1 long red chili pepper, medium heat, deseeded and chopped

4 Tbsp Greek yogurt

Zest of 1 lemon

Juice of ½ lemon

Salt (optional)

1 tsp sesame seeds

Place the avocado and oil in a food processor fitted with the steel blade and pulse to break up the avocado into smaller pieces, 10 seconds or so. Add the feta, herbs, garlic, chili pepper, yogurt, and lemon zest and juice. Pulse until the mixture is combined and has a rustic, slightly chunky texture. If you want to thin it out, add a bit more lemon juice, about 1 teaspoon at a time. If you'd like it thicker, add some more yogurt, about 1 teaspoon at a time. Adjust to taste with salt, if desired. You might not need any depending on the type of feta you are using. Sprinkle the sesame seeds on top. Serve.

# shrimp and lobster bisque

SERVES 6
PREP TIME 30 minutes
COOK TIME 1 hour,
10 minutes

Do you automatically think of *Seinfeld* when you hear "lobster bisque"?! I can still picture the Soup Nazi's blackboard with *lobster bisque* written out, and Elaine getting a hold of his secret stash of recipes. This may not be his recipe, but it's still pretty darn good! It's inspired by soup from a diner in Lee, on the I-90 in Massachusetts. Their lobster bisque is chock-full of lobster meat, so I don't skimp either. I use a combination of lobster and shrimp, for budget-friendly flavor. Perfect for dinner parties, and easily halved if you just want to serve two.

1½ lb (680 g) raw shrimp, deveined, shell on (about 24–30 jumbo shrimp)

2 fresh or frozen lobster tails (thawed if frozen)

2 Tbsp olive oil

½ yellow onion, chopped

2 shallots, chopped

½ bulb fennel, diced, fronds reserved

2 cloves garlic, minced

1 tsp thyme

1 tsp anise seeds, crushed

¼ cup sherry (see Note, page 34)

¼ cup brandy

2 tsp Worcestershire sauce

½ tsp sweet paprika

½ tsp white pepper

3 Tbsp tomato paste

1 cup heavy cream

3 Tbsp butter, cubed

1 tsp salt

¾ tsp Espelette pepper

2 tsp pink peppercorns, crushed

Set aside 6 whole shrimp. Peel the rest of the shrimp, reserving the shells and tails. Cut the shrimp into smallish bite-size pieces. Chill the whole shrimp and shrimp pieces in an airtight container in the fridge until needed.

In a large pot over medium heat, combine 1½ cups of water with the shrimp shells and tails and the lobster tails. Cook until the shells turn slightly red, about 3 to 4 minutes. Let cool in the water. Once cooled, set aside the lobster tails from the pot, strain the shell stock from the remaining shells, and return the strained shell stock to the pot.

Working with one lobster tail at a time, insert the tip of a chef's knife near the end of the tail shell, and press firmly until it cracks down and through the shell. Pull the shell back on both sides to crack it open. (Or place the lobster tail on its side and use both hands to press down on the tail until the shell cracks.) Remove the meat and set it aside. Repeat with the second tail.

Return the lobster shells to the shell stock and add about 4 cups water. Bring to a boil over medium-high heat, drop the heat to medium-low, cover, and gently simmer for 40 minutes to bring out the flavors. Meanwhile, shred the lobster meat into bite-size pieces (about the same size as the shrimp pieces) and chill in the fridge until needed.

*recipe continues*

NOTE

Fortified wines such as sherry, port, Madeira, and marsala have brandy or pure alcohol added to them after fermentation. They can range from dry to smoky caramel to raisiny and sweet. They are a wonderful addition to soups, sauces, stews, and even desserts—just don't invest in a vintage bottle for cooking. An open bottle can last in the pantry for over a year.

When the stock is ready, strain it into a large bowl and discard the shells. (The lobster meat and the shell stock can be prepared the day before and stored in the fridge. Just bring the stock and meat to room temperature before moving on to the next step.)

In a saucepan over medium heat, warm the oil. Sauté the onions, shallots, fennel, garlic, thyme, and anise until softened, about 5 minutes. Slowly add the sherry and brandy, then stir in the Worcestershire, paprika, and white pepper. Cook for 1 minute. Stir in the tomato paste, followed by the shell stock. Simmer for 8 minutes. Add the cream and butter, and let the butter melt into the soup. Remove from the heat.

Use an immersion blender or, working in batches, purée the soup in a blender, keeping a towel over the lid to keep any steam from hitting you. Blend until smooth. Return the soup to the pot if need be. Taste and season with the salt and Espelette pepper.

Turn the oven to broil and place the reserved whole shrimp on a baking sheet. Broil the shrimp for 2½ to 3 minutes, turn them over, and continue broiling until they are a lovely pinky red, another 2½ to 3 minutes. Set aside.

Bring the soup to a simmer over medium-low heat and add the shrimp pieces and lobster meat. Simmer until the shrimp are firm and opaque and the lobster meat is warmed through, about 3 to 4 minutes.

Ladle the soup into individual bowls and place a broiled shrimp gently in the center of each. Garnish with crushed pink peppercorns and fennel fronds.

# niçoise tuna melt

SERVES 4

PREP TIME 20 minutes

COOK TIME 10 minutes

Truly, the tuna melt is one of life's simple joys. I don't know who first decided that melted cheese over tuna salad was a good move, but I'm so glad they did. So how do you improve on this classic? Take inspiration from one of the best salads ever invented: salade niçoise! I took most of the elements of the salad and combined them with the tuna melt ingredients. A spiced-up lemony mayo dressing brings it all together. *Recipe pictured on page 20*

### Tuna Melt

2 eggs

4 large slices crusty bread, like sourdough

2 (each 5 oz/140 g) cans tuna packed in water

5¼ oz (150 g) cherry tomatoes

¼ cup kalamata olives

2 Tbsp finely diced red onion

2 Tbsp capers, well drained

½ tsp chili flakes

1 Tbsp chopped parsley

6 oz (170 g) mix of thinly shaved or sliced medium marble and fontina cheeses (or your favorite melty cheeses)

Pepper

### Dressing

⅓ cup mayonnaise

1 tsp lemon juice

1 tsp Seasoning Salt (page 264)

### For the Tuna Melt

Fill a small saucepan with ½ inch of water. Bring to a boil over medium-high heat, add the eggs, and cover. Prepare a bowl with ice cubes and cold water. Steam the eggs for 8 minutes, then use a spider or slotted spoon to transfer them to the ice-water bath.

Preheat the oven to 375°F.

Lay the bread on a baking sheet. Drain the tuna and place it in a bowl. Break the tuna up into bite-sized pieces. Chop the tomatoes into bite-size pieces and add to the bowl. Slice the olives into three or so rings and add to the bowl. Add the onions, capers, and chili flakes.

### For the Dressing

In a small bowl, combine the mayonnaise, lemon juice, and seasoning salt.

Add the dressing to the tuna mixture and gently toss to coat. Peel the eggs (see Note, page 67), and roughly chop into bite-size pieces. Add to the tuna and toss once more. Season with more seasoning salt, if desired.

Spoon the tuna salad onto the four slices of bread. Save any remaining tuna for a snack. Sprinkle with the parsley and place the cheese slices on top. Bake until the cheese bubbles and turns golden, about 10 minutes. Feel free to place them under the broiler for a minute or so if you want a bit more color. Season with pepper before serving.

# cinnamon and sumac sautéed brussels sprouts

SERVES 4
PREP TIME 5 minutes
COOK TIME 20 minutes

**B**russels sprouts. The misunderstood veggie we all loved to hate when we were kids. Even most adults couldn't stomach the typical way these little baby cabbages were served back in the day: gray, mushy, and bitter. Of course, plenty of thick, gooey cheese sauce helped hide them and make them more palatable. These days, they are enjoying a renaissance thanks to bacon, pancetta, pomegranate arils, fresh herbs, and not cooking the heck out of them! Here's my take on them. The first time I made this dish, Jim remarked, after taking his first forkful, "How can anyone not like Brussels sprouts?" My work is done. *Recipe pictured on page 282*

2 Tbsp pine nuts

1 lb (450 g) Brussels sprouts, root end trimmed and halved

2 Tbsp butter or olive oil

½ tsp ground cinnamon

½ tsp sumac

½ tsp salt

¼ tsp pepper

2 cloves garlic, minced

1 Tbsp grated lemon zest

1 Tbsp lemon juice

Olive oil, for drizzling

In a large nonstick sauté pan over medium heat, toast the pine nuts, stirring occasionally to avoid charring, until golden and fragrant, about 5 minutes (but keep an eye on them). Transfer to a bowl.

In the same pan over medium-high heat, add ⅓ cup of water and the Brussels sprouts, cover tightly, and cook until just tender, about 8 to 10 minutes, depending on their size, stirring once to keep them from scorching on the bottom. Add the butter, cinnamon, sumac, salt, and pepper. Cook, uncovered, for 3 minutes, stirring often. If the water has evaporated before the sprouts are fork-tender, add another tablespoon or two.

Stir in the garlic and lemon zest and juice, and cook until the Brussels sprouts are fork-tender or are still firm but offer little resistance when pierced with a knife, about 30 seconds. Larger Brussels sprouts may take more time, of course, so you may want to add another teaspoon of butter and 1 to 2 tablespoons more water. Taste and adjust any seasonings. Finish with a drizzle of olive oil. Sprinkle the pine nuts on top and serve.

# minty, creamy peas and shallots

SERVES 4
PREP TIME 20 minutes + steeping
COOK TIME 20 minutes

Shelling peas was one of my favorite childhood chores in the garden—only because I got to eat peas as I shelled. It took way longer to fill the bowl using my method, but I didn't mind! Each unopened pod was an enthralling mystery. Would it have sweet peas or something less than sweet? That's why I had to sample each one! These days, spring seems to start later, so fresh peas may be harder to come by, but greenhouse peas, already shelled, are often at our produce stores. And if not, good ol' frozen peas work just fine for this recipe. Over the years, I have added more and more mint to this recipe because it really deserves to shine and not sit discreetly in the background. This is a really minty pea side dish that I could totally inhale on its own.

*Recipe pictured on page 20*

1 cup half-and-half or light (18%) cream

½ cup packed mint leaves, divided

2 Tbsp olive oil

1 Tbsp butter

4 shallots, cut into ¼-inch rings

1 lb (450 g) fresh or frozen shelled peas (thawed if frozen)

½ tsp sugar

Salt and pepper

Place the cream in a small pot. Roughly tear half of the mint leaves into small pieces and pinch them as you add them to the cream. Pinching will release some of the oils—just smell your fingers afterwards! Bring to a gentle simmer over medium-low heat. Watch it to ensure it doesn't start to boil. As soon as it reaches a simmer with steam rising, remove the pot from the heat and allow the mint and cream to steep at room temperature for 1 to 2 hours (2 hours if you want it really minty). (If not serving right away, transfer to an airtight container and store in the fridge for up to 1 day. Allow it to come to room temperature before moving on to the next step.) Strain the mint cream into a small bowl and set aside. Discard the mint leaves.

In a large skillet over medium heat, warm the oil and butter. Add the shallots and cook until just turning soft, about 3 minutes. Add the peas, and then pour in the cream. Add the sugar and stir. Cook gently until the peas are cooked through and the cream is just thick enough to coat the back of spoon, about 8 to 10 minutes. Season with 1 teaspoon each of salt and pepper. Adjust the seasoning to taste.

Remove from the heat. Chop the remaining mint leaves and stir them into the sauce. Add a final grind of pepper.

**NOTES**
If you can't find Castelvetrano olives, you can use any milder green pitted olives. Avoid using heavily brined or salty olives. You don't want to overpower the herbs and pangrattato. Any remaining pangrattato is fabulous over scrambled eggs or avocado toast.

# olive and spring herb linguini with lemon pistachio pangrattato

SERVES 4
MAKES ½ cup pangrattato
PREP TIME 20 minutes
COOK TIME 30 minutes

Can olives finally get some love and move to center stage? Yes, they can! Bright, green Castelvetrano olives have the perfect flavor profile for starring in a pasta dish. They aren't too briny or salty, but rather have a bright, light, grassy taste. They play well with all sorts of fresh green herbs and leeks, as they do in this dish. And to top it off, a fun lemon and pistachio pangrattato, or breadcrumb "sauce," adds the perfect amount of crunch.

### Pangrattato

1 Tbsp olive oil

½ cup breadcrumbs (I use fresh or panko)

Zest and juice of 1 lemon

Salt and pepper

¼ cup finely chopped pistachios

### Olive and Herb Pasta

8 oz (225 g) linguini

2 Tbsp olive oil

2 large cloves garlic, minced

3 leeks, white parts only, sliced into half moons

¼ tsp chili flakes

Juice of 1 lemon

Salt and pepper

1 cup pitted Castelvetrano olives, sliced into rings (see Note, page 38), divided

¾ cup finely chopped mixed spring herbs (such as parsley, dill, mint, thyme), divided

### For the Pangrattato

In a large skillet over medium heat, heat the oil. Add the breadcrumbs, lemon zest and juice, and ½ teaspoon each of salt and pepper. Stir until the breadcrumbs start to turn golden. Add the pistachios. Continue to stir until the breadcrumbs are crispy and golden brown, about 2 to 3 minutes, lifting the pan from the heat if the breadcrumbs start to scorch. Season with more salt and pepper. Set aside. This can be made in advance.

### For the Olive and Herb Pasta

Bring a pot of salted water to a boil over high heat. Prepare the pasta according to the package directions. Reserve ½ cup of the pasta water, then drain the pasta. Set aside.

In a large skillet over medium-low heat, heat the oil. Add the garlic and leeks. Sauté until softened and turning golden, about 8 minutes. Add the chili flakes and lemon juice, then ½ teaspoon each of salt and pepper. Taste and adjust the seasoning as desired. Add half of the olives, and half of the herb mixture. Stir in the sauce, keeping the heat at medium-low.

Add some of the reserved pasta water to the sauce to keep it from getting too thick. Toss in the pasta. Add more to thin the sauce out and keep the pasta from getting too dry. Toss in ¼ cup of the pangrattato. Remove from the heat. Scatter the remaining olives and herbs over the pasta. Set out on a serving platter and drizzle with a bit more oil and another 2 tablespoons of the pangrattato (see Note).

# spinach and ricotta crespelle

SERVES 4
PREP TIME 30 minutes + resting
COOK TIME 50 minutes

This is how you turn one of my therapeutic dishes, crepes (or in Italian, *crespelle*), into something a little bit different and rather comforting at the same time. Think of this as a Moroccan manicotti. But instead of stuffing manicotti, you spoon the just-spicy-enough savory ricotta filling, softened greens, barberries, and pine nuts down the middle of savory crespelle, which are then easily rolled up. The harissa marinara sauce is epic and makes a great base to lay the crespelle on. This is a dinner you will come back to time and again!

**Spinach and Ricotta Filling**

2 Tbsp dried barberries

8 oz (225 g) baby spinach (about 7 cups packed)

2 heaping Tbsp pine nuts

2 tsp olive oil

1 yellow onion, minced

1 oz (25 g) pancetta, finely chopped

2 cloves garlic, minced

8 oz (225 g) Simple Fresh Ricotta (page 273) or store-bought ricotta

¾ cup grated Parmesan

1 tsp harissa powder

1 tsp pepper

½ tsp salt

½ tsp chili flakes

½ tsp ras el hanout

1 egg, beaten

**For the Spinach and Ricotta Filling**

Bring a large pot or kettle of water to a boil. Place the barberries in a small bowl and cover completely with the boiling water. Let sit, uncovered, for at least 20 minutes. Meanwhile, place the spinach in a large bowl and add enough boiling water to just cover. Let sit for 1 minute and then drain. Wrap the spinach in a large kitchen towel and give it a good squeeze over the sink. Keep squeezing until all the liquid has been released. Use a sharp knife to chop the leaves into small pieces. Wipe the bowl dry and add the spinach.

Warm a skillet over medium heat. Add the pine nuts and toast, tossing occasionally, until fragrant, about 5 minutes. Watch carefully so they don't scorch. Transfer them to a small bowl.

In the same skillet, now over medium-high heat, warm the oil, and then add the onions and pancetta. Once softened, about 6 minutes, add the garlic and sauté everything until the garlic is golden and the pancetta is starting to crisp, about 3 minutes. Let cool slightly before proceeding.

Add the onion mixture to the spinach. Drain the barberries and add them to the spinach, along with the pine nuts. Add the ricotta, Parmesan, harissa, pepper, salt, chili flakes, and ras el hanout. Taste and adjust the seasoning as desired. Add the egg and gently mix everything together.

*recipe continues*

## Crespelle

3½ cups Harissa Marinara Variation (page 267)

8 (5- to 6-inch) Basic Crepes (page 276)

1½ cups finely grated mozzarella or fontina, or a combo

1 Tbsp chopped parsley, for garnish

2 tsp chopped mint, for garnish

1 tsp rose harissa powder, for garnish

## For the Crespelle

Preheat the oven to 350°F. Pour half of the marinara sauce into a 9- × 13-inch baking dish or a baking dish that will hold all the crespelle. Alternatively, use personal-sized baking dishes that hold two crespelle each.

Place a crespelle on your cutting board and spoon 3 to 4 tablespoons of the spinach and ricotta filling across the middle of it. Roll up firmly and set into the sauce, seam side down. Repeat with the rest of the crespelle.

Cover the rolls with the rest of the sauce. Cover the baking dish with foil and bake for 20 minutes. Uncover and sprinkle the mozzarella over top. Bake until the cheese has melted and turned a bubbling golden brown, another 20 minutes, or 15 if you're using personal-sized baking dishes. If desired, place under the broiler for about 5 minutes to get more color, but keep an eye on it. Remove from the oven and garnish with parsley, mint, and rose harissa.

### NOTES

Source the dried barberries and ras el hanout at your local Middle Eastern markets, gourmet grocery stores, spice shops (I like the Spice Trader in Toronto), or online. The filling can be made a day ahead and stored in an airtight container in the fridge. Just bring it to room temperature before using.

# mustard-infused pot roast

SERVES 6
PREP TIME 15 minutes +
resting
COOK TIME 4 hours

Before the weather has completely warmed up, we always squeeze in one more pot roast. When I was growing up, my parents always had two condiments to accompany a good pot roast: horseradish and mustard. I still need both on the table. One bite with mustard, the next with horseradish. Why choose when you can have both? And while I add mustard to the braising liquid, I still have it on the table when it's time to eat! Start this early in the afternoon so that it will be ready by dinnertime.

3–4 lb (1¼–1¾ kg) well-marbled beef shoulder or boneless chuck roast

2 tsp Italian seasoning

1 tsp salt

1 tsp pepper

1 tsp black peppercorns

2 Tbsp olive oil (approx.)

2 large yellow onions, thickly sliced lengthwise

4 cloves garlic, thinly sliced

2 Tbsp Dijon mustard

1 Tbsp tomato paste

Ensure that the roast is tied off. Depending on how thick it is, you may need to tie it in two or three places so that it will roast evenly. Use paper towels to pat it dry on all sides.

In a small bowl, combine the Italian seasoning, salt, and pepper. Rub this mixture well into the meat on all sides. Crack the peppercorns and use a mortar and pestle, or the bottom of a thick glass on a cutting board, to crush them. Set the crushed peppercorns aside.

In a Dutch oven or heavy-bottomed pot just large enough to hold the roast and vegetables, heat the oil over medium-high heat. Sear the roast on all sides until well browned, about 3 to 4 minutes per side. (Adjust the heat if necessary.) Remove the roast and set aside. Use tongs and paper towel to remove any blackened bits from the pot and wipe it clean.

Add the onions to the pot, and more oil if necessary, and cook until they begin to soften, about 5 minutes. Add the garlic and cook for another minute. Add the peppercorns, Dijon, and tomato paste. Stir to coat and deglaze any bits stuck to the bottom of the pot.

*recipe continues*

1½ cups beef stock (approx.)

½ cup red wine

4 sprigs thyme

4 sprigs rosemary, divided

1 bay leaf

1½ lb (680 g) mini potatoes, scrubbed

1 (12 oz/340 g) bunch carrots, left whole, leaves trimmed

6 stalks celery, sliced into 3-inch pieces

2 Tbsp chopped parsley, for garnish

Mustard and/or horseradish, for serving

Return the roast to the pot. Add the stock and red wine, followed by the thyme, rosemary, and bay leaf, and cover. As soon as the liquids have come to a rolling simmer (just below boiling), drop the heat to low, for a gentle simmer. Simmer for about 15 minutes. Check to see the mixture is still simmering and adjust the heat accordingly. Continue to cook, covered, for 2 hours. Check once, at around the 1½-hour point, to make sure the liquids haven't reduced too much. If they have, add a bit more stock.

Arrange the potatoes, carrots, and celery around the meat. Cover and continue cooking for 45 minutes, checking the liquids again. Check to see if the meat is fork-tender. If the meat needs to cook a bit longer, transfer the vegetables, except for the onions, to a baking dish and keep warm in the oven (around 275°F should do the trick). Continue to cook the meat until fork-tender.

Once the meat is fork-tender, transfer it to a cutting board, tent loosely with foil, and let rest for 15 minutes. Discard the bay leaves and set the thyme and rosemary sprigs aside for garnish. Stir the remaining juices in the pot. If you like the consistency, pour them into a gravy boat for serving. Otherwise, add more stock to thin out, or cook on medium-high heat until the stock is reduced to your desired consistency.

Cut the roast into large bite-size pieces. If it's tender enough, you'll barely require a knife! Place the pieces on a serving platter, arrange the vegetables around the meat, and garnish the platter with the parlsey, thyme, and 2 rosemary sprigs. Pour the sauce over top. Serve with mustard and/or horseradish, with extra sauce on the side.

NOTES

You can replace the beef stock with a beef bouillon cube (I like Better than Bouillon) dissolved in water, plus more if needed. Store the leftovers in the remaining sauce. They will reheat amazingly in the oven at 300°F and make for the perfect pot roast sammies.

# mum's chicken and rice

SERVES 4
PREP TIME 30 minutes
COOK TIME 1 hour,
5 minutes

Whenever my mum asked what I wanted for dinner, I'd always say her chicken and rice. It wasn't a German classic, but it was the most soothing meal I knew. The sublime way the chicken juices flavored the rice personified "home" for me. It took me forever to capture those flavors once I moved out on my own. I finally discovered the key ingredient—celery! My mum loved cooking with it. The right amount gives this a mild, earthy flavor that brings everything together.

2 tsp sweet paprika

2 tsp dried thyme leaves

Salt and pepper

1 tsp lemon zest

1 tsp onion powder

1 tsp garlic powder

1 Tbsp olive oil

2 Tbsp butter, divided

6–8 chicken thighs, bone in
    and skin on

1 large yellow onion, diced

2 cloves garlic, minced

3 stalks celery, chopped into
    ½-inch chunks

1 cup basmati rice

1¾ cups chicken stock

Olive oil cooking spray
    (optional)

2 Tbsp finely chopped parsley,
    for garnish

NOTE
Searing the meat without seasonings ensures that the seasonings don't burn onto the skin or into the pan.

Preheat the oven to 350°F.

In a small bowl, combine the paprika, thyme, 1½ teaspoons of salt, 1 teaspoon of pepper, the lemon zest, onion powder, and garlic powder. Set this seasoning mix aside.

In a large ovenproof skillet or braiser over medium-high heat, heat the oil and 1 tablespoon of the butter. Add the chicken thighs, in batches if necessary, skin side down. Sear on all sides until just golden brown, about 3 to 4 minutes per side. Transfer to a plate to cool slightly. Remove all but 1 tablespoon of the fat from the skillet.

Place the skillet over medium heat. Add the onions and sauté until they just start to soften, about 10 minutes. Add the garlic and stir for another minute. Add the celery and 1 teaspoon each of salt and pepper. Cook until just softened, about 3 minutes.

Meanwhile, once the chicken thighs have cooled, pat away any remaining fat and rub the seasoning mix into all sides.

Add the rice and remaining butter to the skillet and stir to coat. Place the chicken evenly on top of the rice. Pour the stock and ½ cup of water around and between the chicken thighs, but not over top of them. Increase the heat to medium-high and bring to a simmer. Let it bubble for 30 seconds. Cover with a lid, or seal tightly with foil, and bake in the center of the oven for 35 minutes. Remove the lid or foil. If you want the skins to be crispy, spray the chicken with a little olive oil cooking spray. Bake until the liquid is absorbed and the internal temperature reaches 165°F, about 10 minutes. Remove from the oven and let stand for 5 minutes. If serving from the skillet, gently fluff up the rice around the chicken. Garnish with parsley before serving.

# ginger and miso sticky roast chicken

SERVES 4
PREP TIME 10 minutes +
marinating
COOK TIME 50 minutes

This recipe started out as a salad dressing for my winter slaw (page 187). But I quickly realized that my Miso-Ginger Dressing (page 266) belonged on more than just cabbage! I started drizzling it over grilled pork and chicken. It then morphed into a marinade, and then this recipe was born. This marinade of complex flavors, with the dressing's Japanese miso and Thai sriracha hanging out wonderfully with the soy sauce, honey, and ginger, creates a balance of sweet, sour, salty, and sticky—all the good stuff. It immediately got two thumbs up from Jim!

6 large chicken thighs, bone in and skin on

Salt and pepper

¼ cup Miso-Ginger Dressing (page 266)

¼ cup soy sauce or tamari

2 Tbsp Dijon mustard

1 tsp flakey finishing salt

2 Tbsp chopped scallions, for garnish

1 Tbsp sesame seeds, for garnish

Coconut rice, for serving (optional)

Pat the chicken thighs dry and season with salt and pepper. Place them in a dish that holds them snugly but without crowding (an 8- × 10- inch baking dish is ideal).

In a bowl, whisk together the dressing, soy sauce, and Dijon. Pour this marinade over the chicken and turn to coat well. Cover and place in the fridge to marinate for at least 1 hour or overnight.

Preheat the oven to 425°F. Line an 8- × 10- inch baking dish or 10-inch cast-iron skillet with parchment paper or foil.

Remove the chicken from the marinade and place the thighs in the dish in a single layer, skin side up. You want them to be snug but not crowded. Pour any remaining marinade over the chicken.

Bake until the chicken is cooked through and the internal temperature reaches 165°F, about 45 minutes. The skin will be nicely browned. If you want it extra crispy, turn on the broiler and broil until the skin is beautifully burnished, 1 to 2 minutes. Keep an eye on it!

Arrange the chicken on a platter. Immediately scatter the flakey salt over top. Transfer the remaining liquid to a small pot, spoon off the fat, and cook over medium-high heat until reduced by up to half, making a lovely sauce. Pour the sauce over the chicken thighs or serve it on the side. Sprinkle with scallions and sesame seeds. Serve with coconut rice, if desired.

# (queen) margherita chicken and spaghetti

SERVES 4
PREP TIME 20 minutes
COOK TIME 1¼ hours

This is one of those comfort foods that ticks all the boxes: Pizza, yes. Chicken, yes. Pasta, yes. Ooey-gooey cheese, YES! Named after Toronto's Queen Margherita Pizza (which makes a fabulous Neapolitan pizza), this dish has the Margherita components covered with red tomatoes, white mozzarella, and green basil, plus an added oomph thanks to the La Bomba. Creating a rustic pizza sauce in the pan and then nestling the seared chicken thighs in it is just the start. Roast it all in the oven, broil the scattered fresh mozzarella over the finished chicken, and serve it all over spaghetti. Tell me, what could be better? I'm waiting!

6–8 chicken thighs, bone in and skin on, or 4 whole chicken legs

Salt and pepper

2 Tbsp olive oil, divided

4 oz (115 g) guanciale or pancetta, diced

¼ cup thinly sliced red onion

4 cloves garlic, thinly sliced

1 Tbsp capers, drained well

1 Tbsp La Bomba

2 tsp Italian seasoning

½ tsp chili flakes

1 (28 oz/796 ml) can whole tomatoes

½ cup basil leaves, divided

2 tsp sugar

Heaping ½ cup whole cherry tomatoes

Heaping ½ cup halved cherry tomatoes

Preheat the oven to 400°F. Line a plate with paper towel.

Pat the chicken dry and season all sides with 2 teaspoons of salt and 1 teaspoon of pepper.

Heat a large ovenproof skillet over medium-high heat. Warm 1 tablespoon of the oil for a few seconds. Add the guanciale and sauté, stirring frequently, until it's well browned and just crisp, about 3 minutes. Transfer to the prepared plate. Leave the oil in the skillet.

Add the chicken to the skillet, in batches if necessary. Sear until well browned on the bottom, about 5 to 6 minutes. Turn over and repeat. Transfer the chicken to a large plate. Remove all but 1 tablespoon of the fat from the skillet.

Add the onions, garlic, capers, La Bomba, Italian seasoning, and chili flakes to the skillet and sauté over medium-high heat for 1 minute. Stir in the whole tomatoes and their juices, ¼ cup of the basil, the sugar, and ½ teaspoon each of salt and pepper. Using the back of a wooden spoon, break up the tomatoes as they cook. Cook until the sauce begins to thicken nicely, about 10 minutes.

*recipe continues*

8 oz (225 g) spaghetti

Small handful each room-
temperature black olives,
hot banana peppers, or other
favorite pizza toppings

8 oz (225 g) fresh fior di latte or
mini bocconcini

Grated Parmesan, for garnish

Nestle the chicken pieces and any juices into the sauce. Scatter the whole and halved cherry tomatoes over and around the chicken pieces and transfer the skillet to the oven. Roast, uncovered, until the chicken reaches an internal temperature of 165°F, about 45 minutes.

Meanwhile, bring a pot of salted water to a boil and cook the pasta according to the package instructions. Drain. Toss the pasta with the remaining 1 tablespoon of oil. Chop the remaining basil leaves and set aside.

Remove the skillet from the oven and scatter your preferred pizza toppings over the chicken. Tear the fior di latte into rough pieces and place evenly over the chicken. If desired, move some of the cherry tomatoes to sit on top of the cheese. Scatter half of the guanciale over the cheese. Turn the oven to broil and place a rack 6 inches or so from the heat. Place the skillet under the broiler and broil until the cheese is bubbling, about 1 to 3 minutes, but watch it carefully!

To serve, transfer the pasta to a platter or divide it among individual plates. Top with the sauce, and then place the chicken and cheese on top. Garnish with the chopped basil leaves and finish with the remaining guanciale, a sprinkle of Parmesan, and a final grind of pepper.

# rhubarb bumbleberry crumble

SERVES 8
PREP TIME 20 minutes + resting
COOK TIME 1 hour

I couldn't let spring go by without at least one rhubarb recipe. Because it's mouth-puckeringly tart, it works well with sweeter fruit. Traditionally, strawberries are rhubarb's best friend. Add apples (avoiding varieties that melt as they bake, like McIntosh, Jonagold, or Red Delicious), blueberries, and raspberries—and we get this bumbleberry crumble. Say that 10 times fast! *Recipe pictured on page 20*

**Bumbleberry Filling**

2 apples (such as Gala or Ambrosia), peeled and chopped

2 cups chopped rhubarb

1½ cups hulled and quartered strawberries

1 cup blueberries

1 cup raspberries

Zest and juice of 1 lime, divided

⅔ cup sugar

4 Tbsp arrowroot starch

1½ Tbsp finely chopped mint

**Crumble Topping**

¾ cup all-purpose flour

½ cup almond flour or meal

¾ tsp baking powder

3 Tbsp light brown sugar

3 Tbsp granulated sugar

½ cup butter, chilled

Vanilla ice cream, for serving

Preheat the oven to 375°F. Spray or grease a 9- or 10-inch deep-dish pie plate or baking dish.

**For the Bumbleberry Filling**

In a large bowl, combine the apples, rhubarb, strawberries, blueberries, and raspberries. Add the lime juice and toss to coat. In a small bowl, combine the sugar, arrowroot, mint, and half of the lime zest. Add the lime zest mixture to the fruit and toss well. Let sit, uncovered, for 10 minutes to release the juices.

**For the Crumble Topping**

Meanwhile, in a medium bowl, whisk together both flours, the baking powder, both sugars, and the remaining lime zest. Grate the butter into the bowl on the large side of a box grater. Rub the mixture together with your fingertips until it has a sandy texture with some larger pea-sized lumps.

**To Assemble**

Transfer the filling to the prepared pie plate. Sprinkle the crumble topping over top, making sure there are lumpy bits throughout. This gives it texture and a shortbread feel.

Place the pie plate on a baking sheet. Bake for 30 minutes. If the topping is getting too browned at this point, cover loosely with foil. Continue baking until the juices are bubbling throughout and the topping is golden brown, 20 to 30 minutes. Remove the baking sheet and transfer the pie plate to a cooling rack. Let rest until the juices settle and thicken slightly, about 30 minutes.

Serve with generous amounts of vanilla ice cream.

# lemon mascarpone chiffon pie

MAKES one 9-inch pie
PREP TIME 1½ hours + chilling
COOK TIME 15 minutes

This is simply a bright, happy pie! Sure, it can be made year-round, but its sunny disposition just sings spring to me. The crust is so easy—it's barely baked. The little baking that does occur gives the sugar and the spiced Dutch speculaas cookie crumbs a caramelized flavor, which is a great contrast to the bright and creamy filling. The filling is no-bake and uses lemon curd, which can be made in advance. And since it's topped with a frothy egg white meringue, this is pretty light. Icing sugar gives the egg whites stability. The *pièce de résistance* is the candied lemon ribbon garnish. After this you'll want to candy all the citrus you can get your hands on!

## Candied Lemon Ribbons

3–4 lemons, scrubbed

1½ cups (340 g) sugar, divided

## Speculaas Crust

1½ cups (175 g) speculaas cookie crumbs or gingersnap crumbs (see Note)

2 Tbsp brown sugar

4 Tbsp butter (approx.), melted and slightly cooled

## Lemon Chiffon Pie Filling

½ cup (120 g) mascarpone cheese

1 cup heavy cream

½ cup (65 g) icing sugar

1¼ cups Lemony Lemon Curd (page 268)

2 Tbsp lemon zest

## Swiss Meringue Topping

½ cup (115 g) sugar

3 egg whites

### For the Candied Lemon Ribbons

Using a bar zester or vegetable peeler, peel the lemon rind in vertical strips, removing as much of the bitter white pith as possible.

In a small saucepan over medium-high heat, combine the peels with 2 cups of cold water and bring to a boil. If you used a bar zester to remove the peels, set them aside and move on to the next step. Otherwise, refill the pan with cold water, bring to a boil, and drain again. Repeat this process one more time, so it's boiled three times total, to remove the bitterness from the peels. Set the peels aside.

In the same saucepan, combine 1 cup (225 g) of the sugar and ½ cup of water. Set over medium-high heat, bring to a boil, and whisk until the sugar dissolves. Carefully drop in the peels, drop the heat to medium-low, and simmer, uncovered, until the peels are tender and translucent, about 8 to 10 minutes. Using tongs, remove the peels, allowing the excess sugar to drip back into the pot, and place on wax paper to cool at room temperature. Reserve the simple syrup for tea or the Summer Berry and Lemon Trifle (page 102) if you want.

Place the remaining ½ cup (115 g) sugar in a wide, shallow bowl. Once the peels are cool to the touch, add them to the sugar and toss with your fingertips until they are evenly and thoroughly coated. Remove one peel at a time, shake off the excess sugar, and place on a wax paper–lined plate until needed. Reserve the unused sugar (even if there are lemon bits in it) for a cup of tea.

*recipe continues*

### For the Speculaas Crust

Preheat the oven to 350°F.

In a bowl, stir together the cookie crumbs and sugar to combine. Add the melted butter and stir to combine again. The mixture should hold together when you pinch a small amount between your fingers. If it's too dry, add more melted butter, 1 teaspoon at a time, until it holds together.

Transfer the crumb mixture to a 9-inch pie plate (no, no need to grease it first!). Using your fingers, spread out the crumbs to evenly line the bottom and the sides, and press down to create an evenly packed pie crust. You can use the bottom of a measuring cup to help smooth out the crust. Chill, uncovered, in the fridge for 10 minutes.

Place the pie plate on a baking sheet and bake until the sugars have started to melt and the crust is lightly browned, about 8 minutes. The melted sugar will hold the crumbs together once it cools and add a caramel flavor to the crust. Cool on a cooling rack for at least 40 minutes. If the sides of the crust have slid down ever so slightly, use the back of a spoon to gently push them back up while the crust is still warm.

### For the Lemon Chiffon Pie Filling

Using a stand mixer fitted with the whisk attachment, or a handheld mixer and a large bowl, whisk the mascarpone on low speed until smooth. Add the cream and whisk on low speed until frothy. With the mixer running, add the icing sugar in a slow stream, then whip on medium-high speed until stiff peaks form. Gently fold in one-third of the lemon curd and all the zest. Continue folding in the curd, a little at a time, until just blended. Spoon the filling into the crust and smooth it out to have a nice even top. Chill in the fridge, uncovered, for at least 4 hours.

### For the Swiss Meringue Topping

In the upper part of a double boiler, or using a stainless steel bowl set over a pot of simmering water, heat the sugar and egg whites, stirring constantly, until the sugar has dissolved and a thermometer reads 140°F. Remove the bowl from the water bath and use a handheld mixer to beat the mixture until stiff peaks form.

### To Assemble

Spread the meringue over the cooled pie, making swirls with an offset spatula. If you want to brown the meringue, use a kitchen torch or make sure the meringue covers the filling right up to the edge of the crust, place the pie on a baking sheet, and broil on the upper rack of the oven until browned, about 30 seconds. Let it cool slightly. Scatter as many candied lemon ribbons as you like over top to decorate.

NOTES

Leftover candied lemon ribbons can be stored in an airtight container at room temperature for several weeks. They can be placed on top of glazes on cakes or cookies for decoration, or even used as a garnish for a yogurt bowl or salad, to name a few options.

If you're so inclined, you can just serve the meringue naked, without browning it or adding the candied lemon ribbons—the pie will still taste amazing!

# cardamom-scented carrot cake

MAKES one 9-inch double-layer cake

PREP TIME 20 minutes + chilling

COOK TIME 1 hour

We are not huge cake eaters over here. It's not that we don't love a good chocolate cake, Victoria sponge, or fruit-filled torte. It's just that there are only the two of us. So I rarely make cakes unless I know we'll have help eating them! This all changes when it comes to carrot cake. I could make this moist, spicy carrot cake with a warmly spiced cream cheese icing every month and Jim would be a happy camper. The cardamom and bitters add true depth to the cake, which is full of wonderful ingredients like pecans, pineapple, and, of course, carrots. A layer of orange marmalade adds a nice surprise to this layer cake. Practically health food! And yes, I will eat it for breakfast.

## Carrot Cake

2 cups (300 g) flour

2 tsp baking soda

2 tsp ground cardamom

2 tsp ground cinnamon

¼ tsp salt

3 eggs

¾ cup kefir or buttermilk

¾ cup neutral oil

1 cup (225 g) granulated sugar

¼ cup (50 g) golden brown sugar

2 tsp vanilla extract

5 good dashes cardamom bitters

2 cups (245 g) shredded carrots

1 cup (100 g) sweetened shredded coconut

1 cup (120 g) finely chopped pecans

¾ cup (170 g) canned crushed pineapple and juice

### For the Carrot Cake

Preheat the oven to 350°F. Prepare two 9-inch springform pans by lining the bottom and sides with parchment paper, securing the sides so the parchment is trapped inside and outside of the pan. Spray the sides with cooking spray.

In a bowl, sift together the flour, baking soda, cardamom, cinnamon, and salt. In a large bowl, whisk together the eggs, kefir, oil, sugars, and vanilla. Add the bitters. Add the dry ingredients to the wet. Mix with a wooden spoon until incorporated.

In the bowl that the dry ingredients were in, combine the carrots, coconut, pecans, and pineapple. Fold the carrot mixture into the egg and flour mixture until evenly incorporated. Pour the mixture into the prepared pans. Tap the pans on the counter to release any air bubbles.

Place the pans on a large baking sheet, and bake until a skewer comes out clean, about 50 minutes to 1 hour. Allow the cakes to cool in the pans on a cooling rack for 20 minutes. Remove the sides of the pans and cool completely on the rack, then chill in the fridge for at least 1 hour, or cover with plastic wrap and chill in the fridge overnight, before icing.

*recipe continues*

### Allspice Cream Cheese Icing

3–3½ cups (390–455 g) icing sugar

1 (8 oz/250 g) package cream cheese, softened and cubed

½ cup (110 g) butter, softened and cubed

¾ tsp ground allspice

½ tsp ground cinnamon

1 tsp vanilla extract

2 Tbsp milk (as needed)

3 Tbsp Spiced Seville Orange Marmalade (page 269)

4–5 Tbsp toasted large-flake coconut, for garnish

### For the Allspice Cream Cheese Icing

Place the icing sugar in a bowl and use a whisk to break up any clumps (or run it through a sieve).

In a stand mixer fitted with a paddle attachment, mix the cream cheese, butter, allspice, cinnamon, and vanilla on medium speed until combined and completely smooth. Add the icing sugar, ½ cup at a time, mixing after each addition. Stop when the icing has reached your desired thickness and sweetness. If it's too thick, add the milk, 1 tablespoon at a time, and mix to thin it.

### To Assemble

Place one cake on your cake stand or plate and spread the marmalade to cover the top surface, just avoiding the edges. Spread a layer of frosting past the marmalade to the edges, and then place the second cake on top. Using an offset spatula, spread the frosting, as thick as you would like, over top of the cake (or, cover the cake entirely if you'd like—there's enough icing to do so!). Garnish with the toasted flaked coconut.

Chill in the fridge for at least 30 minutes before serving.

### NOTES

These cakes can be baked in advanced, wrapped in plastic wrap, and stored in an airtight container in the freezer for up to 3 months. Just thaw in the fridge before icing.

If I'm just baking for two, I use two 7- or 8-inch pans. I pour the rest of the batter into a greased 12-cup muffin tin and bake at 375°F until a toothpick inserted into the center comes out clean, 20 to 30 minutes. You can store these in an airtight container at room temperature for a couple of days, or wrap each one in plastic wrap and store in a freezer-safe bag in the freezer for up to 3 months. Use the leftover canned pineapple for smoothies!

## Breakfast
Grilled Peaches with Almond Grits

Prosciutto and Egg Salad Sammie

## Appetizers
Agua Fresca Cocktail

Toasted Dukkah with Sourdough Cubes

Chermoula Lamb Lollipops

Mediterranean-Inspired Marinated Feta

## Soups and Sammies
Chicken and Lime Soup, aka Honeymoon Soup

Chicken and Yellow Zucchini Avgolemono-Style Soup

Lake Perch Fish Sammies

## Salads and Sides
Nectarine, Blue Cheese, and Little Gem Salad

Pan Bagnat Salad

German Cucumber and Fresh Pea Salad with Pea Shoots

Elote-Style Greek Fingerling Potatoes

## Mains
Buttermilk-Brined Fried Chicken

Mum's Saturday Steak Tartare with Rosemary Potato Chips

Coffee and Bourbon Baby Back Ribs

Rose Harissa Lamb Chops with Chili Fregola

## Desserts
Summer Berry and Lemon Trifle

Spiced Blueberry Skillet Pie

Black Forest Cherry and Cocoa Nib Crumble Bars

SUMMER

I may be one of the few people who has a dubious relationship with summer. It's not that I don't love all the activities or the late sunsets. I just don't work well in the heat! I still love summer and its charm, though, thanks to so many childhood memories . . .

I can still taste the excitement of the last day of grade school, participating in the school's mini Summer Olympics with ribbons and prizes, or playing euchre and signing yearbooks in high school. When school was done, we hopped on our bikes and rode off into the sunset for a few glorious months of NOTHING! Sure, there may have been work in the garden—picking beans, raspberries, tomatoes, and cucumbers—but there was also time for climbing trees and eating cherries, sitting between the currant and gooseberry bushes and snacking until the belly ached, and canning peaches with my mum.

Summer was wearing sundresses, drinking Kool-Aid, camping, going to the beach, walking barefoot all day, running under the sprinkler to cool down, sleeping under the stars when it got too hot inside, snacking on watermelon, and enjoying the annual corn roast. It was the sound of my dad cutting the grass every Saturday morning. After a wicked thunderstorm broke the humidity and hopefully made the heat more bearable, I could do my most favorite thing: find a willow tree, spread out a blanket, and read a book. While lying there, I'd gently pluck out the blades of grass until the white roots appeared and eat the tender, sweet white grass. Then, when I was older, I'd enjoy summer concerts under the stars: Queen, Harry Connick Jr., Air Supply, Manhattan Transfer, John Cougar, the Monkees, Chris de Burgh, and road trips to see Billy Joel (more than once!).

But back to the garden. My mum realized that while I didn't like a lot of cooked veggies as a kid, I'd gladly eat them raw. So she always left out a bowl of leafy spinach, cucumbers, or peppers from the backyard for us to graze on through the day. And I'd get to eat my favorite meal all summer long: thickly sliced beef-steak tomato on crusty bread spread with a very generous layer of mayo and plenty of cracked black pepper. Seriously, we all would just slice away at the ripened tomatoes and call it dinner.

These days, weekly trips to the farmers' markets mean not only feasting on those beefsteak tomatoes but also stocking up on local Niagara peaches, nectarines, and grapes. The strawberries and cherries here in Ontario are wonderful on their own and also great in salads with those tomatoes and peaches. Zucchini and summer squash can be added to pastas, fritters, and baked goods, both sweet and savory. Is there anything better than fruit or veg in season?!

◀ *Clockwise from top left: Mediterranean-Inspired Marinated Feta (page 74), Summer Berry and Lemon Trifle (page 102), Nectarine, Blue Cheese, and Little Gem Salad (page 83), Mum's Saturday Steak Tartare with Rosemary Potato Chips (page 94)*

# grilled peaches with almond grits

SERVES 2
PREP TIME 5 minutes
COOK TIME 25 minutes

When I was a kid, peaches came with a coat. A fuzzy, itchy coat. Sometimes it was so bad that my chin chafed for minutes after eating them. But it was worth enduring the fuzz for the sweet, juicy flesh inside, even if those juices were dribbling down a chafed chin! Getting the flesh off the pit was also near to impossible. You could suck on the peach pit for half an hour, but there would always be strings of peach flesh hanging on for dear life. These days, peaches are much less work, but when you find a juicy, sweet, tender one, like the ones grown in Ontario's Niagara region, it is to be treasured. This simple preparation really lets them shine. If you don't have a grill pan, use a skillet!

## Peaches

2 medium-ripe freestone peaches, rubbed clean of any stray fuzz

Olive oil, for brushing

1 Tbsp brown sugar

## Grits

1½ cups almond milk

1 Tbsp light brown sugar

½ tsp salt

½ tsp ground cardamom

1⅓–1½ cups almond meal

¼ cup Salted Bourbon Caramel Sauce (page 270)

2 Tbsp coarsely chopped hazelnuts

### For the Peaches

Preheat a grill pan or cast-iron skillet over medium heat. Run a sharp knife along each peach's seam to halve them. Cut each one in half again to create wedges. Remove the pit and brush all sides, including the skin side, with oil. Place the peaches cut side down on the grill and cook undisturbed until grill marks appear, about 2 minutes. Turn the peaches and grill the other cut side until grill marks appear, about 2 minutes. Finally, flip and grill the skin side until the skins are charred and the peaches are soft, 2 to 3 minutes more. Remove from the grill. Sprinkle the sugar over them. Set aside.

### For the Grits

In a pot over medium-high heat, bring the almond milk, sugar, salt, and cardamom to a boil. When it's boiling, add 1⅓ cups of almond meal in a stream, whisking to avoid lumps. Drop the heat to a simmer and continue to stir until it begins to thicken, about 10 to 15 minutes. If you find it too thin, feel free to add extra almond meal, 1 tablespoon at a time, to get it to the thickness you want (I like mine creamy, so I cook about 1⅓ cups of almond meal). Remove from the heat. As it cools, it will continue to absorb more liquid. If you find that it thickens up too much for your liking, just add about 1 tablespoon of almond milk to thin it out.

### To Serve

Divide the grits between two bowls and arrange the peaches on top. Drizzle with the caramel sauce and finish with the hazelnuts.

# prosciutto and egg salad sammie

MAKES 1 sammie
PREP TIME 15 minutes
COOK TIME 15 minutes

This is for my sister, Anita. When she came home after giving birth to her son, Sam, I asked what I could make her for lunch. She had a sudden hankering for an egg salad sandwich. Great. I love making and eating egg salad sandwiches. So I went about making the perfectly diced egg salad with just enough mayo filling tucked into two slices of whole wheat bread. She ate it most appreciatively. Only later did I find out that she told my brother-in-law, Carl, that she thought the sandwich wouldn't arrive until dinnertime! She had never seen anyone take so long to make a sandwich. I guess I was a little overly zealous about making sure that the eggs were uniformly diced. Lesson learned. I promise this won't take as long as the sandwich I made for Anita.

1–2 eggs

2½ Tbsp mayonnaise

Salt and pepper

⅛–¼ tsp Espelette pepper or your favorite ground pepper blend (like harissa)

2 slices prosciutto (or more, depending on their size)

2 slices rye or multigrain sourdough

2 leaves Bibb or Little Gem lettuce

Flakey finishing salt

**NOTE**
To peel an egg with ease: Crack and peel both ends of the egg. Gently peel off a line of shell from one end to the other, creating a seam. Then gently and easily peel the remaining shell away in one or two fell swoops.

Fill a small pot with no more than ½ inch of water. Cover and bring it to a boil over medium-high heat. Add the eggs, cover the pot, and cook for 8 minutes, for jammy eggs. Meanwhile, prepare a bowl with ice cubes and cold water. Transfer the eggs with a spider or slotted spoon to the ice-water bath. Let cool.

In a small bowl, combine the mayonnaise, salt, and Espelette pepper (start with ⅛ teaspoon of the Espelette). Taste and add more salt, Espelette, or black pepper if necessary.

Line a plate with paper towel. In a small pan over medium heat, sauté the prosciutto until nicely browned but not dried out, about 4 to 5 minutes. Transfer to the prepared plate.

If desired, lightly toast the bread. This helps bring it to a fresh texture, even popping it in the toaster to warm it through.

To assemble the sandwich, spread the mayo on one side of each slice of bread. Layer the lettuce and prosciutto on one slice. Peel the eggs (see Note). Roughly chop the eggs into four to eight pieces and place them on the prosciutto. Lightly smash the eggs with a fork, if desired. Depending on the size of your bread, you may have some egg left over—perfect for snacking. Season with a little flakey salt and more pepper. Set the other slice of bread on top.

# agua fresca cocktail

MAKES 1 pitcher agua
fresca, 1 agua fresca
cocktail
PREP TIME 15 minutes

When I was growing up, we had all sorts of melons in the garden. Eating them is one of my favorite summer memories. Someone would inevitably ask, "What is your favorite melon?" I was always so torn. I thought nothing could be better than really sweet watermelon, but then the cantaloupes would start ripening and I was enraptured by them, and then came the honeydew! I'm sure there are so many other melons that I haven't even discovered yet. So let me just say that I have loved every type I've tasted! This recipe is perfect for turning melons into the best summer thirst quencher: agua fresca. You can enjoy it on its own or turn it into a refreshing summer cocktail. Either way, thank you, Mexico, for this treat.

### Agua Fresca

8 cups packed seeded melon, in 1-inch cubes

⅓ cup cane sugar (see Note)

1 Tbsp lime zest

1 cup cold filtered water (approx.)

⅔ cup lime juice (about 5 or 6 limes)

¼ cup runny honey (see Note)

Ice

### Cocktail

½ cup agua fresca (see above)

2 Tbsp sparkling lemonade

1 oz (30 ml) gin

Ice

Lime wedge, for garnish (optional)

Watermelon spear, for garnish (optional)

### For the Agua Fresca

In a blender, purée the melon, sugar, lime zest, water, lime juice, and honey until smooth. You may need to do this in batches. If you find it's too thick, just add more water, about 1 tablespoon at a time, and blend again. This keeps in the fridge for up to 2 days. Just stir before serving. If you're serving the agua fresca on its own, pour the juice into a pitcher and add the ice. Otherwise, see the next step for making the cocktail.

### For the Cocktail

In a cocktail shaker, combine the agua fresca, lemonade, and gin. Serve over ice in a martini glass, a rocks glass, or even a wineglass. Garnish with a lime wedge and melon spear, if desired.

### NOTES

Feel free to adjust the sugar and honey depending on how sweet your melon is.

Agua fresca works perfectly as a cocktail base for tequila, vodka, or gin cocktails. Or try pouring about 3 tablespoons into a champagne flute and topping with sparkling wine or sparkling lemonade for a fresh brunch drink.

# toasted dukkah with sourdough cubes

MAKES about 1 cup dukkah
PREP TIME 15 minutes
COOK TIME 15 minutes

Ever since our friends who had lived in Egypt served this to us about 12 years back, it has been one of my favorite appetizers! I mean, a bowl of toasted spices, nuts and seeds, a bowl of olive oil, and a platter of bread? So simple, yet effective! Our friends explained that all we had to do was take a cube of bread and press it gently into the oil and then the dukkah blend. I still remember that first cube I popped in my mouth! The kick, the heat, the sweetness from the almonds, the play of all those spices at once . . . It was a game changer for my tongue.

¾ cup whole blanched almonds, pistachios, or hazelnuts

2 tsp ground turmeric

2 Tbsp sesame seeds

2 tsp cumin seeds

1 tsp nigella seeds

1 tsp celery seeds

1 tsp coriander seeds

4 tsp harissa powder or other chili powder

1 tsp onion flakes or onion powder

1 tsp pepper

Pinch of cayenne

½ tsp salt

⅔ cup olive oil

3–4 thick slices of sourdough or crusty bread, cubed

Preheat the oven to 350°F. Spread out the almonds on a baking sheet. Roast until they are just starting to turn golden brown and become fragrant, about 10 minutes. Let cool completely.

In a dry skillet over medium to medium-high heat, toast the turmeric and all of the seeds, giving the skillet a few shakes, until just fragrant, about 5 minutes. Let cool.

Transfer the almonds to a food processor and grind until they are small enough to cling to the oil-soaked bread. Do not grind them too fine, though, or they will release their oils. Add the ground almonds to a bowl.

Using a mortar and pestle, in batches as needed, pound the cooled seeds, harissa, onion flakes, pepper, and cayenne until combined. Add the salt. Taste and adjust the seasonings, if desired. Add to the almonds and mix to combine. You've just made dukkah.

Place about ⅔ cup of the dukkah in a dipping bowl. Pour the oil into a separate bowl. To eat, follow my friends' guide above, and wait for the party to start in your mouth.

NOTE

Store the leftover dukkah in an airtight container in the fridge for up to 3 weeks or in the freezer for up to 6 months. Just bring to room temperature before using. Dukkah also works great sprinkled on watermelon, on grilled veggies, or on olive oil–grilled bronzed flatbreads, and as a coating for chicken or fish.

# chermoula lamb lollipops

SERVES 6 as an appetizer,
4 as a main
PREP TIME 20 minutes +
marinating
COOK TIME 10 minutes

Anything named "lollipop" can't help but be delicious and fun! Being tender lamb chops, they become juicy, succulent morsels in no time. Adding the chermoula sauce, a Moroccan dipping sauce using cilantro, cumin, coriander, paprika, lemon, and chili pepper, takes it up a notch. This delicious appetizer can easily become a meal when served with Levantine-Inspired Salad (page 232) and Elote-Style Greek Fingerling Potatoes (page 89).

## Lamb Lollipops

1½ Tbsp salt

1½ Tbsp pepper

2 racks of lamb, frenched, trimmed, and cut into chops

3 cloves garlic, minced

1 Tbsp minced thyme

1 Tbsp minced rosemary

½ tsp chili flakes

¼ cup olive oil

## Chermoula Sauce

2 cloves garlic, minced

½ cup packed parsley, finely minced

½ cup packed cilantro, finely minced

½ tsp ground cumin

½ tsp ground coriander

½ tsp smoked paprika

Juice of 1 lemon

½–1 small red chili pepper, deseeded and minced

¼–½ tsp salt

2–3 Tbsp olive oil

Zest of 1 lemon, for serving

Flakey finishing salt

### For the Lamb Lollipops

Place the salt and pepper in a small, flat dish, large enough for a lamb chop to sit on comfortably, and combine. Coat the chops by gently pressing each side into the salt and pepper mixture. Place the lambs in a large freezer bag or a pan that can hold them snugly.

In a small bowl, combine the garlic, thyme, rosemary, and chili flakes. Stir in the oil. Pour the herby oil mixture over the chops, covering all sides. You can stand the chops up so that all the meat is submerged. Marinate in the fridge for at least 3 hours or overnight. Bring back to room temperature before grilling.

Preheat a large cast-iron skillet, grill pan, or grill to medium-high heat. Sear the chops, in batches if necessary, until nicely browned. For medium-rare, sear for about 2 minutes per side; for medium, add 30 seconds per side. Transfer the chops to a platter.

### For the Chermoula Sauce

In a bowl, whisk together the garlic, parsley, cilantro, cumin, coriander, paprika, and lemon juice until blended. Add half the red chili, ¼ teaspoon of salt, and 2 tablespoons of oil. Taste and add more chili and up to ¼ teaspoon more salt if desired. Add up to 1 tablespoon of oil if it is too thick. (This can be prepared a few hours in advance and stored in the fridge. Bring it to room temperature before using. It's also great on any meat or fish, or as a dipping sauce for crudités or flatbread.)

### To Serve

Sprinkle the chops with the lemon zest and finish with the flakey salt. Serve with the chermoula sauce on the side.

# mediterranean-inspired marinated feta

SERVES 6
PREP TIME 20 minutes + marinating

Feta—the perfect tangy cheese for a hot summer's day. This recipe calls for cubed feta and shallots, marinated in olive oil, chilies, mint, oregano, and lemon. For best results, ask your cheesemonger for good-quality feta that isn't too creamy or crumbly. The cubes need to hold their shape. Add the marinated feta to a mezze platter for a great casual way to entertain. *Recipe pictured on page 62*

12¼ oz–14 oz (350–400 g) feta

1 cup olive oil

2 cloves garlic, minced

2 shallots, sliced into thin rings

2 Tbsp finely diced preserved lemon, rinsed (see Note)

2 tsp minced chili peppers, deseeded

¼ cup packed finely chopped mint

2 Tbsp chopped oregano, cilantro, or parsley

Pepper

Yogurt Flatbread (page 274) or pita bread, for serving

Cut the feta into 1-inch cubes. Place them in a wide, shallow dish or container that will allow the marinade to just cover the feta.

In a bowl, combine the oil, garlic, shallots, lemons, chilies, mint, and oregano. Pour this marinade over the feta to just cover it. Cover the dish with a lid or plastic wrap. Allow the feta to marinate in the fridge for at least 2 hours or up to 1 week.

Serve the cheese in the same dish, if you like, or transfer it to a lovely shallow serving plate and drizzle a few spoonfuls of the marinade on top. Season with pepper before serving. Serve with flatbread on the side.

NOTES
You can replace the preserved lemon with the zest of 2 lemons, the juice of ½ lemon, and 1 teaspoon of salt.

For a great mezze platter, serve the feta with pita, hummus, stuffed grape leaves, grilled meats, crudités, etc.

The marinade is also amazing on its own as a dip for pita bread, as a marinade for grilled chicken or pork, or as a salad dressing (just thin it out with some more lemon juice or sherry vinegar).

# chicken and lime soup, aka honeymoon soup

SERVES 6
PREP TIME 20 minutes
COOK TIME 30 minutes

Toward the end of our honeymoon in Cancún, we first tried this soup at one of the fancier restaurants along the strip. We both loved its intense flavor and light, bright nature. So much so, we decided it was worth splurging to eat there again, just to enjoy the soup one more time. When I got home, it took me a little while, but I finally got the flavors and ingredients to work for us. It tasted like Cancún! Jim dubbed it our "Honeymoon Soup" and the name has stuck. It isn't tortilla soup, even though there is a tortilla garnish. It's more of a chicken and lime soup, a much lighter, more summery soup if you will.

### Tortilla Strips

1 cup vegetable oil

3 small corn tortillas, sliced into thin strips

1 tsp salt

½ tsp chili powder

### Lime Broth

6 cups chicken stock

½ tsp ground coriander

½ tsp ground cumin

1 Tbsp chopped cilantro

1 Tbsp chopped oregano

1 tsp red wine vinegar

2 Tbsp lime juice

¼ tsp chili powder

¼ teaspoon salt

¼ teaspoon pepper

**For the Tortilla Strips**

Line a plate with paper towel.

In a wok, or a skillet with tall sides, over medium heat, warm the oil. Working in batches, fry the tortilla strips until just golden and crisp, about 2 minutes. Using a spider or slotted spoon, transfer the strips to the prepared plate. Sprinkle the strips with the salt and chili powder. Let the oil cool, and then strain it into a jar or container. Store in a dark, dry space for one more use. Reserve the skillet, leaving any residue oil but wiping out any burnt bits.

**For the Lime Broth**

Place the stock, coriander, and cumin in a stockpot. Bring to a boil over high heat, then drop the heat to a rolling simmer, and simmer for 5 minutes. Add the cilantro and oregano. Simmer for another 5 minutes. Add the vinegar and lime juice. Season with the chili powder, salt, and pepper. Taste and adjust the seasoning if desired. Cover and set aside.

*recipe continues*

## Chicken and Vegetables

2 Tbsp olive oil

1 large (about 12 oz/340 g)
   boneless chicken breast,
   patted dry and thinly sliced

Salt and pepper

1½ tsp chili powder

1 yellow onion, sliced lengthwise
   into thin rounds

2 cloves garlic, thinly sliced

½ large green bell pepper,
   deseeded and thinly sliced
   lengthwise

2 Roma tomatoes, deseeded and
   thinly sliced

3 Tbsp chopped cilantro, for
   garnish

2 Tbsp finely diced jalapeño
   pepper, for garnish
   (optional)

Lime wedges, for garnish

## For the Chicken and Vegetables

In the reserved skillet over medium-high heat, warm the oil.
Season the chicken on both sides with salt and pepper. Add to the
skillet and sauté until browned, about 2 minutes per side. Sprinkle
with the chili powder and push the chicken to the sides of the
skillet. Place the onions and garlic in the center of the skillet and
sauté for 1 minute. Add the bell pepper and sauté for 2 minutes.
Add the tomatoes and sauté for 1 minute. Finish with a final
¼ teaspoon each of salt and pepper. Add the chicken and combine.
Remove from the heat.

## To Serve

Divide the chicken and vegetable mixture among the serving
bowls. Ladle the broth over top. Garnish with a handful of the
tortilla strips, cilantro, and jalapeño, if using. Serve with the lime
wedges on the side.

# chicken and yellow zucchini avgolemono-style soup

SERVES 4
PREP TIME 15 minutes
COOK TIME 20 minutes

Yellow is such a happy color. Since I was little, it's been right up there with green for me. This soup takes the yellow from summer squash (or yellow zucchini), lemon, and turmeric to create a light but filling soup. It kind of morphed from a fresh vegetarian soup to a chicken soup to an avgolemono-inspired soup during my experiments in the kitchen. Finishing the soup with eggs and more lemon makes it pleasantly creamy and thick. You just can't be in a bad mood when eating this soup.

1 large yellow zucchini, skin on

2 Tbsp olive oil, divided

1 small yellow onion, minced

2 cloves garlic, minced

Zest and juice of 1 lemon

2 tsp ground turmeric

1 tsp salt

½ cup basmati rice

5 cups chicken stock, divided

1 cooked chicken breast (poached, roasted or broiled), shredded

2 eggs

2 Tbsp lemon juice

Flakey finishing salt

Pepper

2 Tbsp chopped parsley, for garnish (optional)

Slice the zucchini into rounds and then finely dice them.

In a large pot over medium-high heat, warm 1 tablespoon of the oil. Add the onions and garlic, and sauté until just softened, about 5 minutes. Add the zucchini and stir. Add the remaining 1 tablespoon of oil, the lemon zest, turmeric, and salt. Stir to coat the veggies. Add the rice and stir until completely coated. Add 4 cups of the stock and then the lemon juice. Bring to a boil and then drop the heat to medium-low. Cook, uncovered, for 15 minutes, stirring occasionally to ensure the rice isn't sticking to the bottom of the pot. Meanwhile, warm the final cup of stock in a small pot over medium heat, not going past a gentle simmer.

At the 15-minute mark, check the rice to see if it's almost, but not quite, tender. It might need another couple of minutes. Once it's almost tender, add the chicken and cook until the rice and zucchini are tender, about 5 minutes. Keep warm on low heat.

In a bowl, whisk together the eggs and the 2 tablespoons of lemon juice. Add ¼ cup of the warmed stock to the egg-lemon mixture and whisk to temper the eggs. Slowly add more stock, ¼ cup at a time, until combined. Pour this into the soup and stir firmly to blend. Do not bring it to a boil or the eggs will scramble.

Remove the soup from the heat. Season to taste, starting with ½ teaspoon each of the finishing salt and pepper. This soup tastes even better slightly cooled. Serve with parsley, if desired.

# lake perch fish sammies

SERVES 4

MAKES 8 to 12 sliders

PREP TIME 1 hour + chilling

COOK TIME 20 minutes

I'm putting it out there: Lake Erie yellow perch is like the candy of the fresh fish world. So tender and practically sweet. Even people who don't like fish like lake or yellow perch. There is something of an obsession over it in Southern Ontario. But of course, you can source it elsewhere in North America. Just ask your fishmonger. Otherwise, substitute with some fresh pickerel or walleye. Serve this with french fries or chips. I have to admit, Jim and I like store-bought frozen crinkle fries—they remind us of our childhoods. So a baking sheet of freezer french fries is fine by me! For best results, make the coleslaw and tartar sauce a day ahead.

## Coleslaw

1¼ cups shredded green cabbage

1¼ cups shredded red cabbage

1 large carrot, coarsely grated

1 shallot, chopped

⅓ cup mayonnaise

1 Tbsp sour cream

1 Tbsp runny honey

1 Tbsp apple cider vinegar

½ Tbsp lemon juice

1½ tsp dry mustard powder

1½ tsp Seasoning Salt (page 264)

## Tartar Sauce

1 cup mayonnaise

⅓ cup finely diced dill pickles

1 Tbsp pickle or lemon juice

1 Tbsp capers, chopped

1 tsp dry mustard powder

1 tsp chopped dill

¼ tsp salt

¼ tsp pepper

⅛ tsp cayenne pepper (optional)

### For the Coleslaw

Place the cabbage, carrots, and shallots in a bowl. In a separate bowl, mix together the mayonnaise, sour cream, honey, vinegar, lemon juice, mustard powder, and seasoning salt. Taste the dressing and adjust to taste. Add to the slaw and mix together until everything is well combined. Transfer to an airtight container and chill in the fridge for at least 4 hours or overnight.

### For the Tartar Sauce

Place all the ingredients in a blender and blend until creamy with a bit of texture. Use a bit more pickle juice to thin it out, if desired. Transfer to an airtight container and chill in the fridge for at least 1 hour or overnight.

### For the Lake Perch Fish

Using a wok or high-sided cast-iron Dutch oven, heat 1½ to 2 inches of oil to 375°F, monitoring the temperature with a thermometer. If you don't have a thermometer, the oil will shimmer when it's ready and you can test the oil with some batter as directed on page 82. Make sure any long handles are pointed away from you. Line a baking sheet with paper towel.

*recipe continues*

**Lake Perch Fish**

Neutral oil, for frying

1 cup flour, divided

2 tsp Seasoning Salt (page 264), divided

6 oz (175 ml) local craft lager (½ bottle), divided

1 lb (450 g) lake or yellow perch fillets (see Note)

Flakey finishing salt

**For Serving**

12 slider buns

Butter

French fries or Rosemary Potato Chips (page 94) (optional)

Meanwhile, in a shallow bowl, whisk together ¼ cup of the flour and 1 teaspoon of the seasoning salt. Set aside. Place the remaining ¾ cup flour (110 g) and remaining 1 teaspoon of seasoning salt in a separate bowl. Whisk half of the beer into it until you have a batter with a thin consistency that just coats the back of a spoon. Let it rest for about 10 minutes and sip the beer while you wait! If the batter is still thick, add a bit more beer, 1 tablespoon at a time. Otherwise, you run the risk of the coating turning soggy when the fish is being fried and while it sits afterwards.

Working with one fillet at a time, dip the fish in the dry mixture, shake off any excess, and then dip into the batter. You may see some of the fish peeking through the batter, which is fine. Repeat with the other fillets.

If you don't have a thermometer, gently drop ¼ teaspoon of the batter into the oil. The batter should bubble up immediately. If not, continue to heat the oil and try again.

When you're ready to fry, working in batches, use a spider to add two or three fillets to the hot oil. Fry until the coating is a lovely golden brown, about 2 minutes on each side. Monitor the oil and keep it between 340°F and 360°F while the fish is frying. You may need to give it a few minutes to come back to temperature between batches. Drain on the prepared baking sheet, and sprinkle with salt.

**To Serve**

Slice the buns and spread them with butter. In a skillet over medium-high heat, or using the oven set to broil, lay the buns cut side down (or cut side up for the broiler), until toasted. This should only take a few minutes.

Spread some tartar sauce on the bottom bun. Add the fish, and top with 2 tablespoons of coleslaw. Cover with the top bun. Repeat. Serve with french fries, if desired.

**NOTES**

If you're using a fish other than perch, cut the fillets to just larger than your slider bun. Thicker fish, like walleye or pickerel, will take a few minutes longer to fry. It's better to have too much batter than not enough, so feel free to use the rest for more fish (sometimes I'm able to use it for up to another pound of fish!).

# nectarine, blue cheese, and little gem salad

SERVES 4 to 6 as a side,
2 as a main
PREP TIME 20 minutes +
overnight chilling
COOK TIME 10 minutes

San Francisco, one of our favorite cities, has one of the best food scenes around. It's right in the epicenter of the Farm to Table movement, you have your pick of restaurants showcasing local farms, orchards, and artisans in the most imaginative ways. One summer took us to Nopa, a groovy restaurant in the NoPa (North of Panhandle) district. Our salad was so amazing that Jim ordered a second! He asked if I could make my own localized version at home, so here it is. A true celebration of all the Niagara stone fruit, which is second to none! Feel free to use peaches, or even 2 to 3 plums or apricots per person, in place of the nectarines. Be sure to make the dressing the night before. *Recipe pictured on page 62*

## Dressing

¼ cup sour cream

¼ cup mayonnaise

3 Tbsp buttermilk

½ tsp Worcestershire sauce

½ tsp Dijon mustard

¼ tsp garlic powder

¼ tsp sugar

¼ tsp Seasoning Salt (page 264)

¼ tsp pepper

1 oz (25 g) crumbly blue cheese

2 tsp lemon juice, divided

## Salad

⅓ cup walnut halves

2–3 heads Little Gem lettuce, leaves separated (see Note)

2 just-ripe nectarines

½–¾ cup Bronx, muscat, or Thompson grapes

2 oz (50 g) blue cheese

Pepper

### For the Dressing

In a bowl, whisk together the sour cream, mayonnaise, buttermilk, Worcestershire sauce, Dijon, sugar, garlic powder, seasoning salt, and pepper. Finely crumble the cheese and stir it into the dressing. Stir in 1 teaspoon of the lemon juice. Season to taste. Cover and chill in the fridge overnight before using, to help the flavors meld. Bring back to room temperature and add the remaining 1 teaspoon of lemon juice before using.

### For the Salad

Preheat the oven to 350°F. Spread out the walnuts on a baking sheet. Roast until they are just starting to turn golden brown and become fragrant, about 10 minutes. Alternatively, toast them in a skillet over medium heat for about 5 minutes, stirring constantly. Watch closely. Let cool completely.

Arrange the lettuce on a platter. Drizzle some of the dressing over top. Slice the nectarines into 8 or 10 slices. Arrange the nectarine slices over the lettuce, followed by the grapes and then the walnuts. Crumble the marinated cheese over the fruit. Drizzle the salad with the remaining dressing. Season with a bit more pepper.

### NOTES

You can replace the Little Gem lettuce with Boston, bib, or romaine heart lettuce. Leftover dressing is great with the Buttermilk-Brined Fried Chicken (page 91), or as a dip for crudités.

# pan bagnat salad

SERVES 6
PREP TIME 20 minutes + chilling
COOK TIME 10 minutes

One of the most loved street sandwiches in the Mediterranean is a glorified tuna and veggie salad sandwich pressed in a crusty roll: the pan bagnat. It translates to "bathed bread" because of how the tuna juices and olive oil soak into the bread. Turning it into a salad is a fun way to enjoy the flavors without the bread. Every grandmère uses her own favorite veggies. This recipe uses mine (even though I'm not a grandmère!).

3–4 eggs (or as many as you want)

Dressing

½ cup olive oil

Zest and juice of 1 lemon

2 Tbsp red wine vinegar

1 tsp sugar

1 tsp Seasoning Salt (page 264)

1 tsp Dijon mustard

½ tsp chili flakes

Salad

½ bulb fennel, cored and sliced

½ bunch radishes, halved

2 mini cucumbers, halved lengthwise and sliced

¼ red onion, thinly sliced

1 stalk celery, sliced diagonally

½ cup halved cherry tomatoes

2 heads Little Gem, quartered

2 heads endive, quartered

¼ head radicchio leaves

1 (5 oz/140 g) jar Italian water-packed tuna, drained

¼ cup halved black olives

1 Tbsp capers, drained

Flakey finishing salt

Pepper

1 lemon wedge

Place a steamer basket in a pot filled with 1 inch of water. If you don't have a steamer basket, just fill the pot with ½ inch of water. Cover and bring the water to a boil over medium-high heat. Meanwhile, prepare an ice-water bath.

Add the eggs to the steamer basket or the pot in a single layer, cover, and steam for 8 minutes for jammy eggs or 10 minutes for hard-boiled. Immediately transfer to the ice-water bath to stop any residual cooking. Peel (see Note on page 67) and chill in the fridge, covered with cold water in an airtight container, until needed, up to 3 days. Quarter the eggs when you're ready to assemble the salad.

**For the Dressing**

In a small bowl, whisk together the dressing ingredients. Taste and adjust the seasonings, if desired.

**For the Salad**

In a large bowl, combine the fennel, radishes, cucumbers, onions, celery, and tomatoes. Pour 2 tablespoons of the dressing over the vegetables and gently toss to coat.

Arrange the lettuce, endive, and radicchio on a platter. Drizzle more dressing. Arrange the dressed vegetables over the greens and gently toss. Separate the tuna into large chunks. In the same bowl used for the vegetables, add the tuna, olives, capers, and about 1 tablespoon more dressing. Gently toss. Arrange the tuna mixture over the veggies. Place the eggs on top.

Finish with a final tablespoon of dressing. Sprinkle with flakey finishing salt and pepper and an extra squeeze of lemon juice.

**NOTE**
It's better not to overdress salads in general! Any remaining dressing can be stored in an airtight container in the fridge for up to 1 week.

# german cucumber and fresh pea salad with pea shoots

SERVES 4

PREP TIME 20 minutes + draining

My mum made the best salads, especially in the summer. I may have been biased, but her creamy German salads were just so delicious. I think it was the touch of sugar she added to the dressing that made them extra tasty. This is my homage to her salads of my youth. I have combined her cucumber and pea salads and added some pea shoots! Store-bought pea shoots weren't even an option back then, but they should have been. My family never even thought to raid the garden to use them for a garnish. So, let's take advantage of them now!

### Salad

1 English cucumber (see Note)

Salt

1½ cups freshly shelled peas

¼ cup pea shoots or
   microgreens, divided

### Dressing

½ cup sour cream

2 Tbsp chopped dill

1 clove garlic, minced

1–2 Tbsp white wine vinegar

1 tsp sugar

½ tsp salt

½ tsp pepper

¼ tsp Espelette pepper

### NOTE

You can replace the English cucumber with a garden cucumber, but if the skin is tough, peel it before proceeding.

### For the Salad

Cut the cucumber in half crosswise, then cut each section in half lengthwise. If the seeds are plentiful, use a spoon to scrape them out. Using a mandoline or the single slicing section of a box grater, cut or shave the cucumber into thin slices. Place these in layers in a colander set over a bowl. Evenly sprinkle each layer with ¼ teaspoon of salt. Let sit for 40 minutes to let the salt draw out the excess water from the cucumbers.

Meanwhile, in a saucepan over medium-high heat, bring well-salted water to a boil. Prepare an ice-water bath. Quickly blanch the peas in the boiling water for 10 to 20 seconds. They should be just tender but still pop in your mouth. Transfer to the prepared ice-water bath to stop the cooking. Rinse under cold running water. Transfer to a serving bowl. Add half of the pea shoots. Toss and set aside.

### For the Dressing

In a small bowl, whisk together the sour cream, dill, garlic, 1 tablespoon of the vinegar, and the seasonings. If it's too thick, add the remaining 1 tablespoon of vinegar. Season to taste. Don't be shy, as the vegetables are mild and will need some oomph.

### To Serve

Drain the cucumber slices and pat dry, removing the excess salt with the paper towel. Add the cucumbers to the peas. Pour the dressing over top and gently toss to coat. Garnish with the remaining pea shoots. Add a final crack of black and Espelette pepper.

# elote-style greek fingerling potatoes

SERVES 6
PREP TIME 15 minutes +
chilling
COOK TIME 50 minutes

Unfortunately, I can't eat corn. But I still want to enjoy all the fun and flavors of elote, grilled Mexican street corn. One night, I was grilling some Greek roasted fingerling potatoes when I realized that if I skewered these creamy, lemony potatoes and grilled them, I could pretend they were corn! And they would taste amazing with elote sauce. This may be a strange fusion, but who cares, it sure tastes great! For best results, make the Greek-inspired elote sauce earlier in the day and feel free to finish by grilling the potatoes on an indoor grill pan or even under the broiler.

### Elote Sauce

2 Tbsp mayonnaise

2 Tbsp Greek yogurt

¼ cup finely crumbled feta + more for serving

1 clove garlic, finely minced

1 Tbsp finely chopped oregano leaves

1 Tbsp finely chopped parsley leaves

1 tsp Aleppo pepper + more for serving

### Greek Potatoes

1½ lb (680 g) fingerling potatoes, skin on, halved lengthwise

1 cup chicken stock, or 1 Tbsp Faux Chicken Bouillon Powder (page 265) dissolved in 1 cup boiling water

⅓ cup olive oil

3 Tbsp lemon juice

3 cloves garlic, minced

2 tsp oregano leaves

1½ tsp salt

### For the Elote Sauce

Several hours before you plan to eat, place all the sauce ingredients in a small bowl and whisk to combine. Cover and chill in the fridge to allow the flavors to meld.

### For the Greek Potatoes

Preheat the oven to 400°F. Arrange the potatoes in a roasting pan large enough to hold them in one layer. In a bowl, combine all the remaining ingredients and pour over the potatoes. Toss to coat the potatoes. Arrange the potatoes cut side up and roast for 15 minutes. Flip the potatoes and roast for another 15 minutes. Turn them over one last time and roast for 10 minutes. They should be tender and starting to turn golden brown, and much of the liquid will have evaporated. If your potatoes are on the larger side, they may take another couple of minutes.

### For the Charred Lemon

While the potatoes are roasting, preheat the grill to 375°F.

Wash the lemon and pat it dry. Roll it back and forth on a hard surface a couple of times to release its extra juices. Cut the lemon crosswise into four even rounds removing the ends so that both sides of flesh are exposed. Remove any visible seeds. Using a silicone brush or a paper towel, brush the cut sides with a bit of olive oil. Sprinkle the cut sides with fine sea salt. Set aside until the potatoes are ready for the grill.

*recipe continues*

**Charred Lemon**

1 lemon

Olive oil, for drizzling

Fine sea salt, for sprinkling

Flakey finishing salt

**To Grill**

Transfer the potatoes to a large baking sheet to cool enough to handle. Thread them onto six metal skewers and drizzle with some of the remaining liquid from the roasting pan. Grill the potatoes until evenly crisped and starting to char, 5 minutes per side.

While you're grilling the potatoes, grill the lemons as well. Grill without moving them until one side chars evenly, about 3 minutes. Turn to char the other side, about another 3 minutes.

Transfer the skewers to a serving board and sprinkle with the flakey finishing salt. Spoon the elote sauce over the cut side of the potatoes. Sprinkle with some feta and Aleppo pepper. Serve with the charred lemon slices on the side.

# buttermilk-brined fried chicken

SERVES 4
PREP TIME 25 minutes + marinating
COOK TIME 30 minutes

I'm going to share one of my guilty pleasures with you. No judging, please. Here goes: I love KFC. I may only have it twice a year, but when I have a hankering for it, nothing else will satisfy me. It's most likely my salt craving kicking in. When I was growing up, there was always fried chicken in a big cardboard bucket when the family got together. All of us cousins emptied the bucket in mere moments. And these days, if we're all at a summer barbecue or picnic, someone can always be counted on to bring a bucket to add to the spread. This is my bones-free version . . . no bones about it, you'll love it! The brine has all the same spices as the dredging flour. Adding layers of flavor leads to optimum results.

## Brine

1 cup buttermilk

1 egg

1 Tbsp smoked sweet paprika

1 Tbsp Seasoning Salt (page 264)

1 tsp Italian seasoning

½ tsp cayenne pepper

8 boneless, skinless chicken thighs

## To Fry

Neutral oil

### For the Brine

Whisk the buttermilk, egg, paprika, seasoning salt, Italian seasoning, and cayenne in a bowl. Transfer to a large freezer bag (or lidded container) that can hold all the chicken. Seal and set aside. Slice the chicken thighs diagonally into strips about 1½ inches wide. Place the chicken in the bag and mix to coat thoroughly and evenly. Set the bag in a bowl and place in the fridge for at least 2 hours or overnight, turning occasionally to let all the meat brine evenly.

### To Prepare the Fryer

When you're ready to fry, half-fill a Dutch oven or wok with oil. Set it over medium to medium-high heat and heat the oil to 350°F. Monitor the temperature so it doesn't go higher. Make sure any long handles are pointed away from you.

Meanwhile, preheat the oven to 200°F. Place a cooling rack over a large baking sheet and set aside. Place another cooling rack over a baking sheet and put it in the oven.

*recipe continues*

## Dredge

1¾ cups flour

¼ cup cornstarch

2 tsp baking powder

1 Tbsp Seasoning Salt (page 264)

2 tsp Italian seasoning

1 tsp cayenne pepper

Flakey finishing salt

Barbecue sauce or hot sauce

## To Dredge

In a baking pan, combine the flour, cornstarch, baking powder, seasoning salt, Italian seasoning, and cayenne. Take 3 tablespoons of the buttermilk brine from the bag with the chicken and drizzle it into the flour dredge. Toss it about loosely with your fingers. This will create chunks of coating that will adhere to the chicken.

Remove the chicken pieces from the bag, letting the excess liquids drip away, transfer all the chicken to the flour and toss to coat. Using your fingers, press the coating right into the chicken to create a thick layer. Transfer the chicken pieces one by one to the cooling rack set over the baking sheet on the counter.

Once the oil has come to temperature, using tongs, take the first few pieces of chicken, shaking off any excess flour, and gently lower them into the oil (this will lower the oil temperature to about 325°F). Let them sit in the oil undisturbed for the first few minutes so the coating doesn't fall off, then cook on both sides, turning occasionally, until crunchy and golden brown and they have an internal temperature of 165°F, about 6 to 8 minutes in total. Transfer the chicken to the cooling rack over the baking sheet from the oven, immediately season generously with flakey salt, and then pop into the oven to keep warm. Repeat with the remaining chicken, working in batches and keeping the temperature of the oil at 325°F. You may have to give it a few minutes to return to temperature between batches. Reserve the oil (see Note).

Serve with your desired sauce.

### NOTE

For extra-crispy skin, the chicken can be fried earlier in the day, kept in the fridge, and reheated in the Dutch oven. Use the reserved oil and bring it to 350°F before adding the chicken. It will only take a few minutes on each side to warm through and make the skin extra crispy. Alternatively, any leftovers warm up just great in a 325°F toaster oven. I always make extra, because these pieces work great with waffles and maple syrup for brunch.

# mum's saturday steak tartare with rosemary potato chips

SERVES 4
PREP TIME 30 minutes
COOK TIME 40 minutes

Every Saturday lunch growing up was steak tartare. My mum would make an easy breezy version she had learned back in Europe. Her tartare wasn't fancy, just high-quality ground sirloin, onions, salt, pepper, and an egg yolk. I couldn't imagine anything better. This recipe is a nod to this tradition, with inspiration from a steak tartare I had in Paris. And adding homemade rosemary potato chips is just fun. It's a rustic and relaxed dish. A mandoline is your friend here. *Recipe pictured on page 62*

## Rosemary Potato Chips

4 large or 6 medium Yukon gold or yellow-flesh potatoes, skin on

1½ tsp olive oil

1 Tbsp minced rosemary

Salt and pepper

## Steak Tartare

1 Tbsp capers, drained and rinsed, + extra for garnish

1 Tbsp Dijon mustard

1 tsp Maggi or Worcestershire sauce (see Note)

2 egg yolks, as fresh as possible

1 lb (450 g) beef tenderloin, freshly ground (see Note)

2 Tbsp shallot, minced

2 Tbsp finely chopped parsley

1 Tbsp olive oil

Salt and pepper

1 tsp Tabasco sauce (optional)

### For the Rosemary Potato Chips

Preheat the oven to 400°F. Grease two baking sheets with cooking spray or oil.

Using a mandoline or a good knife, slice the potatoes into ⅛-inch-thick rounds. Place them in a bowl of cold water. When you're ready to bake, drain and pat them dry with a tea towel. Place the potatoes in a large bowl, working in batches if necessary, and toss with the olive oil, rosemary, and about ¼ teaspoon of pepper, so they are evenly coated but not too oily. Right before they go into the oven, toss with ¼ teaspoon of salt.

Lay the rounds, in a single layer and evenly spaced, on the baking sheets. Bake in the center of the oven for 10 minutes. Using a spatula, turn them over and bake for another 10 minutes. Repeat the flipping process every 10 minutes until the chips are crispy, dried, and golden around the edges, about 35 to 40 minutes. If the smaller ones are browning more quickly than the others, they can be moved to a cooling rack. Remove from the oven and immediately sprinkle with more salt to taste. Cool all the chips on a cooling rack. Set aside.

### For the Steak Tartare

In a bowl, mash together the capers, Dijon, and Maggi. Add the egg yolks and use a fork to mix everything together until a thick sauce forms. The sauce can be made earlier in the day. Just keep it in the fridge, covered, until needed.

Preheat the oven to 300°F. Return the chips to the baking sheets and reheat the chips for about 3 or so minutes before serving.

While the chips are reheating, place the beef in a nonreactive bowl. Add the Dijon-Maggi sauce, the shallots, parsley, and oil. Mash everything together with a silicone spatula. Season with salt and pepper (I use about ½ teaspoon of each, as the Maggi sauce is salty) and Tabasco, if desired. Garnish with a scattering of capers. Serve immediately with the potato chips on the side.

**NOTES**

Maggi liquid seasoning is a flavor enhancer with an intense umami flavor that home cooks throughout the world swear by (my mum was a huge fan!) because it adds instant richness to broths or stocks. Interestingly, the lovage in your garden has a similar flavor.

Please use only pasteurized eggs. Source the best, freshest beef possible the day of serving from your local butcher. Tell them you need a tender cut (tenderloin, also known as filet mignon) for tartare. They can freshly grind it for you, which is a timesaver— and that's what my mum did. If you want to do it yourself, chill the meat in the freezer for about 30 minutes before chopping. Using a very sharp chef's knife, mince the beef small enough to enjoy as a dip. Turn any leftovers into burgers or Frikadellen (page 202)!

# coffee and bourbon baby back ribs

SERVES 4
PREP TIME 40 minutes +
overnight marinating
COOK TIME 4¼ hours

I never had barbecued ribs when I was growing up. They were just not on my parents' radar. The first time I experienced sticky, messy ribs, I was totally floored. The flavor was amazing, the meat was so tender, and although it was impossible to eat them in a ladylike manner, I devoured them! Through the years I have tried all sorts of methods to achieve the most tender, fall-off-the-bone meat. I was also determined to create the perfect sauce. I took a recipe I relied on and started adding flavors to bring out the smokiness of a good barbecue, namely coffee and raw cocoa. Both have that pleasantly bitter quality needed to take the dry brine from sweet to special. Feel free to grill this outdoors all summer, or indoors under the broiler during the colder months (unless you're Canadian and you refuse to let a little thing like the weather stop you from turning on the grill!). You can make the BBQ sauce ahead of time, and you will need to dry brine the ribs overnight.

## Bourbon BBQ Sauce

1 Tbsp butter or olive oil

1 small yellow onion, finely minced

4 cloves garlic, finely minced

2 tsp cayenne pepper

2 tsp dried thyme leaves

1 cup beef broth (see Note, page 98)

1 cup ketchup

¾ cup apple cider vinegar

⅓ cup hot sauce

3 Tbsp bourbon

3 Tbsp unsulfured molasses (don't use blackstrap, you may find it too bitter)

2 Tbsp Worcestershire sauce

### For the Bourbon BBQ Sauce

In a saucepan over medium-high heat, melt the butter. Add the onions, garlic, cayenne, and thyme, and sauté, stirring occasionally, until the onions are softened, about 8 to 10 minutes. Add the broth, ketchup, vinegar, hot sauce, bourbon, molasses, and Worcestershire sauce, and bring it to a boil. Drop the heat to medium-low and simmer, uncovered, stirring occasionally, until the sauce has thickened, about 40 minutes. Let cool, transfer to an airtight container, and store in the fridge until needed (see Note, page 98).

### For the Dry Brine

In a small bowl, mix together the sugar, salt, coffee, pepper, harissa, paprika, cocoa powder, and mustard powder. Store in an airtight container at room temperature until needed (see Note, page 98).

Place the ribs on one or two large rimmed baking sheets. Rub a generous amount of dry brine mix all over them, pressing it into every nook and cranny. Cover with foil and refrigerate overnight.

*recipe continues*

## Dry Brine

1 cup packed dark brown sugar

3 Tbsp salt

2 Tbsp finely ground instant coffee or espresso (if using instant coffee, you may need to crush it into a finer grind)

1 Tbsp pepper

1 Tbsp harissa powder

1 Tbsp sweet paprika

2 tsp raw cocoa powder

2 tsp dry mustard powder

3 racks baby back ribs, silver membrane removed (see Note)

## To Cook

Preheat the oven to 275°F.

Spoon away any liquids that collected overnight on the baking sheets, and then cover the ribs with the foil again. Bake until the meat is tender but not yet falling off the bone, about 3¼ hours.

If you're grilling, around the 2¾-hour point, preheat the grill to 400°F or moderately hot. Bring the BBQ sauce out of the fridge and keep it close at hand. After 3¼ hours in the oven, grill the ribs, basting lightly with the sauce and flipping them over regularly, until you have your desired crust and the meat is fall-off-the-bone tender, about 10 to 15 minutes.

If you're broiling, take the ribs out of the oven after 3¼ hours. Turn the oven to broil and set a rack in the upper third of the oven. Brush the ribs with the BBQ sauce. Broil the ribs, flipping and brushing them regularly with the sauce, until you have your desired burnish and the meat is fall-off-the-bone tender, about 10 to 15 minutes. Keep an eye on the ribs to avoid over-charring.

Let the racks rest on a cutting board for 5 to 8 minutes. To serve, cut the ribs into smaller sections for easy handling, and serve with any extra sauce on the side for dipping or brushing.

**NOTES**

For the beef broth, you can use a bouillon cube dissolved in boiling water. Ask your butcher to remove the silver membrane from the ribs.

If you want to make just one or two racks instead of three, I'd still suggest making the entire batch of rub and sauce. You can refrigerate the unused sauce in an airtight container for up to 1 week or in the freezer for up to 6 months. The rub can be stored in an airtight container in a cool, dark spot for up to 4 months— though the freezer works great to store it even longer. This way, you are ready to go the next time you get a hankering for ribs.

# rose harissa lamb chops with chili fregola

SERVES 4
PREP TIME 15 minutes +
resting
COOK TIME 30 minutes

Jim thought he didn't like lamb until he discovered Greek cuisine here in Toronto, which has an amazing Greek food scene. Eventually he hopped on the lamb chops train, and now lamb is probably our favorite meat to grill. It sears quickly, stays nice and juicy, and has such a great flavor. Whether in the Chermoula Lamb Lollipops (page 73), traditional Greek lamb chops, or this very recipe, lamb is always a festive and rich, flavorful meat to serve friends for relaxed al fresco dining. I serve it in this recipe with a bright, lightly dressed fregola—a Middle Eastern toasted pasta that is delicious served warm or at room temperature.

## Fregola

1 cup fregola pasta, Israeli couscous, or orzo

2 Tbsp olive oil

1 Tbsp diced preserved lemon, rinsed (see Note, page 74)

1 tsp chili flakes

½ tsp cracked black pepper

¼ cup chopped mint

## Lamb Chops

8 (1-inch-thick) loin lamb chops

1½ tsp dried thyme

1½ tsp dried oregano

2 tsp rose harissa powder, divided

1 tsp salt

1 tsp cracked black pepper

1–2 Tbsp olive oil

5 Tbsp butter, divided (if using a skillet)

Lemon juice

Flakey finishing salt

### For the Fregola

Cook the fregola per the package instructions in salted boiling water. Don't remove too early or it will be too chewy. Drain and rinse under cold running water until it has cooled down and isn't sticking. Place in a bowl, drizzle with the oil, and toss to coat. Add the preserved lemon, chili flakes, and pepper and toss to coat. Add the mint and toss again. Season to taste.

### For the Lamb Chops

Pat the lamb chops dry and place them on a large plate. In a small bowl, mix together all the herbs and spices. Rub this mixture on all sides of the lamb chops. Let them rest while you do the next step.

Preheat a large cast-iron skillet over medium-high heat or an outdoor grill to 375°F to 400°F for at least 15 minutes before grilling.

If you're using a skillet, add 1 tablespoon of oil and the butter and swirl to coat the bottom. If you're using an outdoor grill, brush it with 2 tablespoons of oil.

*recipe continues*

Labneh Tzatziki (page 266), for
serving

Levantine-Inspired Salad
(page 232), for serving

If you're using a skillet, add the chops and cook on one side until browned, 3 to 4 minutes. Flip and cook until an instant read thermometer shows an internal temperature of 125°F for medium-rare chops or 130°F for medium, another 3 to 4 minutes depending on the thickness of the chops. If your chops are thicker and you want to cook them longer, reduce the heat to low, and add 4 tablespoons of butter. Let it melt around the chops, continuously spooning the melted butter over the chops until they reach your desired doneness.

If you are using a grill, grill the chops for 4 to 5 minutes on each side, or until desired temperature is achieved.

Transfer the chops to a platter and tent with foil. Let them rest for 10 minutes to let the juices settle. Drizzle with lemon juice and sprinkle with salt and the remaining rose harissa.

To Serve

Divide the fregola among the plates and place the lamb chops on top. Serve with labneh tzatziki and salad on the side.

NOTES

To add extra flavor to the fregola, add 1 tablespoon of the Faux Chicken Bouillon Powder (page 265) to the water the pasta is boiled in. The fregola can be made up to 1 day in advance. To reheat, transfer the fregola to a greased saucepan and place over medium-low heat until warmed through. Add a fresh squeeze of lemon before serving.

If you don't have preserved lemon, use the zest of a large lemon and ¼ teaspoon salt.

# summer berry and lemon trifle

SERVES 12
PREP TIME 45 minutes +
chilling

This is pure summer in a bowl, the perfect easy showpiece for your next picnic, shower, or barbecue. The components can all be made in advance and stored in the fridge until it's time to assemble (see Note). If you only have six people to feed instead of twelve? Easy, just divide everything in half and use parfait glasses or fun small bowls. Don't feel obliged to use the limoncello—but then again, my parents never thought to hold back dessert from us just because there was liquor in it. And look how we turned out . . . Well, maybe don't look too hard! *Recipe pictured on page 62*

1 Lemon Blueberry Basil Yogurt Pound Loaf (page 259), cooled but not glazed

2 cups heavy cream

¼ cup icing sugar

1 tsp vanilla paste or extract, divided

1 (8 oz/250 g) package cream cheese, softened and cubed

1 cup Lemony Lemon Curd (page 268)

2 tsp lemon zest

5–6 cups mixed berries (blueberries, raspberries, strawberries, halved or quartered if large) (see Note)

6 Tbsp limoncello or lemon simple syrup (page 55), divided (optional)

5–6 Pistachio, Apricot, and Dark Chocolate Forgotten Meringues, crushed (page 252)

Slice the cooled cake into 1-inch slices and then cut each slice into bite-size cubes. Transfer to a bowl and set aside.

In a stand mixer fitted with the whisk attachment, or in a large bowl with a handheld mixer, whip the cream on low speed for 1 minute. With the mixer running, slowly add the sugar and ½ teaspoon of the vanilla. Increase the speed to high and whip until stiff peaks form. Store the whipped cream in the fridge while you prepare the rest of the dish.

Clean the mixer and bowl and use the paddle attachment to beat the cream cheese until it's soft and creamy (or you can use your handheld mixer again). Add the lemon curd, lemon zest, and remaining ½ teaspoon vanilla and beat until combined. Fold half of the chilled whipped cream into the cream cheese mixture. Store this in the fridge, uncovered, until 20 to 30 minutes before you're ready to assemble the trifle, just to make sure it's soft enough.

Reserve about ¾ cup of the mixed berries for garnish. To assemble the trifle, in a trifle bowl or large glass mixing bowl, add one-third of the cake cubes. Drizzle with about 2 tablespoons of the limoncello (if using). Top with one-third of the berries and then half of the lemon cheese mixture. Sprinkle one-third of the crushed cookies over the lemon cheese layer. Repeat with half of the remaining cake cubes, 2 tablespoons of the limoncello, half of the remaining berries, the remaining lemon cheese, and half of the remaining crushed cookies.

Top with the remaining cake cubes, limoncello, crushed cookies, and berries. Finish with the plain whipped cream, creating lovely mounds.

Chill the trifle in the fridge for at least 2 hours, and up to 8 hours if you want the flavors to meld even better. If you're chilling it for longer than 4 hours, omit the final layer of cookie crumbs and berries, omit the whipped cream topping, and cover lightly with plastic wrap. When you're ready to serve, finish the layers as instructed and garnish with the reserved berries.

NOTES

You can prepare the cake and whipped cream a day or so before you plan to assemble the trifle. The lemon cheese can be made a day ahead, but no earlier, otherwise it will separate by the time you serve.

Feel free to swap out the fruit with currants or gooseberries, or sliced in-season stone fruit in season.

# spiced blueberry skillet pie

MAKES one 9-inch pie
PREP TIME 45 minutes +
chilling + resting
COOK TIME 1 hour

During the summer, Jim says that if I only make blueberry pie he'd be fine. But then he says the same thing about apple pie when autumn rolls around! I understand, so both pies are on regular rotation in their peak seasons. I think what we both love about a good blueberry pie is its intense, dramatic, and jammy blueberry (or, as we call it, blooby-ness) filling. But sometimes a simple blueberry pie can be rather one-noted: sweet but a tad flat. Enter spices. Nutmeg, allspice, cinnamon, and urfa biber take blueberries to a new place thanks to their smoky, savory, and earthy nature. Now we have some depth in our pie! I make this in a 9-inch cast-iron skillet, but if you don't have one, feel free to use a traditional pie plate.

5 cups (750 g) blueberries

Zest and juice of 1 lemon

⅔–1 cup (150–225 g) sugar, depending on how sweet the berries are

¼ cup (35 g) arrowroot starch

2 tsp ground cinnamon

1 tsp urfa biber

½ tsp ground allspice

¼ tsp ground nutmeg

5–6 dashes Angostura bitters

1 recipe No-Fail Pie Pastry (page 277) (replace ¾ cup of all-purpose with rye flour), divided into 2 disks and chilled

2 Tbsp ground almonds

2 Tbsp butter

1 egg, whisked with a bit of water

2 tsp turbinado sugar

In a large bowl, combine the berries, lemon zest, and 1 tablespoon of lemon juice. In a small bowl, combine the sugar (start with ⅔ cup and taste as you go along), arrowroot starch, and the dry spices. Add the dry mixture to the berries and gently toss to combine. Shake the bitters over the berry mixture. Let rest at room temperature for about 15 minutes. Meanwhile, bring the first disk of dough to room temperature for 10 minutes.

Spray the bottom of a 9-inch cast-iron skillet with nonstick cooking spray or use a paper towel to rub the bottom with a thin layer of oil. (If you're using a pie plate, there's no need to grease it.) Roll out the first disk of dough (see page 277) to a circle about 12 inches in diameter (it should hang over the edges of the skillet) and transfer to the skillet. Let the sides ease down into the pan so that it won't shrink when baking. Trim the edges, leaving a good inch of pastry hanging over the edge.

Bring the second disk of dough to room temperature for 10 minutes.

Meanwhile, evenly cover the bottom of the pie shell with the ground almonds. Add the blueberry filling, packing it down gently to create an even top. Break the butter into small pieces. Dot the surface of the filling with the butter. Place the filled pie in the fridge while you work with the second disk of dough.

*recipe continues*

Roll out the second disk of dough and prepare a top crust or lattice, and/or cookie cutouts as desired (pages 278 to 279 and see Note). Top the pie with the pastry and decorate and crimp as desired. Return the pie to the fridge while the oven comes to temperature.

Place one oven rack in the bottom third of the oven and one in the middle. Preheat the oven to 400°F and keep it on for 30 minutes.

Remove the skillet from the fridge and brush the pastry with the egg wash. Sprinkle the turbinado sugar over top. Place the skillet on a baking sheet and bake the pie in the lower third of the oven until the crust is starting to turn golden, about 25 minutes. Drop the heat to 375°F and bake the pie on the center rack until the juices are bubbling all over and the crust is a lovely golden brown, about 30 to 35 minutes. If the crust is browning too quickly, lightly drape some foil over it, or use a pie crust guard if the edges are the only parts that are browning too quickly.

Let the pie rest at room temperature for at least 4 hours, but preferably overnight to guarantee that the filling has settled and set correctly. Never bake a fruit pie thinking you will eat it an hour later!

NOTE
For the pie in the photo, I made life easy for myself. I folded the excess pastry from the sides back over the fruit filling, rather like a galette. Then I used the remaining disk to create cutouts and a lattice to decorate the top. I used the cutout leaves to hide the seam where the sides and the lattice met.

# black forest cherry and cocoa nib crumble bars

MAKES 12 to 16 bars
PREP TIME 30 minutes
COOK TIME 1 hour

When I was little, I'd climb the cherry tree and gorge on its fruit till my stomach ached. I was totally enthralled by cherries. I'd turn them into pretend earrings, and I obsessed over the cherry-red wool twin set that Nan from the Bobbsey Twins books received as a present. Today, I have to buy twice as many as I think I need, to account for snacking. Sweet dark-red cherries are the best, from the slight crunch into the skin to the indulgence of the juicy interior. Pitting cherries turns the kitchen counter into a crime scene, but it's worth it! These bars are a twist on a classic shortbread crust with crumble topping. The kirsch and chocolate are a nod to a Black Forest torte. The cocoa nibs add crunch and cut through the sweetness perfectly. Sliced up, these make a great picnic treat. You can also add the traditional whipped cream topping—just add one more cherry on top!

## Cherry Filling

5 cups (700 g) cherries, pitted and halved

1 Tbsp lemon juice

¼ cup + 3 Tbsp (70 g) flour

1 Tbsp raw cocoa powder

2 tsp arrowroot starch

1 cup sugar

¼ tsp salt

1 tsp vanilla paste or extract

1 tsp kirsch liqueur

2½ oz (70 g) finely chopped 85% dark chocolate

2 tsp cocoa nibs

### For the Cherry Filling

Preheat the oven to 375°F. Spray a 9- × 13-inch baking pan with cooking spray and line it with a large sheet of parchment paper, making sure the parchment hangs over the sides.

Place the cherries and lemon juice in a large bowl and gently toss to combine. In a separate bowl, whisk together the flour, cocoa powder, and arrowroot starch. Add the sugar, salt, vanilla, and kirsch, and mix to combine. Pour this mixture over the cherries and stir with a wooden spoon to combine. Fold in the chocolate and cocoa nibs and set aside at room temperature.

### For the Crust and Streusel Topping

In a large bowl, whisk together the flour, granulated sugar, cocoa powder, baking powder, and salt. Cut the butter into cubes. Add the cubed butter to the flour and use a pastry blender to mix until coarse crumbs, with a variety of sizes of crumbly bits, have formed.

*recipe continues*

## Crust and Streusel Topping

3 cups (450 g) flour

1 cup (225 g) granulated sugar

2 Tbsp raw cocoa powder

1 tsp baking powder

¼ tsp salt

1 cup (220 g) butter, chilled

1 egg

1 tsp vanilla paste or extract

1 tsp kirsch liqueur

¼ cup (60 g) turbinado sugar

In a small bowl, whisk together the egg, vanilla, and kirsch. Add to the flour and butter mixture and gently combine. The mixture should be crumbly, yet hold together if you press it between your fingers. Transfer half of the crust mixture to the prepared baking pan and pat down firmly to create an even crust. Spread the cherry mixture evenly over top. Crumble the remaining crust ingredients over the cherry layer for your streusel topping. Use your hands to gently pat the streusel into the cherry layer. Sprinkle the turbinado sugar over the streusel topping.

Place the baking pan on a baking sheet and bake until the top is golden brown and cherry juices start to bubble up, about 55 minutes to 1 hour. Let cool completely on a cooling rack before cutting into bars. You can leave the bars in the pan for easy travel if you're taking this to a potluck or picnic, for example.

## Breakfast
Eggs Benedict Hash Bowls
Pumpkin, Beemster, and Sage Spelt Muffins
Crème de Marrons and Chocolate Bostock

## Appetizers
Autumn Sangria
Savory Harvest Pear Tart
Brie en Croute with Serrano Ham, Fig, and Hazelnuts

## Soups and Sammies
Cream of Aleppo Roasted Tomato Soup with Welsh Rarebit Tartines
Gerrard Street Mulligatawny Soup with Spiced Apple Croutons
Hot Turkey Sandwich with Cranberry Sauce and "Stuffin"

## Salads and Sides
Italian Sausage Sourdough "Stuffins"
Forelle Pear and Kohlrabi Salad with Gorgonzola and Pecans
Cinnamon Root Veg and Apple Purée
Spinach Spätzle with Sautéed Onions and Gruyère
Harissa Hasselback Scalloped Potatoes

## Mains
Two-Hour Roasted Turkey with Cider Sage Gravy and Cranberry Sauce
High Park Autumn Perogies
Eritrean Zigni
Pappardelle with Fennel and Italian Sausage Bolognese and Ricotta
Anniversary Chèvre-Stuffed Chicken Breasts

## Desserts
Salted Caramel Apple Strudel
Baked Apple Presents
Double-Ginger Pear Pie

AUTUMN

With the first chill in late August, I know my favorite time of the year is soon to follow: autumn, that dreamy, magical season that never seems long enough, can make my imagination wander.

"Life starts all over again when it gets crisp in the fall," wrote F. Scott Fitzgerald, and these words truly sing to me. Any energy that the lethargic heat of summer melts away gets kicked back into action. Maybe because it reminds me of back to school! I have the most vivid memories of back-to-school shopping and getting excited by new colored pencils, plaid skirts, wooly sweaters, and knee socks that matched my turtlenecks. Yes, I was a geek, but I owned it!

There's also a desire to capture all of autumn's rich colors, which envelop us with big fuzzy bear hugs. The carpets of gold as the sunburnt leaves cover the late-summer grasses. The moody foggy mornings, bright bluer-than-blue midday skies, and early setting suns that turn the skies a fiery red. Windy swirls of brown and red leaves lead us down the sidewalks, giving us all a crisp and crunchy soundtrack. Walks to school meant looking for aspen, sugar maple, and oak leaves to bring home and press between the pages of encyclopedias. Wool plaid blankets, tweedy yarns, jarred plum butter, burnt orange pumpkins, and bushel baskets of red apples still make me giddy. Yes, my favorite color is October.

Every year, the extended family would go apple picking at the apple orchards in Southwestern Ontario. The hay bale mazes, caramel apples, barrels of cider, wagon rides, and feeding the goats and sheep all made for the perfect day. We would come home with bushels of apples for baking apple pies. Some of us were assigned pastry duty, others peeling and slicing, and another group would fill the pie shells. We all went home with plenty of pies for the freezer.

Jim and I love traveling at this time of year. Every city looks beautiful dressed in autumn. We enjoy exploring winding lanes, austere castles, bustling cafés, and intriguing museums without the heat or summer crowds. We often stop for steaming cups of apple cider or hot chocolate, and look forward to soul-soothing meals. Speaking of meals, in autumn we are in the mood to braise, roast, and bake at home, making a turkey dinner (page 141), soups (page 125), or pie (page 159). Longer days in the kitchen, with jazz tunes wafting around to add to the ambience, even if it's stormy outside.

There is a simple honesty to autumn. The birds fly south with their honking "See you soon" farewells. The trees slowly change to gray as their final leaves are released. Yes, winter is coming, but it's because the land needs a good sleep so it can put on a show next year. So light a candle, cozy up with a blanket, and savor that slice of Salted Caramel Apple Strudel (page 154), whose aroma is second to none. Soak up all of autumn. It will keep you warm during winter.

◄ *Clockwise from top left: Salted Caramel Apple Strudel (page 154),*
*Pumpkin, Beemster, and Sage Spelt Muffins (page 117),*
*Savory Harvest Pear Tart (page 121),*
*Harissa Hasselback Scalloped Potatoes (page 140)*

# eggs benedict hash bowls

SERVES 4
PREP TIME 30 minutes
COOK TIME 45 minutes

I don't know about you, but if eggs Benedict is on the menu, I'm almost guaranteed to be ordering it. It's one of those dishes where the whole is greater than the sum of the parts. The English muffin soaks up the gooey egg yolk and the tangy hollandaise sauce, and the peameal bacon adds a wonderful, earthy saltiness. Since Jim loves a good spicy potato hash, I add it to a bowl in place of the English muffin and top it with the poached egg and hollandaise. Credit where credit is due: the hollandaise in this recipe is inspired by Helen Rennie's flavorful recipe, which, bonus, doesn't separate ever!

## Hollandaise Sauce

2 shallots, thinly sliced

½ cup dry white wine

½ cup butter, cubed

½ tsp lemon juice

2 egg yolks

Salt and white pepper

Cayenne pepper

2 tsp chopped dill or chives (optional)

### For the Hollandaise Sauce

Cook the sliced shallots and wine in a small saucepan over high heat until the liquid has reduced by half, about 5 minutes. Remove from the heat and use a slotted spoon or tea strainer to remove the cooked shallots. Reserve the reduced wine in the pot. There should be 3 tablespoons of liquid. If not, add water to make up the balance.

Add the butter to the reserved cooking liquid and cook over medium-high heat until the butter has almost melted. Drop the heat to medium-low, add the lemon juice, and whisk briskly to blend the fats and water. Add the yolks, one at a time, whisking between additions, until thickened, about 2 minutes. If it thickens too quickly, the eggs may start to scramble, so watch the heat and remove the pot from the heat if necessary. If it isn't thickening, increase the heat a bit.

Season with about ¼ teaspoon each of salt and pepper and a pinch of cayenne. Taste and adjust the seasoning as desired. I usually add a bit more lemon juice. Add the dill, if desired. Store in a thermos or insulated travel mug, or pour into a glass jar with a lid, close, and sit it in a bowl of warm water to keep the sauce warm while you prepare the hash.

*recipe continues*

### Hash

2 Tbsp olive oil, divided

8 oz (225 g) peameal (Canadian) or regular bacon, diced

1½ lb (680 g) Yukon gold or yellow-flesh potatoes, cut into ¾-inch chunks

½ tsp garlic powder

½ tsp onion powder

¼ tsp paprika

½ tsp salt

¼ tsp pepper

⅓ cup chopped scallions or chives

4½ oz (125 g) baby spinach, long stems removed

### Poached Eggs

1 Tbsp white wine vinegar or apple cider vinegar

4 eggs

2 Tbsp chopped chives, to garnish

Side salad or fruit, for serving (optional)

### NOTE

The bacon and the seasoned potatoes can be prepared the day before and stored in an air-tight container in the fridge. Just bring them back up to room temperature before sautéing with the onions and spinach and continuing the recipe as directed. If you don't want poached eggs, just fry some sunny-side up!

### For the Hash

In a large skillet over medium heat, warm 1 tablespoon of the oil. Add the bacon and cook until just golden, about 2 minutes per side. Transfer the bacon to a plate, reserving the fat. Return the skillet to medium heat and add the remaining 1 tablespoon of oil. Once the oil is hot, add the potatoes in a single layer. Cook without stirring until they start to turn golden, about 4 to 5 minutes, then flip them with a spatula. They should release easily. Continue frying, stirring occasionally, until they are crispy and cooked through, about 10 minutes. Add more oil if looks like they're at risk of sticking, and drop the heat if they're browning too quickly. In the final minute or so of cooking, sprinkle with the garlic powder, onion powder, paprika, salt, and pepper, and combine.

Stir in the bacon and any of the juices that collected on the plate, the scallions, and spinach until combined. Season with more salt and pepper. Cover partially with a lid and keep warm over low heat while you poach the eggs.

### For the Poached Eggs

Half-fill a large saucepan with water. Bring it to a boil, then drop the heat to a gentle simmer. Add the vinegar.

Crack 1 egg into a tea strainer placed over a small bowl or cup. Let it sit for about 15 seconds to strain off any loose bits of egg white.

Once the water is simmering, use a wooden spoon to stir it vigorously around the outer edge in a circle. When you have a good spin going, gently submerge the edge of the tea strainer into the center of the vortex and tip the egg into the water. The spinning water will wrap the egg white around the yolk. Let it simmer until the egg whites have solidified and the yolk is cooked to your liking, about 2 minutes, depending on the heat of the water and how firm you like your eggs. Using a slotted spoon, remove the egg and place it on a paper towel–lined plate. Bring the water back to a gentle simmer if need be and repeat, one at a time, with the remaining eggs.

### To Assemble

Divide the hash among the bowls and place a poached egg on top of each. Drizzle with hollandaise sauce and sprinkle with chives. Serve with a side salad or fruit, if desired.

# pumpkin, beemster, and sage spelt muffins

MAKES 12 muffins
PREP TIME 20 minutes
COOK TIME 25 minutes

A ren't grab-and-go breakfasts the best?! Having a batch of these irresistible muffins ready for the week solves the morning belly growls for those rushed days. All the perfectly paired ingredients just sing autumn, and the harissa and cayenne bring warmth and a slight kick. These are best eaten slightly warm, but if you're going on a hike, bike ride, or even a wander through a hay bale maze, they'll still taste fabulous when cool. *Recipe pictured on page 112*

1 cup (150 g) all-purpose flour

1 cup + 1 Tbsp (130 g) spelt flour

6 Tbsp old-fashioned oats, divided

1 Tbsp light brown sugar

2 tsp baking powder

¾ tsp salt

¼ tsp baking soda

1½ Tbsp chopped sage

½ Tbsp finely chopped rosemary

½–¾ tsp harissa powder

4 Tbsp (55 g) butter

2 Tbsp buckwheat honey

1¼ cups (300 g) puréed pumpkin (not pumpkin pie filling)

½ cup skyr

2 eggs

1 Tbsp Dijon mustard

6 Tbsp (75 g) grated Beemster, divided (or substitute Gouda, Jarlsberg, or medium Cheddar)

6 Tbsp (75 g) grated Gruyère, divided

1 Tbsp poppy seeds

Preheat the oven to 375°F. Line a 12-cup muffin tin with liners.

In a large bowl, mix together the flours, 3 tablespoons of the oats, the sugar, baking powder, salt, and baking soda. Add the sage, rosemary, and ½ teaspoon of the harissa and mix to combine.

In a small pot over medium-low heat, melt the butter and honey. As soon as it has melted, remove it from the heat. In a medium bowl, combine the pumpkin, skyr, eggs, and Dijon. Stir in the butter-honey mixture. Add 3 tablespoons of each cheese and stir to combine.

Make a well in the dry ingredients and add the wet ingredients to it. Use a wooden spoon to combine, being careful not to overmix (some exposed flour is fine). Divide the batter equally among the prepared muffin liners. Combine the remaining 3 tablespoons of rolled oats, the remaining 3 tablespoons of each cheese, and the poppy seeds, and sprinkle on top of the muffins, gently patting the muffin batter so they adhere.

Bake on the center rack of the oven until the muffins are golden brown and a skewer inserted in the center of one comes out relatively clean (a bit of cheese is fine), 20 to 25 minutes. Cool slightly in the pan on a cooling rack.

NOTE
You can store these in an airtight container at room temperature for a couple of days, or wrap each in plastic wrap and store in a freezer-safe bag in the freezer for up to 2 months. Thaw in the fridge overnight and warm in a 300°F oven for 5 to 10 minutes.

# crème de marrons and chocolate bostock

SERVES 4
PREP TIME 20 minutes
COOK TIME 25 minutes

Think of this little "pastry" as a cross between French toast and an almond croissant. You can easily make these with store-bought brioche or challah. But it's also the perfect use for those few stale slices of homemade loaf sitting around. The slices are brushed with a simple syrup or a thinned-out jam or jelly. Topped with a layer of chestnut spread, chocolate, and sliced almonds, this bakes until the frangipane puffs up and the nuts are golden brown. Add a mug of steaming café au lait, and you have a perfect brunch.

**Simple Syrup**

⅓ cup sugar

5–6 dashes chocolate bitters

**Frangipane**

½ cup sugar

2 Tbsp softened butter

1 egg, at room temperature

3 Tbsp flour

⅔ cup ground almonds or almond meal

¼ tsp salt

3 Tbsp crème de marrons (sweetened chestnut spread—not unsweetened chestnut purée!)

**Bostock**

4–8 slices thick-cut, day-old, slightly stale brioche

¼ cup shaved dark chocolate

½ cup sliced almonds

Icing sugar, for dusting (optional)

### For the Simple Syrup

In a small saucepan, combine the sugar with ⅓ cup water. Bring to a boil, without stirring, over medium heat, drop the heat to low, and cook until the sugar mixture has completely melted, about 5 minutes. Remove from the heat and stir in the chocolate bitters. Let cool.

### For the Frangipane

Using a bowl and a wooden spoon or handheld mixer, mix the sugar and butter until combined, creamy, and almost fluffy. Add the egg and continue to mix thoroughly until smooth. Add the flour and almonds and mix to combine. Add the salt and then the crème de marrons, and mix until totally creamy. (This can be made the night before and stored in an airtight container in the fridge. Just bring it back to room temperature and stir before using.)

### For the Bostock

Preheat the oven to 400°F. Using a pastry brush, spread half of the simple syrup over one side of each slice of brioche. Turn each slice over and spread with the remaining syrup. Using an offset spatula, spread about a ¼-inch layer of the frangipane over the top of the bread, going right to the edges. Evenly sprinkle the chocolate shavings over top and scatter the sliced almonds over the chocolate.

Lay the brioche on a baking sheet and bake on the center rack of the oven until golden brown and crisp on the outside, 15 to 20 minutes. The nuts should be fragrant and burnished, but not scorched. Let cool for 5 minutes before dusting with icing sugar, if desired. Enjoy!

**NOTE**
Ensure that the bread has dried
by spreading the slices out on a
lined baking sheet and
letting them sit for
a few minutes.

# autumn sangria

MAKES 1 pitcher
PREP TIME 15 minutes +
overnight chilling

This is the best way to enjoy all the goodness of autumn in a glass. Don't make this an hour before company comes and expect it to taste good. It won't. Let the autumn fruits hang out together in the fridge overnight, giving them the time they deserve to sweeten the wine and liquors. The symbiosis of the fruit and liquor shines the next day, creating a balanced sangria. The fruit sugars will gently sweeten the liquids, and the fruit will become appropriately soaked. Rosemary adds just enough of an herby savoriness to remind us that it is autumn. The added treat is that you get to snack on the fruit afterwards. Serve this with the Brie en Croute with Serrano Ham, Fig, and Hazelnuts (page 123) or the Savory Harvest Pear Tart (page 121) for a wonderful way to entertain good friends.
*Recipe pictured on page 122*

1 Honeycrisp or Gala apple

1 red pear

2 red or blue plums

½ cup blackberries

3 sprigs rosemary

4 oz brandy

2 oz triple sec (Cointreau works well)

1 (25 oz) bottle rioja, merlot, or malbec

2 cups sparkling water

½–1 cup tonic water

Ice

The day before you plan to serve this, cut the apple and pear into thin slices. Place them in a large pitcher. Pit and thinly slice the plums and add them to the pitcher. Add the blackberries and rosemary.

Add the brandy, triple sec, and wine. Stir everything together. Cover with plastic wrap and chill in the fridge overnight. This will get the fruit to flavor the wine and vice versa, creating a balanced blend of flavors.

The next day, when you are ready to serve, stir in the sparkling water and ½ cup of the tonic water. Taste and add more tonic as needed. To serve, fill your glasses with ice and then use a ladle to add some of the wine and liquor-soaked fruit to each glass.

# savory harvest pear tart

SERVES 6 to 8 as an appetizer
PREP TIME 25 minutes
COOK TIME 20 minutes

This savory tart has some sweet overtones in more ways than one! It's a perfect first course or appetizer. Ripe (but not too ripe) Bosc or red-skinned pears will withstand the heat and maintain their shape while poaching and baking. Combining the sweet pears with the herbs, mustard, and cheeses creates the best sweet-savory matchup.
*Recipe pictured on page 112*

2 large red or Bosc pears, halved, cored, and cut into ¼-inch-thick slices

1 cup pear nectar (see Note)

1 Tbsp thyme leaves

½ (1 lb/450 g) package puff pastry, thawed (1 sheet)

1 egg

1 Tbsp milk

2 tsp sesame seeds

2 Tbsp Dijon mustard

¾ cup grated Gouda or Jarlsberg, divided

¾ cup grated medium Cheddar, divided

Pepper

2 sprigs thyme, leaves only

Place a rack in the bottom third of the oven. Preheat the oven to 375°F.

In a skillet over medium heat, simmer the pear slices in the pear nectar until just softened but still with some bite, about 3 minutes. Using a slotted spoon, transfer the pears to a large bowl. Increase the heat to medium-high and cook the nectar until it's reduced to 2 tablespoons and is thick and syrupy, about 4 to 5 minutes. Pour the nectar over the pear slices. Add the thyme leaves and gently toss to combine.

Unroll the puff pastry on the parchment sheet it came in and place it (parchment and all) on a baking sheet. It should be roughly 10 × 11 inches. Using the tip of a sharp knife, score the pastry, careful not to cut all the way through, around the four edges to create a ½-inch-wide frame.

In a small bowl, whisk together the egg and milk. Brush this egg wash over the outside edges of the pastry. Carefully sprinkle the washed edges with the sesame seeds.

Spread a thin, even layer of the Dijon over the surface of the pastry, right up to the score marks. Evenly sprinkle ½ cup of the Gouda and ½ cup of the Cheddar over the Dijon. Top the cheese with the sliced pears, layering them to fit and leaving a 1-inch-wide border on all sides. Sprinkle the remaining cheeses over top, avoiding the border.

Bake in the bottom third of the oven until the cheeses are bubbling and the edges are crisp and browned, about 20 minutes. Season with pepper and thyme. Rest for 3 minutes. Cut into 6 to 8 slices.

**NOTE**
Nectar is thicker than pear juice and has a more intense flavor. Find it in the juice or European aisle of your grocery store.

# brie en croute with serrano ham, fig, and hazelnuts

SERVES 6 to 8

PREP TIME 20 minutes

COOK TIME 25 minutes

Camembert is the cheese I remember the most from my childhood. I had a love-hate relationship with strong cheeses. My little palate hadn't yet developed an appreciation for their pungency. So, when our parents first brought Brie home, my sister and I inhaled it in mere moments. These days I keep both cheeses in the fridge. This recipe wraps the melty goodness of Brie and a dash of salt and sweet from the Serrano ham, luscious fig preserves, and crunchy hazelnuts in the best fragrant gooey mess! And yes, you can easily use Camembert for this recipe as well.

3 Tbsp hazelnuts

1 (1 lb/450 g) package puff pastry, thawed (2 sheets)

8–9 thin slices Serrano ham or prosciutto

1 (7- to 9-inch) wheel of Brie

3 Tbsp fig preserves

2 Tbsp chopped rosemary

1 tsp pepper

1 egg, whisked with a bit of water

Crusty bread, crackers, and grapes or sliced plums, apples, or pears, for serving

Preheat the oven to 425°F. In a skillet over medium heat, toast the hazelnuts until they are just starting to brown and smell fragrant, about 5 minutes. Keep an eye on them, as they can turn from brown to burnt in the blink of an eye. Let cool slightly and roughly chop. Set aside.

Roll out one sheet of the puff pastry to create about a 12-inch square. Place it on a parchment paper–lined baking sheet. Line the surface of the pastry with the ham. Place the wheel of Brie in the center and fold the ham slices up and around the Brie to envelope it. Spoon the fig preserves on top. Sprinkle the toasted hazelnuts, rosemary, and pepper over the preserves.

Roll out the other sheet of pastry to a 12-inch square. Quickly brush the exposed pastry that the Brie is sitting on with water. Carefully place the second sheet of pastry directly over the Brie, letting it fall around the sides. Gently press the sides down into the first sheet of pastry, then along the bottom to seal in the Brie. Trim away the excess, leaving a 1-inch border on all sides. Reserve the excess pastry. Crimp the border with a fork. Brush the pastry's surface with the egg wash.

If desired, roll out the excess pastry and make some pastry cutouts (see page 279), such as rustic leaves. Adhere these to the center of the pastry with a bit of water. Brush with the egg wash.

Bake until the pastry is puffed and golden brown, 22 to 25 minutes. Let it sit for about 5 minutes before slicing. Serve with a knife, crusty bread, crackers, and fresh fruit.

# cream of aleppo roasted tomato soup with welsh rarebit tartines

SERVES 4
PREP TIME 20 minutes
COOK TIME 1 hour,
20 minutes

Tomato soup and grilled cheese sandwiches, the quintessential meal of childhood. Who are we kidding? We still love this meal! But how do you make it fresh and unexpected? Enter Aleppo pepper, for a bit of fruity heat, and Welsh rarebit because it takes melted gooey cheese to the next level. I first had rarebit, a creamy, cheesy tartine, at a little pub in Devon, England. It traditionally contains beer, but I'm using La Bomba instead! Under the grill, the cheese, egg, and cream topping puffs up and turns golden brown. This is a comforting meal for a hungry family when the winds are blowing the russet leaves off the trees and the skies are turning a somber shade of gray.

## Roasted Tomato Soup

2½ lb (1 kg) Roma or plum tomatoes (I prefer the meatier Roma)

1 yellow onion, roughly chopped

4 cloves garlic, peeled

2 sprigs rosemary

4 Tbsp olive oil

1 tsp salt

1 tsp pepper

½ tsp Aleppo pepper, + more for sprinkling

3–4 cups chicken or vegetable stock

2 Tbsp tomato paste

2 bay leaves

4 Tbsp butter

½ cup Crème Fraîche (page 272) (optional)

### For the Roasted Tomato Soup

Preheat the oven to 450°F.

Quarter the tomatoes and spread them out on a baking sheet. Add the onions, garlic, and rosemary. Drizzle everything with the oil and toss to combine. Arrange everything into one layer. Sprinkle with the salt, pepper, and Aleppo pepper, and roast until wonderfully caramelized, about 40 minutes.

Transfer to a large stockpot. Stir in 3 cups of the stock, followed by the tomato paste, bay leaves, and finally the butter. Increase the heat to medium-high and bring to a boil. Drop the heat to medium-low and simmer, uncovered, for 30 minutes.

Discard the bay leaves and rosemary. Remove the pot from the heat. Using an immersion blender, or working in batches in a blender (it should be no more than half full; hold the lid down with a towel), blend to your preferred consistency. For a velvetier result, blend until smooth; for a more rustic result, blend until chunky. Return the pot to low heat. Add the crème fraîche and a bit more stock, about 1 tablespoon at a time, if you find it too thick. Season to taste. Keep on low heat while you prepare the rarebit.

*recipe continues*

## Welsh Rarebit

4 slices sourdough bread

1 egg yolk

Heaping ⅔ cup grated Cheddar cheese

⅓ cup Crème Fraîche (page 272)

½ tsp Dijon or regular mustard

2–3 dashes of Worcestershire sauce

Salt and pepper

3–4 Tbsp La Bomba

## For the Welsh Rarebit

Lightly toast the bread. While it's toasting, place the egg in a medium bowl and beat well. Add the cheese, crème fraîche, mustard, and Worcestershire sauce. Use a fork to blend well and break up the cheese. Taste and season with salt and pepper.

Turn the oven to broil. Spread about 1 tablespoon of La Bomba across each slice of toasted bread. Divide the cheese mixture among the slices, spreading it out to the edges. Depending on how large your bread slices are, there may be plenty of the cheese mixture or it may spread more thinly, but don't worry, it will still work. Place on a baking sheet and broil until the cheese is bubbling and turning a lovely golden brown, about 5 minutes but keep an eye on it. Let cool slightly before eating.

## To Serve

Divide the soup among four bowls. Serve with a sprinkling of Aleppo pepper over top and the Welsh rarebit on the side.

### NOTE

If you are making the soup without the Welsh rarebit and you want to make it vegan, feel free to swap out vegan butter for the butter, and coconut cream for the crème fraîche.

# gerrard street mulligatawny soup with spiced apple croutons

SERVES 6
PREP TIME 30 minutes
COOK TIME 35 minutes

For years during the cooler months I used to feed a hungry crowd for lunch once a week. It was always soup, crusty warmed baguettes, and freshly baked cookies or brownies. It was a way to get together with friends for a quick bite before we continued our busy day. One day I made a batch of mulligatawny soup, an eastern Indian chicken and rice soup, with flavors inspired by one of my favorite restaurants on Gerrard Street in Toronto's Little India neighborhood. It was such a hit that I'd regularly get requests for the "curry soup." I've since updated my original recipe with some crisp, spiced apple croutons, which add a lovely sweet, crunchy contrast to the creamy soup. This recipe can be a vegetarian delight if you replace the chicken with red lentils (see Note, page 128).

## Mulligatawny Soup

2 Tbsp butter

2 yellow onions, chopped

1 Tbsp tomato paste

⅓ cup shredded unsweetened coconut

3 cloves garlic, minced, divided

1 Tbsp minced ginger, divided

3 Tbsp flour

1½ Tbsp curry powder

2 tsp ground cumin

¼–½ tsp cayenne pepper

5 cups low-sodium chicken stock

2 carrots, chopped

1 stalk celery, chopped

1 very ripe banana, cut into 1-inch pieces

Salt and pepper

### For the Mulligatawny Soup

In a large Dutch oven over medium heat, melt the butter. Add the onions and tomato paste, and stir until the onions are softened and golden, about 3 minutes. Stir in the coconut and cook until fragrant, about 1 minute. Add half of the minced garlic and ginger, the flour, curry powder, cumin, and ¼ teaspoon of the cayenne. Stir until combined. Whisking constantly, gradually add the stock. Add the carrots, celery, and banana. Increase the heat to medium-high and bring to a boil. Cover, drop the heat to low, and simmer until the vegetables are tender, about 20 minutes.

Add the remaining garlic and ginger to the pot. Using an immersion blender, or working in batches in a blender (it should be no more than half full; hold the lid down with a towel), purée the soup. Taste and season with salt and pepper, and more cayenne if desired. Keep on low heat while you prepare the croutons.

*recipe continues*

### Spiced Apple Croutons

2 Tbsp butter

½ tsp ground ginger

1 tsp crushed cumin seeds

1 Granny Smith apple, peeled and cut into ½-inch cubes

### To Serve

About 1½ lb (680 g) chicken breasts, cooked then shredded (about 3 cups) (see Note)

2 cups cooked basmati rice

Plain yogurt, for garnish

Chopped cilantro, for garnish

### For the Spiced Apple Croutons

In a skillet over medium-high heat, melt the butter, and then add the ginger and cumin seeds. Stir to spread out evenly. Add the apples and sauté on all sides until golden and coated in the ginger and cumin.

### To Serve

Divide the chicken and rice among the soup bowls. Slowly ladle soup over top. Garnish with a dollop of yogurt and sprinkling of cilantro. Finish with the spiced apple croutons.

#### NOTES

The chicken can be poached, roasted, or grilled before shredding. Use rotisserie chicken to make life simpler! You can also use cooked turkey instead of chicken.

For a vegetarian version, replace the chicken with 2 cups of cooked red lentils, and the chicken stock with vegetable stock; the rice is optional.

This soup is so versatile, you can also garnish it with roasted curry-spiced chickpeas. Just rinse, drain, and dry one 14-ounce (398 ml) can of chickpeas, toss with ¾ tablespoon olive oil, ½ teaspoon cumin seeds, ¼ teaspoon coriander seeds, and 1½ teaspoons curry powder, and roast on a baking sheet in a 400°F oven until golden brown, about 20 minutes. These can be made in advance and stored in the fridge until needed.

Store leftover rice and soup in separate containers in the fridge for up to 2 days, as this will avoid thickening the soup with the rice. To serve, combine the soup and rice in a pot and cook over medium-low heat until heated through.

# hot turkey sandwich with cranberry sauce and "stuffin"

MAKES 2 sammies
PREP TIME 10 minutes
COOK TIME 10 minutes

The next best thing to a good roast turkey dinner is all the ways you can enjoy the leftovers from a good roast turkey dinner. Like hot sandwich meals. Remember those? Across the street from my high school was Maria's, the best old-fashioned diner, which served my favorite: a hot turkey sandwich. We would also enjoy french fries and gravy, BLTs, minestrone soup, slices of pie, and all-day breakfasts. But back to hot sandwich meals. There's nothing like slices of bread layered with warmed roast turkey (or roast beef or even meatloaf) and smothered in gravy, with a side of mashed potatoes, peas, and carrots. This is my take, which is a great way to use leftovers from a delicious Thanksgiving spread. I have given you a rough guide on how much to use for two sandwiches, but this is really a case of use as much as you want! Thanks, Maria's, for the memories.

1 cup Cider Sage Gravy (page 143)

6–8 slices Two-Hour Roasted Turkey (page 141), cold, cut into ¼-inch-thick slices

1 Italian Sausage Sourdough "Stuffin" (page 132), cut into four slices

2–4 slices bread (crusty sourdough, multigrain, and whole wheat all work well) (see Note)

4 Tbsp Cranberry Sauce (page 142)

Warm the gravy in a shallow skillet or pan over medium-low heat until runny. If it has thickened, add a splash of water. Add the turkey and cook, covered, until the turkey is almost but not quite warmed through, about 3 minutes. Add the stuffing slices on top, cover again, and let everything warm up for another 1 to 2 minutes.

Meanwhile, lightly toast the bread. Do not over-toast. You just want it warmed through and lightly crisped.

To serve, divide the toasted bread between two plates. Spread a layer of cranberry sauce on each slice, then add the turkey and stuffing on top. Drizzle with all the excess gravy. Done!

NOTES
If your bread is on the small side, use 2 slices per person.

Yes, you could serve the cranberry sauce on the side. But try it inside the sandwich. It's really good! If you have leftover scalloped potatoes (page 140), warm them up and serve them on the side!

THE LEMON APRON    131

# italian sausage sourdough "stuffins"

MAKES 12 muffins
PREP TIME 20 minutes
COOK TIME 1 hour

Stuffing . . . muffins . . . stuffins! These are portable versions of my most favorite turkey dinner side. Making the stuffing as muffins ensures that each person gets that glorious crispy crust on a plate mounded with turkey, potatoes, and vegetables, with the gravy puddling into all the nooks and crannies. I contend, though, that the turkey is just the conduit to the gravy and stuffing. If forced to choose, I'd take the stuffing over the mashed or roasted potatoes. The best stuffing starts with slightly stale bread. I love a good sourdough for its slight tangy flavor and airy texture. The rest of the ingredients should be a perfect balance of savory and sweet. The sweet and slightly hot sausage, earthy celery, and herbs take care of the savory. Pecans, onions, and cranberries take care of the sweet and also add great texture. Make extra. These are great on their own, or sliced and layered in the required day-after turkey sammie (page 131)! *Recipe pictured on page 136*

6 cups crusts removed and cubed (½-inch pieces) stale sourdough bread (see Note)

9½ oz (270 g) spicy Italian sausages, casings removed

1 yellow onion, cut into ¼-inch pieces

2 stalks celery, cut into ¼-inch cubes

1 tsp olive oil (optional)

1 tsp dried rosemary leaves

1 tsp dried thyme leaves

1 tsp dried sage

½ cup dried cranberries, coarsely chopped

½ cup pecans, lightly toasted and chopped (page 134)

1 Tbsp chopped sage

Preheat the oven to 350°F.

Place the bread cubes in a large bowl. In a skillet over medium-high heat, sauté the sausage meat, breaking it up with a wooden spoon. Let it sit without stirring too often until brown and crisp, about 10 minutes. Drain, reserving a bit of fat in the pan, and transfer the meat to the bowl with the bread.

Drop the heat to medium and, in the same pan, sauté the onions and celery until softened and just turning golden, about 8 minutes. If the sausage did not release enough fat, add 1 teaspoon or so of oil as needed to the pan. Crush the dried herbs in the palm of your hand to release the oils, add to the skillet, and stir to combine. Transfer the seasoned onion mixture to the bowl. Mix in the cranberries, pecans, and fresh herbs.

Add ½ cup of the stock to the bowl and quickly fold everything together. Wait a moment to let the bread soak up the liquid. Adding another ½ cup of stock, quickly fold everything together, and wait a moment. If the mixture is moist and holds together, continue with the next step. Otherwise, add no more than ¼ cup or so of stock, 1 tablespoon at a time, ensuring it doesn't turn into a soggy mess.

2 tsp chopped rosemary

2 tsp chopped thyme

1–1¼ cups chicken or turkey stock

Salt and pepper

2 eggs, beaten

Season with 1 teaspoon each of salt and pepper. Taste and adjust the seasoning as desired. Add the eggs and mix to combine.

Generously spray the cups of a 12-cup muffin tin with cooking spray. Divide the mixture among the cups. Bake until the tops are lightly browned and crunchy, 35 to 40 minutes. There should be a slight springiness when you press on one. Let cool for a minute. Using a sharp knife and small offset spatula, carefully remove the muffins from the tin. Serve.

**NOTES**

If your bread is fresh, cut it into cubes the night before you plan to make these. Spread the cubes out on a baking sheet. Let sit at room temperature overnight, covered with a tea towel (or in a 175°F oven the morning of for 10 to 15 minutes). Check regularly and turn over if necessary. This will make the bread stale and allow it to hold its own.

You can also bake the stuffing in a greased 9- × 13-inch baking pan or a baking sheet lined with parchment paper for optimum crust formation. The cooking time will be reduced, so start checking at about the 20-minute mark.

To make the day before serving, bake in a baking dish covered with foil at 350°F for 25 minutes. Let cool, cover the dish with fresh foil, and refrigerate overnight. The next day, reheat in a 350°F oven for 15 to 20 minutes, then remove the foil to brown the top for 10 to 15 minutes.

Leftovers will keep for up to 3 days in an airtight container at room temperature. They can be reheated at 325°F for a few minutes to warm through.

# forelle pear and kohlrabi salad with gorgonzola and pecans

SERVES 4
PREP TIME 15 minutes
COOK TIME 5 minutes

This is a wonderful autumn salad. Using red leaf lettuce, frisée, and radicchio makes for the perfect crispy base. Slicing the firm, sweet, crunchy pear and kohlrabi ahead of time and tossing them in a bit of the dressing helps keep them from turning brown before serving. Adding toasted pecans and gorgonzola rounds out the flavors, and sprinkling on pomegranate arils as a topping adds a tart sparkle (they really are like jewelry, aren't they!). While I can't abide dried fruit in salads, fresh fruit is wonderful. Slice up a couple of figs as well, if you're feeling it. This salad can be turned into a complete meal if you add some sliced roasted beets and rotisserie chicken! *Recipe pictured on page 137*

¼ small red onion

½ kohlrabi

2 forelle pears or 1 red pear

4 Tbsp Champagne Mustard Vinaigrette (page 265), divided, + more for serving

½ cup pecans

3 oz (85 g) red or butter lettuce

3 oz (85 g) frisée

1 oz (25 g) radicchio

3 sprigs thyme, leaves only

Pepper

¼ cup crumbled Gorgonzola, for garnish

2 Tbsp pomegranate arils, for garnish

Slice the onion lengthwise and put the slices in a bowl. Discard the outer skin of the kohlrabi and cut the flesh into ¼-inch-wide slices, then into ¼-inch-long batons. Add these to the bowl. Halve and core the pears, cut them into thin lengthwise slices, and add to the bowl. Drizzle with 2 tablespoons of the vinaigrette. Set aside.

In a skillet over medium heat, toast the pecans, turning occasionally, until browned and fragrant, about 5 minutes. Watch them carefully so they don't burn. Remove from the pan and set aside.

Tear the lettuce, frisée, and radicchio into bite-size pieces and arrange them on individual serving plates or a large serving platter. Drizzle with the remaining 2 tablespoons of dressing and toss gently. Spoon the onions, kohlrabi, and pears evenly over the greens. Scatter the thyme leaves over top. Season with pepper, and top with the pecans, Gorgonzola, and pomegranate arils. Drizzle a bit more dressing over top.

# cinnamon root veg and apple purée

SERVES 6
PREP TIME 15 minutes
COOK TIME 50 minutes

Sure, mashed potatoes reign supreme as far as Jim is concerned. But there is another mash that runs a close second, and it's the perfect accompaniment to a roast pork, chicken, or even turkey dinner (page 141). I'm talking root vegetables. All the autumn scents of cinnamon and ginger add magic to this brilliant combo of root veg and apples. Use whatever root vegetables you can find—turnips, yuca, kohlrabi, even celeriac—and any kind of apple on hand. If you are using root veg with less natural sweetness, you may want to increase the apple to balance the flavors. The garlic and peppercorns keep this dish from being too sweet. For a richer finish, stir in ¼ cup heavy cream at the end of cooking. This may have autumn vibes, but it works as a super side all the way through to spring. *Recipe pictured on page 136*

2 sweet potatoes or yams, peeled and cut into ¾-inch cubes

2 carrots, cut into ¾-inch cubes

2 parsnips, cut into ¾-inch cubes

2 apples, cut into ¾-inch cubes

1 red onion, coarsely chopped

3 cloves garlic, chopped

1-inch piece ginger, peeled and chopped

2 cinnamon sticks

2 Tbsp olive oil

Salt and pepper

¾ cup chicken stock, or 1½ tsp Faux Chicken Bouillon Powder (page 265) dissolved in ¾ cup boiling water

¾ cup fresh apple cider

1 tsp crushed red peppercorns, for garnish

Preheat the oven to 425°F. On a large baking sheet, combine the sweet potatoes, carrots, parsnips, apples, onions, garlic, ginger, and cinnamon sticks. Drizzle with the oil, season with 1 teaspoon each of salt and pepper, and toss to evenly coat. Arrange everything in a single layer. You may need two baking sheets.

Bake on the center rack (if you're using two baking sheets, place one in the top third and one in the bottom third of the oven and rotate them halfway through cooking) until the mixture starts to turn golden brown, about 25 to 30 minutes. The potatoes, carrots, and parsnips may not be soft yet, even if the apples are. That's okay.

Transfer everything to a large stockpot. Add the stock and cider. Bring to a boil over high heat, then drop the heat to medium and simmer, uncovered, until all the vegetables are softened, about 8 to 10 minutes. There should still be some liquid in the pot.

Discard the cinnamon sticks. Transfer the mixture to a blender, or use an immersion blender, and blend until it's as smooth as you like. If it's too thick to blend, add more stock or cider, 1 tablespoon at a time. Return to the pot. Season with salt and pepper. Serve garnished with the red peppercorns.

# spinach spätzle with sautéed onions and gruyère

SERVES 4 to 5 as a main, or 8 as a side
PREP TIME 30 minutes + resting
COOK TIME 30 minutes

This rustic version of mac 'n' cheese, called Käsespätzle, is pure German comfort food. *Käes* means cheese and *Spätzle* are little handmade dumplings or noodles. Does that make them cheesy dumdles or noodlings? The easiest way to shape the thick batter is to run it through a spätzle maker. This handy gadget sits on top of a pot of boiling water, allowing the batter to run down through holes to create little dumplings that fall into the water. I don't often recommend a single-use gadget to take up room in your cupboard, but this one can't be beat! If you don't have one, though, don't fret. You can also push the batter through a colander placed over the water. This dish uses the beloved star ingredients of French onion soup, namely golden-brown onions and melty cheese. I've updated it by adding spinach to the spätzle batter. It makes for a hearty main dish or a sublime side to a chilly-weather roast. Kids will love it (tell them it's what Kermit, Oscar, or some puppet eats).
*Recipe pictured on page 136*

## Spätzle

12 oz (340 g) baby spinach

4 eggs

1 tsp salt

¼ tsp white pepper

¼ tsp ground nutmeg

2 cups flour

3 Tbsp butter, melted

2 tsp Dijon mustard

1 tsp grainy mustard

¼ cup milk (as needed)

Butter or olive oil, for coating

### For the Spätzle

Place the spinach leaves in a large bowl. Bring a kettle of water to a boil and pour it gently over the leaves until they are covered. Let sit for 30 seconds. Transfer the leaves to a colander. Working in batches, place them in a tea towel and squeeze the water out over the sink. Don't fuss over getting every last bit of water out.

Place the spinach leaves and the eggs in a food processor fitted with the steel blade. Add the salt, pepper, and nutmeg. Pulse until the spinach is finely chopped, about 2 minutes. Add the flour and process, stopping to scrape down the sides as needed, until the batter is thick and smooth, about 4 minutes. Add the melted butter and both mustards, and process to combine. If you find the batter is very thick, add the milk, 1 tablespoon at a time, until it's thick but falls off a spoon without effort. It shouldn't drip or stream off the spoon, though, so it's a bit of a balancing act. Cover the bowl with plastic wrap and let the batter rest for 20 minutes.

## Käsespätzle

4–5 Tbsp butter, divided

1 large Spanish onion, halved and then sliced lengthwise

2 cups grated cheese (Emmenthal, Gruyère, and Jarlsberg all work well) (see Note)

Salt and pepper

2 Tbsp chopped parsley, for garnish

Bring a large pot of salted water to a boil over high heat. Place a Spätzle maker or large colander with medium-sized holes over the pot. Working in batches, spoon about ¼ cup of the batter into the Spätzle maker, pushing the batter through the holes by moving the trough back and forth, or through the holes of the colander into the boiling water.

When the dumplings rise to the surface, after about 1 minute, use a slotted spoon or spider to transfer them to a serving bowl. Toss each batch in a touch of butter. Continue until all the batter is used up. Set aside. (The spätzle can be stored in an airtight container in the fridge overnight; just bring them to room temperature before continuing.)

### For the Käsespätzle

Heat 2 tablespoons of the butter in a large sauté pan over medium-low heat. Add the onions and cook until golden brown, stirring regularly to avoid scorching, about 20 minutes. If needed, add 1 more tablespoon of butter.

Push the onions to the edges of the pan, increase the heat to medium-high and add the Spätzle, along with 2 tablespoons more butter. Stir and cook until warmed through and starting to turn a lovely golden brown, about 4 to 5 minutes. Drop the heat to medium if you see them starting to scorch. Add the cheese, a handful at a time, and stir to melt. Continue until all the cheese is used up. Season with salt and pepper. Depending on the saltiness of your cheese, you may only need 1 teaspoon or so of salt. Garnish with the parsley.

### NOTES

My method of caramelizing onions is not the true way, which traditionally takes up to 50 minutes on low heat. I find that 20 minutes at a higher temperature gives you the golden brown hue and the depth of flavor needed without the onions being overly sweet. Not to mention that it's a timesaver!

I know I say 2 cups of grated cheese, but add more if you like. I like my measuring cup to be heaping with cheese!

# harissa hasselback scalloped potatoes

SERVES 8
PREP TIME 25 minutes
COOK TIME 1½ hours

Jim used to claim he didn't like scalloped potatoes. "We both like mashed, why make anything different?" Jim logic. So for 17 years, I stopped making them, until one night, I made some for company—and Jim took spoonful after spoonful. Apparently, he had just never had *my* scalloped potatoes! This recipe should really be called "The Scalloped Potatoes Jim Didn't Know He Liked"! *Recipe pictured on page 112*

2 tsp butter, softened

6–7 large Yukon gold or yellow-flesh potatoes (try to have them the same size)

2 Tbsp butter, melted

¾ tsp salt

½ tsp pepper

½ tsp garlic powder

½ cup heavy cream or half-and-half

½ cup milk (whole or low-fat)

½ cup shredded white Cheddar

½ cup Parmesan, divided

⅛ tsp ground nutmeg

1 Tbsp chopped thyme

½ tsp harissa powder

Flakey finishing salt

Preheat the oven to 400°F. Coat a 9- or 10-inch cast-iron skillet or round baking dish with the softened butter.

Using a mandoline or very sharp knife, cut 6 of the potatoes crosswise into ⅛-inch rounds. Gently pat them with a paper towel to remove any excess moisture and then place in a large bowl. Add the melted butter, salt, pepper, and garlic powder. Toss to coat.

In another large bowl, mix together the cream, milk, Cheddar, 2 tablespoons of the Parmesan, and the nutmeg. Working in batches, place the potato rounds in the milky cheese mixture, tossing to coat each round well. Arrange them in the prepared skillet in tight concentric circles. If you don't have enough to fill your dish, slice up the extra potato, then coat and fit in enough slices to finish. Pour any remaining mixture evenly over the potatoes. It should reach about halfway up the sides, but no more.

Cover with foil and bake for 45 minutes. Remove the foil and bake for 20 minutes. Meanwhile, combine the remaining Parmesan with the thyme and harissa. Evenly sprinkle the cheese mixture over the potatoes. Bake until bubbling and browned, about 20 minutes. Sprinkle with flakey salt.

**NOTE**
Leftovers reheat perfectly. Just pop them in a 300°F oven for 10 to 15 minutes. Or warm them up in a skillet over medium heat, crack an egg on top, and call it breakfast!

# two-hour roasted turkey with cider sage gravy and cranberry sauce

SERVES 8 to 10
PREP TIME 20 minutes +
chilling overnight +
resting
COOK TIME 4 hours
(stock), 2 hours (turkey
and cranberry sauce),
20 minutes (gravy)

I don't think I can put into words just how much I love a roast turkey dinner. From writing the grocery list to washing the last dish, making this meal gets me downright giddy. I get to cook and share a meal with friends and family (once I made it for 120 people!). It's a happy week for me, thanks to the aromas of the cranberry sauce, stuffing, and pies I make in advance, setting the table with autumn leaves and blooms, and having jazz playing while I cook. The day before, I make the stock. The day of, I'm dealing with the turkey and taters. When I say that a full turkey can be cooked in 2 hours (plus resting time), I'm not joking. The secret's in the prep. By separating the breasts and the legs from the carcass, not only can you make the stock for the gravy in advance, but you also have full control over how long each piece of meat is in the oven. No more worries about drying out the breast meat while waiting for the thigh meat to get up to temperature either. Just remove them once ready! Apples and sage add the perfect autumnal flavor to this meal. For a smaller crowd, you can use a smaller turkey, but the leftovers are a gift that keeps on giving—sandwiches (page 131), soup, enchiladas . . . *Recipe pictured on page 137*

## Turkey Stock

1 (12–15 lb/5½–6¾ kg) turkey, separated into breasts, legs thighs, and wings (see Note, page 143)

2 yellow onions, skins on and coarsely chopped

2 stalks celery, coarsely chopped

1 leek, coarsely chopped

3 bay leaves

10 peppercorns

4 sprigs parsley

5 sage leaves

2 sprigs rosemary

3 sprigs thyme

### For the Turkey Stock

The day before you roast the turkey, place the wings and carcass in a large, heavy-bottomed stockpot. Add the onions, celery, leeks, bay leaves, and peppercorns. Make a bouquet garni by tying the parsley, sage, rosemary, and thyme together with kitchen twine. Fill the stockpot with water until the turkey is just covered. Bring to a boil over high heat, then drop the heat to low and simmer, covered, for at least 4 hours for a flavorful stock. Remove from the heat.

Once it's cool enough to touch, strain the stock into a pot. Let cool completely in the fridge overnight. Remove the fat that has risen to the top and set aside the 2¼ cups stock needed for this recipe; keep refrigerated until ready to use. You can freeze the rest in individual portions for up to 6 months.

*recipe continues*

## Cranberry Sauce

1 (12 oz/340 g) bag fresh or
    frozen cranberries

Zest and juice of 1 large orange
    + more juice as needed

1 cinnamon stick

1 star anise pod

1 tsp ground cinnamon
    (approx.)

1 tsp sugar (approx.)

Sage leaves, for garnish

## Roast Turkey

4 Tbsp coarse salt

2 Tbsp dried rubbed sage

4 carrots, cut into 2-inch pieces

3 yellow onions, quartered

6 stalks celery, cut into 2-inch
    pieces

½ cup butter

½ cup chopped sage leaves

Pepper

⅔ cup cold apple cider or apple
    juice

### For the Cranberry Sauce

Combine the cranberries, orange zest and juice, cinnamon stick, star anise, ground cinnamon, and sugar in a saucepan. Bring to a rolling simmer over medium-high heat and cook until the berries are starting to burst open, about 12 to 15 minutes. Add more sugar or cinnamon, about ¼ teaspoon at a time, if needed. Drop the heat to medium and cook to your desired thickness. Remove the cinnamon stick and star anise from the sauce, and let cool in the pan, then store in an airtight container in the fridge until needed. If you wish to thin it out a bit, add 1 to 2 tablespoons of orange juice. Garnish with the sage before serving.

### For the Turkey

Mix together the salt and dried sage in a small bowl. Place the turkey pieces in two pans just large enough to hold them without crowding and rub well with the sage salt. Let rest at room temperature for 2 hours. This will help create a crisp skin. If the breasts are not attached to any bone, roll them into tight rolls and tie with string every inch or so. This will help the meat cook evenly.

Set a rack in the middle of the oven. Preheat the oven to 425°F.

Divide the carrots, onions, and celery between two roasting pans. Lay the turkey pieces, white in one pan and dark in the other, on top of the vegetables. In a small saucepan over low heat, melt the butter with the chopped sage. Brush two-thirds of this sage butter all over the turkey pieces. Sprinkle with pepper.

Roast the turkey, uncovered, for 30 minutes. Baste with any pan juices and the remaining sage butter. Drop the oven temperature to 375°F and roast for 30 minutes. Pour the cider over the turkey and vegetables, rotating the pans for even cooking. Roast, basting and turning the pan occasionally, until an instant-read thermometer inserted into the thickest part of a breast reaches 165°F, about 40 to 45 minutes, depending on the size and thickness of the meat.

Transfer the breasts to a platter, tent loosely with foil, and let rest until ready to slice. Don't wash the roasting pan.

Continue to roast the legs and thighs, occasionally basting and turning the pan, until an instant-read thermometer inserted into the thickest part of a thigh reaches 165°F, about 20 to 25 minutes. Transfer to the platter with the breasts and tent with foil.

## Cider Sage Gravy

2–2¼ cups turkey stock

¾ cup cold apple cider or apple juice

¼ cup flour

3 Tbsp apple brandy (I like Calvados) (optional)

2 Tbsp chopped sage leaves

Salt and pepper

2–3 Tbsp heavy cream (optional)

## For Serving (mix and match)

Harissa Hasselback Scalloped Potatoes (page 140)

Broccolini Amandine (page 236)

Italian Sausage Sourdough "Stuffins" (page 132)

### For the Cider Sage Gravy

Pour all the pan juices into a 4-cup measuring cup. Spoon off 4 tablespoons of the fat that rises to the surface and place it in a large, heavy-bottomed saucepan. Discard the remaining fat. Transfer the vegetables to a bowl (they are great for snacking or serving).

Place one roasting pan over two burners on your stovetop, scraping all the bits from the other pan into it. Add 2 cups stock and the cider. Bring to a boil over medium-high heat, scraping up all the browned bits. Boil until reduced to 1½ cups, about 7 minutes. Add the liquid to the juices in the measuring cup. If needed, add enough stock to bring the liquid to 3½ cups.

Place the saucepan with the turkey fat over medium-high heat. Add the flour and whisk until the flour smells nutty and starts to brown, about 3 minutes. Whisk in the stock mixture. Cook until the gravy thinly coats the back of a wooden spoon, about 6 minutes, or longer if you want it thicker. Whisk in the brandy, if desired, and add the sage. Season with salt and pepper. Enrich the gravy with cream, if desired, but only if you want to go over the top!

### To Serve

Slice and arrange the turkey slices on a platter. Drizzle with a little of the gravy. Serve with the cranberry sauce and desired sides.

### NOTES

Ask your butcher to separate the breasts from the carcass and to remove the legs, thighs, and wings. Reserve the carcass and wings for the stock.

If you're preparing the turkey and gravy earlier in the day, warm up the gravy and pour some into a baking dish, just enough to cover the bottom. Place the rested, sliced turkey on the gravy. Drizzle with a touch more and cover with foil. When you're ready to serve, reheat at 325°F for 10 to 15 minutes. Keep the rest of the gravy on your stove's back burner to reheat.

# high park autumn perogies

SERVES 4
PREP TIME 30 minutes
COOK TIME 35 minutes

Going out for comfort food means hitting our favorite local spots in High Park for perogies, zhurek, and schnitzel. For quick weekday meals at home, I turn to my trusty bag of perogies stashed in the freezer. Just add sautéed bacon and onions, and sour cream. How can we transform them into an autumn meal? By turning to the sumptuous autumn gourds and berries, and some brown butter sage! The hardest part is cubing the squash, but thankfully you can find prepped squash at most grocery stores. The rest is easy. A quick roasting and making the butter sage sauce, all while the perogies are cooking and next thing you know, you have an impressive meal that elevates a freezer staple to a meal worthy of company.

## Roasted Squash

2 cups (½-inch) cubes squash (such as butternut, acorn, or kabocha)

1 Tbsp olive oil + extra for tossing

½ tsp salt

¼ tsp pepper

¼ tsp ground cinnamon

¼ tsp ground ginger

½ red onion, sliced into thin rounds

## Perogies

16–20 store-bought perogies, thawed

## Brown Butter Sage Sauce

8 Tbsp butter, cubed

16 large sage leaves, patted dry

Pepper

¼ cup dried cranberries

### For the Roasted Squash

Preheat the oven to 400°F.

Place the squash on a baking sheet and sprinkle with the oil and all the seasonings. Toss well to coat, then spread out into one layer. Roast for 25 to 30 minutes, turning the squash and adding the onions halfway through. The squash should be just tender and starting to caramelize.

### For the Perogies

Meanwhile, bring a large pot of salted water to a boil. Cook the perogies according to the package directions. Drain and set aside in a bowl, tossing with a little oil to keep them from sticking together.

### For the Brown Butter Sage Sauce

In a large skillet over medium-low heat, melt the butter until bubbling. Add the sage leaves, spreading them out evenly. After about 3 to 5 minutes, the butter will start to foam and then turn brown. Don't stir. When the foam starts to die down, remove the pan from the heat. The sage will have crisped up around the edges. Using a slotted spoon, gently transfer it to a plate. Add the perogies, squash, and onions to the butter. Gently toss to coat well. Sprinkle with pepper. Scatter the sage and cranberries on top.

**NOTE**

Try cooked ravioli or tortellini in place of the perogies.

# eritrean zigni

SERVES 6
PREP TIME 15 minutes
COOK TIME 1¾ hours

Close Eritrean friends of ours once made us a classic zigni (stewed spiced beef and tomatoes), upping the berbere spice at Jim's request so much that even they couldn't eat it. Jim, as always, refused to collapse under the pressure, trying to ignore the sweat dripping down his forehead. I learned how to make this dish from Rachel, one of those dear friends, but don't worry, the heat is quite tolerable. Traditionally, this is served with injera, a spongy, airy, tangy flatbread made from teff. This cuisine is communal, with a central platter of food. Tear a piece of the injera, wrap it around some of the zigni, and pop it in your mouth. I asked my friend Mihertab for an acceptable substitute if you can't source the injera. He suggested naan or thin flatbreads. This is served with yogurt flatbread, the easiest, softest flatbread to whip up.

4 Tbsp olive oil

2 large yellow onions, chopped

4 cloves garlic, minced

4 Tbsp Berbere Spice Blend (page 264), divided

2 lb (900 g) stewing beef, cut into ½-inch pieces

2 Tbsp tomato paste

1 (28 oz/796 ml) can whole tomatoes

½–¾ cup beef stock (see the Note on page 44)

Salt and pepper

Pinch of cayenne pepper (optional)

Cilantro leaves, for garnish

Yogurt Flatbread (page 274), for serving

Lemon wedges, for serving

In a large Dutch oven or pot over medium heat, warm the oil. Add the onions and sauté until they start to soften and change color, about 3 minutes. Add the garlic and sauté for another minute. Add 2 tablespoons of the berbere spice blend and stir to coat everything.

Increase the heat to medium-high. Add the beef and brown well on all sides, stirring regularly to keep the garlic from sticking to the bottom of the pot. Add the tomato paste and then the remaining 2 tablespoons of berbere spice. Stir to coat everything again.

Place the tomatoes and their juices in a large bowl and crush the tomatoes between your fingers. Add to the pot, along with ½ cup of the stock. Cook until it starts to boil, then drop the heat to a simmer and cover. Simmer for 30 minutes. Partially cover the pot with the lid and continue simmering, stirring occasionally, until the meat is absolutely tender and the stew has thickened, about 45 minutes to 1 hour. If it thickens too much before the meat is tender, add the remaining stock. Season with salt and pepper. To up the heat, stir in the cayenne. Garnish with cilantro. Serve with the flatbread and some lemon wedges.

NOTE
Pile some stewed chopped cabbage, harissa-roasted carrots, and even some dal around the zigni on a platter for a full meal.

# pappardelle with fennel and italian sausage bolognese and ricotta

SERVES 4
MAKES 5 cups of sauce
PREP TIME 30 minutes
COOK TIME 1 hour,
5 minutes

I'd say that Bolognese is desired all year round, but it's especially comforting as the days get cooler, isn't it? It really doesn't get much better than eating pasta with a thick, hearty sauce, cheesy garlic bread on the side, and a fresh salad for dinner. For me, making this meat sauce is as comforting as eating it. There is something so therapeutic about all the chopping and stirring. This sauce is perfect for making on a rainy Sunday afternoon and then freezing until needed. In this recipe I use pappardelle, but use the pasta you want: large rigatoni and spaghetti also work great. Use as much sauce as you need and store the rest.

1 Tbsp olive oil

4 oz (115 g) pancetta or bacon lardons, cut into ¼-inch cubes

1 yellow onion, diced

1 carrot, diced

2 stalks celery, diced

Salt and pepper

½ tsp chili flakes

3 cloves garlic, minced

1 tsp fennel seeds, cracked with a mortar and pestle

½ tsp dried thyme leaves

½ tsp dried basil leaves

½ tsp dried rosemary leaves

1 lb (450 g) ground beef

1 lb (450 g) spicy Italian sausages, casings removed

1 Tbsp tomato paste

¼ cup red wine

In a large, heavy-bottomed pot over medium-high heat, warm the oil. Add the pancetta and sauté until golden and crispy on all sides, about 5 minutes. Add the onions, carrots, and celery. Season with ¾ teaspoon each of salt and pepper, and the chili flakes. Sauté until the veggies are softened, about 5 minutes. Crush the garlic, fennel seeds, thyme, basil, and rosemary between your fingers, then mix in and cook for another minute.

Add the ground beef and sausage meat, and cook until evenly browned, breaking up the meat with the back of a wooden spoon, about 7 to 8 minutes. Add the tomato paste and stir to coat. Cook for 30 seconds to eliminate any acidity from the tomato paste. Deglaze the pot with the wine and cook, stirring to remove pieces from the bottom of the pot. Reduce the liquid by half, about 3 minutes.

*recipe continues*

1 (28 oz/796 ml) jar or can
     crushed or puréed tomatoes

1 large bay leaf

1–2 tsp sugar (optional)

1 Parmesan rind, or 2 Tbsp
     grated Parmesan (see Note)

2 Tbsp heavy cream

8 oz (225 g) pappardelle pasta
     (see Note)

½ cup Simple Fresh Ricotta
     (page 273) or store-bought
     ricotta

Basil leaves, for garnish

Salad, for serving

Garlic bread, for serving
     (optional)

Add the crushed tomatoes and bay leaf. Bring to a boil over high heat and then drop the heat to low to bring everything to a simmer. Cover the pot partially with its lid and let simmer for 45 minutes, stirring occasionally. At the 30-minute mark, taste the sauce. If you find it a tad too acidic, feel free to add a teaspoon or so of sugar, which will help to balance the acid from the tomatoes. If you have a Parmesan rind kicking about, add it now. Otherwise, once the sauce has thickened, stir in the grated Parmesan. Add the cream. Season with more salt, pepper, and chili flakes.

During the final 10 minutes of simmering, prepare the pasta according to the package instructions. Drain. Divide the pasta among the serving bowls.

Remove the bay leaf from the sauce. Serve the sauce over the pasta. Spoon dollops of ricotta on each dish and garnish with basil. Sprinkle with more chili flakes, if desired. Serve with a salad and garlic bread, if desired.

NOTES

The finished sauce will keep in an airtight container in the fridge for up to 4 days. If freezing it, transfer it to an airtight container before adding the cheese and cream. It will last in the freezer for up to 6 months. Just thaw, warm through, and add the cheese and cream as directed. Allow a fistful of dried pasta per person.

Adding a Parmesan rind imparts an extra layer of cheesy goodness—I have a bag of rinds in the freezer for such occasions!

This sauce can also be used for lasagna or a baked pasta dish. For an easy dinner, just combine it with short pasta cooked al dente, add a couple of handfuls of grated cheese and some wilted greens, and spoon it into a greased baking dish. Top with more cheese and bake at 375°F until the top is golden and bubbly, about 40 minutes. To go in a different direction, add canned beans, diced peppers, Mexican spices, and call it chili!

# anniversary chèvre-stuffed chicken breasts

SERVES 2

PREP TIME 20 minutes

COOK TIME 40 minutes

The first time I made this dish early in our married life, I thought it would be just another Wednesday evening meal. (Or was it Thursday?) On the surface, this is a basic pounded, stuffed chicken breast. But the pepper crust and chèvre and fresh herb stuffing add something special. And while the chicken is simmering in the wine and stock, some of the cheese oozes out and combines with the bits of pepper that get stuck to the bottom of the pan. Once these juices get reduced into a dark-amber gravy, the flavors take on a whole new life. Jim wiped his plate clean that first time, saying, "Make this often and don't change a thing!" He learned early on that I can't leave a recipe well enough alone. I pull this dish out when I really want to make Jim happy.

2 (each 8 oz/225 g) chicken breasts

1 (5 oz/140 g) package fresh chèvre, softened

4 Tbsp chopped herbs (see Note)

2½ Tbsp pepper, divided, + more as needed

1 Tbsp olive oil (approx.)

3 Tbsp butter, divided

¾ cup dry white wine

¾ cup chicken stock

1 Tbsp chopped parsley or rosemary

Place a sheet of wax paper on the counter and sit the chicken breasts 2 inches apart on it. Using your hands, start to open them up like a book. It may be that the "tender" is the only part that will fold over. Cut each chicken lengthwise through the thick part of the meat down to the middle, close to where the tender is attached, being careful not to cut all the way through. Butterflying will allow more meat to fold over the tender, so the meat will be more evenly distributed. Cover with another piece of wax paper. Pound the meat with a meat mallet until it has spread out to a uniform thickness of about ¼-inch. Ensure that the wider part of the breast is at the bottom and the "pointier" end at the top.

Divide the chèvre between the lower half of the breasts. Spread it out onto the top half with a small offset spatula, but don't go to the very edges. Evenly sprinkle the herbs over the cheese. Fold the sides of the chicken over the cheese filling. Then take the bottom part of the meat and fold it up and over the cheese, enclosing the side meat. Roll up firmly toward the pointy end, without pulling so tightly that the meat tears (don't worry about natural tears). Once rolled up completely, use toothpicks to secure the end flaps and close any gaps.

*recipe continues*

Place 1½ tablespoons of the pepper in a small plate that will hold the rolled breasts. Place the breasts firmly in the pepper, rolling them gently to cover the sides. Cover the rest of the breasts with the remaining pepper. Depending on the size of the rolls, you may want to use more pepper.

Heat a sauté pan over medium-high heat. Add the oil and 1 tablespoon of the butter and warm until the butter melts. Place the rolls in the pan and sear, without touching, until a good crust develops, about 4 minutes. Gently loosen and turn to sear the next side. Keep turning, adding more oil if necessary, until all the sides are nicely browned. Add 1 tablespoon of butter, the wine, and the stock. Cover and then drop the heat to a gentle simmer. Cook until the meat is cooked through, about 20 minutes. Transfer the breast rolls to a plate.

Increase the heat to medium-high and cook, stirring, until the liquid filled with bits of cheese and peppery goodness reduces to a scrumptious gravy. You can have it as thick as you like, but you need at least ¼ cup. Watch carefully, because it can suddenly reduce to a glaze. Finally, stir in the remaining 1 tablespoon of butter until smooth.

Remove the toothpicks and slice each chicken roll on the diagonal into four equal pieces. Serve with the gravy poured over top, or place some gravy on the bottom of each plate and serve the pieces on top of it. Garnish with the parsley.

**NOTES**

Use any herbs that work well with chicken, such as parsley, rosemary, thyme, tarragon, chervil, sage, or a combo of all of the above. This is a great meal for company. Just double the ingredients and use a larger skillet. Speaking of turning this into a meal, Jim loves this with roasted garlic, shallots, and onions and mashed, scalloped (page 140), or roasted potatoes. A rather monochromatic color scheme, but this is how he likes it! Feel free to switch up the vegetable sides (such as asparagus or broccoli). And wouldn't rice or egg noodles for the starch be yummy?

# salted caramel apple strudel

SERVES 8 to 10
MAKES 2 strudels
PREP TIME 25 minutes
COOK TIME 40 minutes

**W**hat is more quintessentially European than a fruit-filled strudel for dessert? A classic strudel requires a pastry so thin that you can read a newspaper through it. But I am always up for an easier route as long as the outcome will still taste amazing. Step this way, puff pastry, you baking lifesaver. I keep it traditional with a breadcrumb and nut base under the fruit. I finish the filling with a drizzle of my Salted Bourbon Caramel Sauce (page 270) and a sprinkling of fleur de sel. Perfection. Sure, this is NOT a traditional step, but it IS good! An easy faked braid of the pastry over the filling, and next thing you know, you have a fantastic dessert or breakfast treat. Apple Danish, anyone!? *Recipe pictured on page 112*

### Filling

4 large Granny Smith apples, peeled and cut into about ¼-inch-thick slices

¾ cup (170 g) sugar

2 Tbsp butter

2 Tbsp arrowroot starch or cornstarch

2 tsp ground cinnamon

½ tsp salt

¼ tsp ground allspice

¼ tsp ground cloves

⅛ tsp ground nutmeg

Preheat the oven to 375°F. Have one full-sized baking sheet (or two smaller ones) close at hand.

**For the Filling**

In a large bowl, gently mix together the apples, sugar, arrowroot, cinnamon, salt, allspice, cloves, and nutmeg to coat the apples. Set aside.

**For the Strudel**

Working with one sheet of pastry at a time, unroll the pastry on the parchment it was wrapped in. It should be roughly 10 × 11 inches. Place it with a short side facing you.

Scatter 3 tablespoons of the breadcrumbs lengthwise down the center, leaving the edges clear and a 3-inch border on either side of the filling. Evenly sprinkle half the walnuts over the breadcrumbs. Place half of the apple mixture over the breadcrumbs and walnuts. Dot the butter on top of the apple. Evenly drizzle 3 tablespoons of the caramel sauce over top. Sprinkle half of the flour de sel evenly over the filling.

Make incisions about 2½ inches deep and on a slight downward angle on either side of the filling, without actually touching the filling. At 1-inch intervals, you should get about 8 or 9 fringes on each side. Cut right through the pastry and all the way to the outer edge. Fold one piece of pastry across the fruit on a slight angle, pulling gently to cover it. The flap of pastry should just start to meet the other side, but don't force it farther. As long as it covers the apples, you're good.

## Strudel

1 (1 lb/450 g) package puff pastry, thawed (2 sheets)

6 Tbsp fresh breadcrumbs, divided

6 Tbsp chopped walnuts, divided

2 Tbsp softened butter

6 Tbsp Salted Bourbon Caramel Sauce (page 270), divided

1 tsp fleur de sel or flakey finishing salt, divided

1 egg, whisked with a bit of water

2 tsp raw or demerara sugar

Icing sugar, for dusting

Fold the opposing piece over the first one, creating a crisscross and pressing them gently into each other so that they adhere. Continue folding until you have reached the end. Press the top and bottom ends tightly, using some water to seal them together, and tucking any excess under.

Repeat the unrolling, filling, and folding process with the second puff pastry sheet.

Transfer the parchment papers carrying the strudels to the baking sheet(s). Brush the strudels with the egg wash. Sprinkle each strudel with demerara sugar.

Bake the strudels until golden brown, about 35 to 40 minutes (if using two smaller sheets, bake side by side and switch their positioning halfway to bake evenly). Transfer the baking sheet to a cooling rack and let the strudels cool completely. Remove the baking sheet and transfer the strudels directly onto a cutting board using the parchment. Dust with icing sugar. Slice each strudel into four or five portions.

**NOTE**
Leftovers can be stored in an airtight container at room temperature for up to 3 days.

# baked apple presents

MAKES 4
PREP TIME 30 minutes
COOK TIME 50 minutes

Think of this dessert as an apple of gold wrapped in even more gold . . . golden flakey pastry, that is. When my sister and I were kids, my mum would often bake apples for dessert. Hers were a simple treat: apples baked in a small baking dish, with sugar sprinkled on top. They would come out of the oven with their skin wrinkled and slightly burnished, the flesh all soft underneath. I decided that I wanted to hide the apple under a layer of "wrapping paper" to make it more of an apple pie–type of treat. Coring the apples and filling them with a combo of nuts, spices, and dried fruit creates a magical touch. You can add a side of ice cream, or even crème anglaise, as a lovely contrast to the rich and dreamy filling. The best apples for this are the firmer Jonagold, Gala, Honeycrisp, or Granny Smith. My Salted Bourbon Caramel Sauce (page 270) is also wondrous over these!

1 recipe No-Fail Pie Pastry (page 277) (add 1 Tbsp ground cinnamon to the flour before adding the butter), divided into 2 disks and chilled

2 Tbsp unsalted butter

2 Tbsp brown sugar

2 Tbsp chopped walnuts

2 Tbsp dried black currants

2 tsp ground cinnamon

½ tsp ground ginger

½ tsp ground cloves

4 apples, peeled and cored, using a spoon or a melon baller to remove more of the middle to hold the filling (see Note, page 158)

1 egg, whisked with a bit of water

2 tsp raw or turbinado sugar

Ice cream or Crème Anglaise (page 272), for serving

Preheat the oven to 350°F. Bring the pastry to room temperature. Line a shallow baking dish, just large enough to hold the apples without crowding, with parchment paper.

In a small bowl, mix together the butter, sugar, walnuts, currants, cinnamon, ginger, and cloves.

Dust your work surface with flour. Roll out both pieces of pastry to about ⅛-inch thick. Cut out two 7-inch rounds (a small plate is a great template) from each piece of pastry. If you're planning to decorate your desserts, bring together the scraps of pastry and chill in an airtight container in the fridge until needed.

Place an apple upright, with the opening at the top, on the center of each pastry round. Divide the stuffing among all the apples, packing it all the way down. Brush the edges of the pastry with a little water and gently bring them up to cover each apple, pleating and pinching the edges to seal. Remove any excess pastry from the top, give it a final pinch to seal, and then smooth out the top.

If you're decorating, roll out the reserved pastry and use a cookie cutter or knife to cut out 8 leaves. Use a knife to score in veins to add more dimension to the leaves. Dab some water over the top of each apple pastry and stick 2 leaves on top.

*recipe continues*

Brush the pastry with a little egg wash, getting right into the folds. Sprinkle the raw sugar evenly across the pastries.

Place the apples on the prepared dish, at least 1 inch apart. Bake until the apples are tender and the pastry is golden brown, about 45 to 50 minutes. Test with a knife to ensure that the apples are tender. The larger the apples, the longer they may take to bake. If needed, drape the pastry loosely with foil to avoid over-browning. Let cool slightly. Serve warm with ice cream or crème anglaise.

**NOTES**

When you core the apples, be careful not to go all the way down to the bottom. You need a base so the filling doesn't fall out.
To reheat, place the apples in a baking dish and bake at 350°F for 10 to 12 minutes. Try not to use a microwave, as the pastry won't stay flakey.

You can make these ahead. Simply store the unbaked assembled apple presents (before the egg wash and raw sugar) in a sealed container in the fridge for up to 24 hours or the freezer for up to 2 months. If frozen, thaw them in the fridge overnight. Remove the apple presents from the fridge 30 minutes before baking, and proceed as above.

# double-ginger pear pie

MAKES one 9-inch
double-crust pie
PREP TIME 45 minutes +
resting
COOK TIME 1 hour,
5 minutes

Yes, autumn means apples for many of us. Jim could have apple pie all year round. But I think pears make just as good, if not better, pie. They have a subtle beauty and flavor, but are often overlooked as a pie option. So here is a pie that I say rivals any apple pie. It may in fact become your new favorite autumn pie. Jim says it's one of the best pies he's ever had. And he's taste-tested a lot of different pies! The gentle sweetness of the pear and the sweet heat of the ginger really make for a fantastic filling. I recommend using a Bosc or Anjou pear for baking, as they hold their shape when baked. Bartletts tend to soften and turn mushy, so they are better for eating as is. But if you really wanted to include a Bartlett, it would melt wonderfully around the firmer Bosc pears.

---

1 recipe No-Fail Pie Pastry (page 277), divided into 2 disks and chilled

5–6 Bosc pears, enough to make 5½ cups thinly sliced, not overly ripe

2 tsp lemon juice

⅔ cup sugar

3 Tbsp finely chopped candied ginger

2 tsp ground ginger

3 Tbsp arrowroot starch

1 tsp ground cardamom

¼ tsp salt

¼ tsp urfa biber

5–6 dashes Angostura or old-fashioned bitters (don't skimp!)

2 Tbsp ground almonds

1 egg, whisked with a bit of water

Turbinado sugar, for sprinkling

Vanilla ice cream, for serving

Bring one piece of pastry out of the fridge and let rest at room temperature for 10 minutes. Roll it out to 12 inches in diameter and ease it into a 9-inch pie plate pie plate (see page 277). Trim the edge so you have ½ inch of pastry hanging over the edge of the plate. Chill in the fridge while you prepare the filling.

Peel and slice the pears into relatively thin slices, about ⅛-inch thick. Place them in a large bowl, sprinkle with the lemon juice, and stir to coat. In a bowl, mix together the sugar, both gingers, arrowroot starch, cardamom, salt, and urfa biber. Pour this over the pears. Add the bitters and gently toss to coat. Let it rest for 10 minutes. Remove the pie shell and the remaining pastry disk from the fridge.

Scatter the ground almonds over the bottom of the pie shell and add the filling. Use your fingers to tightly fit all the pear slices, like a puzzle, overlapping them as needed to create tight layers. Once they are all in, gently push them down to release any air bubbles. Chill in the fridge while you prepare the top crust.

Roll out the top pie crust, keeping everything well floured. Make a simple top or a lattice crust, and even cookie cutouts to top and decorate the pie (see pages 278 to 279). Top and crimp the pie as desired. Return the pie to the fridge while you preheat the oven.

*recipe continues*

Place a rack in the bottom third of the oven. Preheat the oven to 425°F.

Once the oven is at temperature, place the pie on a baking sheet. Brush the crust with the egg wash and sprinkle with the turbinado sugar. Bake in the lower third of the oven until the crust is starting to turn golden brown, about 30 minutes. Drop the heat to 375°F and move the rack to the center of the oven. Bake until the juices are bubbling all over the pie (not just the outer edges) and the crust is a lovely golden brown, about 30 to 35 minutes. Place the pie on a cooling rack and let cool for at least 4 hours to let the filling set.

To serve warm, preheat the oven to 325°F. Warm in the oven for 10 minutes. Let it cool slightly before slicing. Serve with vanilla ice cream or even the Cinnamon Sugar No-Churn Ice Cream (page 254).

NOTE
You can loosely wrap leftovers in plastic wrap and store in the fridge for up to 5 days, or wrap the cooled pie in several layers of plastic wrap and then alumnimum foil and freeze for up to 2 months.

## Breakfast

Bacon and Sausage Breakfast Bread Pudding with Cinnamon Sugar
Chocolate Hazelnut Cinnamon Swirl Eggnog Scones
Mumbai Fog Latte or Oatmeal

## Appetizers

Sambal Oelek Roasted Shrimp Cocktail
Aleppo Pepper Crab and Cheddar Dip

## Soups and Sammies

French Onion Soup with Short Rib Stock
Winter White Turkey and Vegetable Soup
North African–Inspired Harira Soup
Bathurst Street Sheet Pan Reubens

## Salads and Sides

Baby Kale and Romaine Caesar Salad
Winter Slaw with Orange Yogurt Dressing
Creamed Chard, Kale, and Spinach Greens

## Mains

Seville Orange Marmalade–Glazed Pork Rib Roast with Kumquats
Koshari Stuffed Peppers
Spiced Savoy Cabbage Rolls
Cocoa and Red Wine–Braised Short Ribs with Herbed Polenta
Québécois Tourtière 2.0
German Meat Patties with Stout Gravy and Onion Rings

## Desserts

Chocolate Pecan Date Cake with Butterscotch Sauce
Mincemeat Tart with Citrus Crème Anglaise
Nuremburg Lebkuchen

WINTER

The swirls of snow on a windy day, the white quilt that blankets the fields and trees after a quiet snowfall, the diamond chips that glisten from the snow under the moonlight and street lights, and the shades of somber blues and grays. Snow has that ability to cause us to pause, even stop, and take a breath—a breath that we may even see in the chilled air. Winter is the season to take comfort in sitting inside and reflecting as we plan for the year ahead. It's telling not only the trees and flowers but all of us humans to rest. So let's take advantage of winter's short days and the nesting nature it triggers.

When my sister and I were children, blizzards gave us the beloved Snow Day. I lived for those days when I could run back to bed, a book in hand, and read until dinner. My sister and I did get out to play as well, building snow forts, sledding, or skating on the reedy pond nearby. We would come home red-cheeked, my glasses fogging up as I walked back inside, feeling like I'd earned that steaming hot chocolate (with marshmallows). We would also make paper snowflakes, creating our indoor version of snow. My mum willingly taped all those snowflakes to the windows and kept them there until spring.

Today, if I had to pick between a chalet in a snow-covered forest and a sun-bleached sandy beach, the chalet would win out every time. A chalet means everyone can play outside while the sun is up, skiing and snowshoeing, and maybe doing some snow-fort building. But no matter where I am in winter, rosy cheeks are still the sign of a day well spent, although Scotch by the fire, not hot chocolate, is now my reward of choice. And making paper snowflakes has been replaced with playing cards and board games, watching old movies, and listening to gentle, somber jazz and classical music. Richly colored, autumn jewel-toned blankets, sweaters, and scarves—think fleece, fuzzy socks, Hudson's Bay striped wool blankets, Sherpa slippers, and flannel sheets—make it so easy to stay curled up inside.

Winter also means cozy meals with dear ones. Fondue was a family tradition, and I felt like a big kid being allowed near the pot. Jim and I continued the tradition soon after we were married. Today, we have fondue night with friends at least once every winter. And every time we do, I think of my parents.

Fondue is not the only warm and hearty dish. The Bacon and Sausage Breakfast Bread Pudding with Cinnamon Sugar (page 167) was invented for chalet weekends. The Aleppo Pepper Crab and Cheddar Dip (page 175) and the Bathurst Street Sheet Pan Reubens (page 183) are perfect treats for a casual winter day or even a spiffier occasion. The soups (pages 177 to 181) stick to your ribs. The Québécois Tourtière 2.0 (page 199) is pure comfort and makes for amazing leftovers. Carb loading is a fact of winter. Working them off is for spring and summer. The circle of life!

◄ *Clockwise from top left: Koshari Stuffed Peppers (192), Chocolate Pecan Date Cake with Butterscotch Sauce (206), Spiced Savoy Cabbage Rolls (194), Creamed Chard, Kale, and Spinach Greens (188)*

# bacon and sausage breakfast bread pudding with cinnamon sugar

SERVES 8
PREP TIME 35 minutes + resting
COOK TIME 50 minutes

We were out for breakfast with friends one morning, and one of the guys freaked out when he saw me drizzle maple syrup over my bacon and sausage. You'd think I'd just committed armed robbery! This breakfast pudding is in direct retaliation to that incident. Think of it as the ultimate sweet-savory baked French toast. It's everything you could want on a snowy morning, all trapped in one pan and with a crunchy cinnamon-sugar topping. There's just a hint of heat, which works well with the maple syrup. This serves a crowd, but a smaller group can enjoy the leftovers, as they reheat wonderfully.

## Bread Pudding

1 (about 1 lb/450 g) loaf day-old bread (see Note, page 168)

6¾ oz (190 g) bacon

13¼ oz (375 g) maple breakfast sausage, casings removed

5 eggs

¾ cup packed brown sugar

2 cups milk

2 cups heavy cream

4 Tbsp butter, melted

1 Tbsp vanilla extract

½ tsp salt

½ tsp chili powder

½ tsp cayenne pepper or chili flakes

## For the Bread Pudding

Slice one piece of bread into a 1-inch-thick slice. If it's too soft on the inside, slice the rest of the bread into 1-inch-thick slices and dry out the bread (see the Notes on page 119). Cut the bread into 1-inch cubes. Pack the cubes into a measuring cup and add to a large bowl. Repeat until you have 12 cups of bread cubes.

Cut the bacon into ½-inch pieces and sauté in a skillet over medium heat until crispy and golden brown. Do not overcook; you don't want it dried out. Remove with a slotted spoon and place on a paper towel–lined plate. Reserve 1 tablespoon of the fat in the pan.

Add the sausage to the skillet and sauté carefully over medium to medium-high heat until just crispy and golden brown, breaking it into small pieces with the back of a wooden spoon as you cook. This may take as long as 15 minutes. Don't rush it with too high a heat, or the meat may scorch. Drain on a separate paper towel–lined plate, blotting with paper towel as needed. Add to the bacon.

In a bowl, whisk together the eggs, sugar, milk, cream, butter, vanilla, salt, chili powder, and cayenne. Add three-quarters of the meat mixture to the bread cubes and toss to combine. Pour the egg mixture over the bread and toss gently to start soaking the bread.

*recipe continues*

## Topping

1 Tbsp sugar

2 tsp ground cinnamon

Maple syrup, for serving

Spray a 9- × 13-inch baking pan with nonstick spray. Spoon the bread mixture into the pan and spread out evenly. Press down gently to get the bread to soak up all the liquid. Cover with plastic wrap and let sit for 20 minutes at room temperature.

Meanwhile, preheat the oven to 325°F.

Remove the plastic from the baking dish and sprinkle the remaining meat over top, gently pushing the pieces into the bread. Place the pan on a baking sheet and bake on the middle rack until a toothpick inserted in the center comes out clean, about 50 minutes. Let cool for 10 to 15 minutes.

### For the Topping

In a small bowl, mix together the sugar and cinnamon until evenly combined. Sprinkle generously over the entire top of the pudding. Serve with maple syrup!

**NOTES**

I have used panettone and brioche in this recipe with wonderful results. No matter which bread you decide to use, make sure it's thick-cut and appropriately stale!

You can prepare the meat the day before you plan to cook the bread pudding. Store in an airtight container in the fridge until needed. Just let it come to room temperature before using. Leftovers will keep in an airtight container in the fridge for up to 3 days—but trust me, you'll want to eat all of this up!

# chocolate hazelnut cinnamon swirl eggnog scones

MAKES 8 scones
PREP TIME 30 minutes
COOK TIME 30 minutes

Winter brings on all the cozy feels and bakes. Cinnamon rolls are always a favorite, but sometimes I just want something more immediate. That's where scones and biscuits step in. This recipe offers the best of both worlds: it combines all the spices and gooey center of a cinnamon roll with an easy-to-make, tender scone. Toasted hazelnuts and mini chocolate chips add a bit of crunch, with an eggnog glaze to deliver the finishing touch! Eggnog is one of those indulgences that tastes amazing . . . and then suddenly it's just too rich. The first half of the carton always goes quickly in our house. The remainder then just smiles taunt-ingly at me, saying, "I'm taking up valuable real estate in your fridge. Better use me before I go bad." I have the last laugh, though. I freeze eggnog in portions so that I can make these scones all through the winter.

## Scones

4 Tbsp (55 g) unsalted butter, softened

⅔ cup (100 g) packed brown sugar

1 Tbsp ground cinnamon

2 tsp salt, divided

1½ cups + 2 Tbsp (240 g) flour + more for rolling

3 Tbsp sugar

1 Tbsp baking powder

6 Tbsp (85 g) unsalted butter, chilled

½ cup full-fat eggnog

1 egg

1 tsp vanilla extract

¼ cup (40 g) mini semisweet chocolate chips

⅓ cup (40 g) finely chopped toasted hazelnuts

## For the Scones

Preheat the oven to 375°F. Spray or grease a 10-inch round cake pan or line a cast-iron pan with damp, and crushed parchment paper.

In a bowl, use a fork to mix together the softened butter, sugar, cinnamon, and 1 teaspoon of the salt until smooth. Set aside.

In a large bowl, whisk together the flour, sugar, baking powder, and remaining 1 teaspoon of salt. Grate the chilled butter over the flour and toss until well coated. In a separate bowl, whisk together the eggnog, egg, and vanilla. Add the eggnog mixture to the dry ingredients and use a wooden spoon to stir until just combined.

Transfer the dough to a well-floured surface and pat it flat, knead-ing it several times to bring it together. If the mixture is too dry, add a bit more eggnog, 1 teaspoon at a time, to help. Pat it to about a ½-inch-thick rectangle. Using well-floured hands, fold one third from the longest side into the middle, and then the other third from the other side over the first, creating a narrow rectangle. Using a floured rolling pin, roll out the dough to a 10- × 11-inch rectangle. Place the dough with one short side facing you.

*recipe continues*

## Glaze

¼ cup (60 g) cream cheese, at
  room temperature

1 cup (130 g) icing sugar, sifted

1–2 Tbsp eggnog

Sprinkle the dough with the sugar-cinnamon mixture. Using a small offset spatula, spread the sugar-cinnamon mixture evenly across the dough, leaving a ½-inch border along each short side. Evenly sprinkle the chocolate chips and chopped hazelnuts over the filling.

Starting at the bottom, roll up the dough to create a 10-inch long log. If the dough is stuck to the work surface, use a well-floured bench scraper or metal spatula to help loosen it. Trim away ½ inch of dough from both ends. Slice the log in half crosswise, then cut each half into 4 slices, for a total of 8 slices. Carefully place each slice in the prepared pan, leaving a little space between each one.

Bake until the scones are golden brown and just bubbling, about 25 to 30 minutes. Place the pan on a cooling rack. Meanwhile, make the glaze.

### For the Glaze

Using a handheld mixer and a bowl, beat the cream cheese until softened and smooth. Add the icing sugar and beat in on low speed. Thin the mixture with 1 tablespoon of the eggnog. Add a little more eggnog, about 1 teaspoon at a time, if it's too thick. If you like really thick glaze, add a little more icing sugar.

While the scones are still in the pan, pour the glaze over them and use an offset spatula or spoon to spread the glaze over top. Serve warm.

NOTE

The unglazed scones can be stored in an airtight container in the fridge for 1 to 2 days. Warm them in a 300°F oven for 10 minutes. If you don't plan on eating these all at once, save the remaining glaze until you have reheated the rest of the scones, in a sealed container for 1 to 2 days in the fridge.

[SEE PAGE 217]

*"Good=by, my darlings! God bless and keep us all!"*

# mumbai fog latte or oatmeal

SERVES 2 (for both latte and oatmeal)
PREP TIME 5 minutes each for latte and oatmeal
COOK TIME 5 minutes (latte), 15 minutes (oatmeal)

Winter is when we get to wrap our hands around steaming cups of hot chocolate, café au lait, or this most fragrant latte. Hand me this latte and some buttered toast or an eggnog scone (page 169) or Nuremburg Lebkuchen (page 211), and I'm all set to watch the snow swirling outside. Or why not make this an oatmeal for a lovely wintery breakfast? Yep, steeping the oats in this fabulous concoction and adding foamed milk at the end takes your everyday bowl of oatmeal to a whole new level. Sprinkle some granola over it for the perfect start to a winter morning.
*Recipe pictured on pages vi and 162*

**Mumbai Fog Latte Option**

1 black tea bag

1 cup boiling water

1 cup milk

1 Tbsp honey

2½ tsp Chai Spice Blend (page 264)

½ tsp vanilla extract

2 cinnamon sticks, for serving

**Oatmeal Option**

½ cup water

1 black tea bag

1½ tsp Chai Spice Blend (page 264)

1 cup old-fashioned rolled oats

¾ cup milk, divided

1 tsp vanilla extract

2 tsp runny honey

1 tsp ground cinnamon

Spiced Coffee and Chocolate Granola (page 271)

**For the Mumbai Fog Latte Option**

Steep the tea bag in the boiling water for 5 minutes. Meanwhile, heat the milk in a small saucepan over medium heat. Add the honey, chai spice, and vanilla. Cook, stirring occasionally, until the milk is steaming and the honey has melted.

Divide the tea between two mugs. Place the milk mixture in a blender (a NutriBullet is great for this, but a regular frother will work just as well) and blend until frothy, about 20 seconds. Alternatively, you can just use a whisk to vigorously beat the milk until frothy. Divide the milk between the two mugs. Use the cinnamon sticks as stir sticks.

**For the Oatmeal Option**

In a saucepan over medium heat, bring the water, tea bag, and chai spice to a boil. Drop the heat to low and simmer gently, stirring often, for 3 minutes. Remove the tea bag and add the oats and ¼ cup of the milk. Increase the heat to medium and cook until the oatmeal has thickened, about 8 minutes. Stir in the vanilla and honey.

While the oatmeal is cooking, in a small pan on medium heat, heat the remaining ½ cup of milk until steaming. Place the milk mixture in a blender, or use a regular frother, and blend until frothy, about 20 seconds. Alternatively, you can just use a whisk to vigorously beat the milk until frothy. Add half of the milk, saving the foam, to the oatmeal, stirring to combine. Divide the oatmeal between two bowls. Spoon the remaining foamed milk over top. Sprinkle the oatmeal with the cinnamon and some granola.

# sambal oelek roasted shrimp cocktail

SERVES 8
PREP TIME 20 minutes
COOK TIME 10 minutes

Anytime shrimp shows up to the party, you know it's going to be a good time. Light but full of flavor, and just so versatile, shrimp love to take center stage. Here is a fun and rustic way to serve up a classic shrimp cocktail. Back in the day, shrimp cocktail meant cooked chilled shrimp draped over a martini glass with cocktail sauce inside the glass for dipping. It was a fairly formal dish, since you had to sit at a table to enjoy it properly. I say, place all the shrimp on a platter, with a couple of shallow bowls of dip at either end of the platter. Let everyone feel relaxed as they nibble and visit, sitting on the floor around the coffee table! You can literally pop the shrimp in the oven while everyone is taking off their coats. By the time drinks are served, this appetizer is ready as well. Of course, you can totally serve this as a first course for a fancy dinner.

*Recipe pictured on page 282*

## Shrimp

2 lb (900 g) raw black tiger shrimp, deveined and shells removed (see Note)

1 Tbsp olive oil

Salt and pepper

½ tsp sambal oelek

2 tsp lemon juice

1 Tbsp chopped parsley

## Sambal Oelek Cocktail Sauce

⅔ cup ketchup

⅓ cup chili sauce

2 Tbsp prepared horseradish

3 tsp sambal oelek

1 Tbsp lemon juice

1 lemon, divided into 8 wedges (optional)

### For the Shrimp

Preheat the oven to 400°F. Lay the shrimp on a baking sheet. Drizzle with the oil, and sprinkle with ½ teaspoon each of salt and pepper, and the sambal oelek. Drizzle the lemon juice over top and toss to coat. Bake until just cooked through, about 10 minutes. The flesh will be pink and just firm. Transfer the baking sheet to a cooling rack.

### For the Sambal Oelek Cocktail Sauce

In a bowl, mix together the ketchup, chili sauce, and horseradish. Stir in the sambal oelek, 1 teaspoon at a time, until your desired heat is achieved (I like it full on!). Stir in the lemon juice.

### To Serve

Arrange the warm and tender shrimp on a large platter or wooden board. Place the cocktail sauce in one or two bowls, and place at each end of the platter for communal nibbling. Scatter the lemon wedges around the shrimp for extra zing, if desired.

### NOTE
One pound of shrimp will usually feed four people. Obviously, the larger the shrimp, the fewer everyone will get. I find the 16 to 20 per pound size is best for this recipe.

# aleppo pepper crab and cheddar dip

MAKES 3 cups
PREP TIME 15 minutes
COOK TIME 35 minutes

**I**f the term "comfort food" can be applied to a dip, it should be this one. All the creamy goodness of melted cheeses, plus sour cream and mayo, is only made better by all the chunks of crabmeat they surround! Add a bit of heat, some brightness from lemon juice, and watch this dip disappear on a winter game night or movie night. Don't go to the expense of purchasing high-end crabmeat; canned lump and shredded meat is just fine! This is a great time to pull out your favorite hot sauce, as each type will bring something unique to the dip.

2 tsp olive oil

3 Tbsp minced red onion

8 oz (225 g) cream cheese, at room temperature, cubed

½ cup medium to old grated Cheddar

½ cup grated Parmesan, divided

⅓ cup sour cream

⅓ cup mayonnaise

1 Tbsp finely chopped chives

2 Tbsp lemon juice

2 Tbsp hot sauce (see Note)

¼ tsp salt

6 oz (170 g) cooked lump crabmeat

6 oz (170 g) cooked shredded crabmeat

1 sliced and toasted baguette, seed crackers, or vegetable sticks, for serving

Preheat the oven to 425°F. Lightly grease an 8-inch square or round baking dish (or any baking dish that can hold 4 cups) with cooking spray and set aside. Note that the dip will rise and bubble as it bakes.

Warm the oil in a small pot over medium-high heat. Sauté the onions until softened and lightly golden, about 3 to 5 minutes. Remove from the heat and let sit until cool to the touch.

Using a stand mixer fitted with the paddle attachment, or a large bowl and a wooden spoon, mix together the onions, cream cheese, Cheddar, ¼ cup of the Parmesan, the sour cream, mayonnaise, chives, lemon juice, hot sauce, and salt until creamy but not completely smooth. Set aside a few larger pieces of the lump crabmeat for garnish. Gently fold in the rest of crabmeat.

Evenly spread the crab mixture in the prepared baking dish, scatter the larger pieces of the lump crabmeat over top, and sprinkle with the remaining ¼ cup of Parmesan. Bake until lightly browned on top and bubbly, about 20 to 30 minutes. Serve with toasted baguette slices, crackers, or vegetable sticks.

**NOTES**
Any hot sauce, from chili garlic to gochujang, or piri-piri to harissa, will work. Feel free to heat half of the dip and freeze the uncooked portion (skip the final addition of Parmesan before freezing) in an airtight container for up to 2 months. To serve, thaw the dip and top with 2 Tbsp of grated Parmesan before baking as directed.

# french onion soup with short rib stock

SERVES 6
PREP TIME 50 minutes + chilling
COOK TIME 4½ hours

**B**ack when I was a server, I never grew tired of having French onion soup at break. Jim, however, didn't like it when we first started dating. *Huh?!* But then I encouraged him to try it at one of our favorite Finger Lakes restaurants in Skaneateles, New York. With that first spoonful he was hooked. He'd simply never had a good version before. I came up with this recipe because of that restaurant's version. A good friend says he uses this as his benchmark whenever he has French onion soup. Thanks, Trevor! Try a combination of Gruyère, Emmental, Cheddar, Swiss . . . I make this recipe into a hearty dinner soup by using the short rib meat from the stock in the broth with the onions.

## Short Rib Stock

2 Tbsp olive oil

3 lb (1¼ kg) meaty beef short ribs, cut into 3- to 4-inch pieces

1 large yellow onion, coarsely chopped

2 sprigs rosemary

2 sprigs parsley

3 sprigs thyme

2 stalks celery, coarsely chopped

1 carrot, coarsely chopped

12 black peppercorns

2 bay leaves

4 whole cloves

### For the Short Rib Stock

Warm the oil in a large, heavy-bottomed stockpot over medium-high heat. Working in batches, sauté the ribs until brown on all sides, about 8 minutes in total. Transfer to a plate. Add the onions to the pot and sauté until golden, about 10 minutes. Adjust the heat if they are browning too quickly.

Make a bouquet garni by tying the rosemary, parsley, and thyme sprigs together with kitchen twine.

Return the ribs and any juices to the pot. Add 3½ quarts water, the bouquet garni, celery, carrots, peppercorns, bay leaves, and cloves. Bring to a boil over medium-high heat. Skim off any foam from the surface. Cover, drop the heat to low, and simmer, skimming the foam occasionally, until the ribs are very tender, about 2½ hours. Using tongs, transfer the ribs to a plate. Strain the stock into a large bowl and discard the solids. Let the stock cool, then cover and chill in the fridge until fat solidifies on top, at least 3 hours. Using a spoon, skim the fat layer off, and discard.

Remove the meat from the ribs, cutting away any excess fat. Shred the meat finely. If desired, reserve 1 cup of the shredded meat for the soup. Store the leftover meat in an airtight container in the fridge for up to 4 days or the freezer for up to 2 months. Reserve 6 cups of stock. Freeze the rest in an airtight container for up to 6 months.

*recipe continues*

## French Onion Soup

4 Tbsp unsalted butter

2 lb (900 g) yellow onions, thinly sliced lengthwise

2 tsp cane or granulated sugar

1½ Tbsp all-purpose, whole wheat, or gluten-free flour

½ cup port or other fortified wine (see Note)

2 Tbsp chopped thyme, or 2 tsp dried thyme leaves

½–1½ tsp Maggi or Worcestershire sauce (see Note, page 95)

Salt and pepper

1 baguette, cut on a steep angle into slices as long as your bowls are wide

10–12 oz (280–340 g) grated or shaved cheeses (try a combination of Gruyère, Emmental, Cheddar, Swiss, etc. )

**NOTES**

Fortified wines like port, sherry, and Madeira, can range from dry, to smoky caramel, to raisiny and sweet. Don't invest in a vintage bottle for cooking. An open bottle can last in the pantry for over a year.

The soup can be stored in an airtight container in the fridge for several days or in the freezer for up to 6 months if you haven't add the bread or broiled it.

## For the French Onion Soup

In a large Dutch oven or heavy-bottomed pot over medium-low heat, melt the butter. Add the onions, spreading them out evenly. Sprinkle with the sugar. Stir regularly for even cooking and to avoid any onions sticking to the bottom of the pot. Keep cooking until they are a golden brown and caramel color, about 1 hour.

Evenly sprinkle the flour over the onions and stir to coat. Add the port, the reserved 6 cups of stock, and the thyme. Add ½ teaspoon of the Maggi sauce. Taste and add up to another 1 teaspoon if necessary. Bring to a bubbling simmer over medium-high heat, and then drop the heat to low. Simmer, partially covered, for about 45 minutes. You want the ingredients to combine for the best flavor. Season with salt and pepper, adjusting the pepper first and then the salt. Do not let the salt become the dominant flavor. Add the reserved shredded meat, if desired, and cook until warmed through, about 4 to 5 minutes.

Place a rack in the upper third of the oven and set the oven to broil. When the soup is almost ready, place the baguette slices on a baking sheet and place under the broiler until just golden on both sides, about 2 minutes per side. Set aside. Keep the broiler on.

Place six ovenproof bowls on a rimmed baking sheet. The bowls shouldn't be too wide, or the bread will fall in and the cheese won't make a fabulous crust. Ladle the soup into the bowls, leaving about ½ inch of space and making sure each gets an amazing amount of onions. The higher the soup goes in the bowl, the higher the bread will sit, and the cheese will melt over the sides of the bowl, which is a good thing. Place two or three slices of the bread on top of each soup bowl. You want most of the soup surface covered. Scatter the cheese over each bowl. Place the soups under the broiler until the cheese is melted, bubbling, and crusting up all over, making sure the bread doesn't burn, about 5 minutes depending on the height of the bowls and how close they are to the element. Serve.

# winter white turkey and vegetable soup

SERVES 6
PREP TIME 15 minutes
COOK TIME 45 minutes

This winter soup warms the soul. Earthy vegetables with a gentle amount of seasoning are cooked in my most favorite broth, turkey, paired with easy-peasy turkey meatballs. Barley makes it both hearty and heartwarming, and it's all topped off with an unexpected garnish: seaweed. Seaweed has natural flavor and crunch, with so many great options: nori, hijiki, or dulce. Plus, it's packed full of minerals and nutrients. *Recipe pictured on page vi*

8 oz (225 g) turkey sausages, casings removed

1 Tbsp butter

1 white onion, diced

2 leeks, trimmed, cleaned and cut into half moons

1 bay leaf

3 sprigs thyme

2 small turnips, peeled and cut into bite-size cubes

2 parsnips, peeled and cut into bite-size cubes

¼ tsp ground coriander

⅛ tsp ground nutmeg

Pinch of cayenne pepper (optional)

6 cups turkey stock (page 141) or chicken or vegetable stock

⅓ cup pearl barley, rinsed

2 Yukon gold potatoes, cut into bite-size cubes

½ tsp salt

¼ tsp white pepper

1 Tbsp chopped dill

Seaweed, finely sliced, for garnish

Roll the turkey sausages into 1-inch meatballs. Set aside.

In a large stockpot over medium heat, melt the butter. Add the onions, leeks, bay leaf, and thyme, and sauté for 3 minutes. Add the turnips, parsnips, coriander, nutmeg, and cayenne pepper (if using). Stir to combine, then add the stock and bring to a boil.

Add the barley (see Note) and drop the heat to medium-low. Gently simmer, partially covered, for 20 minutes. Add the turkey meatballs, potatoes, salt, and pepper. Simmer for another 20 minutes, stirring occasionally. Scatter the dill into the soup. Taste and adjust the seasoning as desired. Discard the bay leaf (or leave it in to prove the soup is homemade!).

Divide the soup among the soup bowls and garnish with seaweed.

### NOTES

If you won't eat this soup in one sitting, cook the barley separately. Just add it to a pot of boiling salted water, bring the water back to a boil, then drop the heat to medium and cook, uncovered, until tender, about 20 to 30 minutes. Drain and rinse. Divide the barley among the bowls and ladle the soup on top. Store any unused barley in a sealed container, and the soup in a separate container in the fridge. The next day, they can be combined and reheated.

# north african–inspired harira soup

SERVES 8
PREP TIME 15 minutes
COOK TIME 1 hour

We have so many amazing African and Middle Eastern restaurants here in Toronto. It was at one of the Moroccan ones that I first tried harira soup years ago. This classic Moroccan comfort food dish is a hearty, abundantly spiced soup filled with all sorts of veggies and legumes. Here is my breezy take on it. This version is meat-free, and I omit the classic addition of smen, a preserved butter with a Parmesan flavor, only because it may be too challenging to source. To keep it vegetarian, feel free to use vegetable stock instead of chicken stock. To make it gluten-free, just use rice or rice noodles. This soup is always finished with a squeeze of lemon juice. Served with some fresh flatbread, it's a perfect stick-to-your-ribs winter dinner. For more of an authentic Moroccan flare, serve this soup with dates on the side. *Recipe pictured on page 282*

2 Tbsp olive oil

1 large carrot, finely diced

2 stalks celery, finely diced

1 yellow onion, finely diced

4 cloves garlic, minced

Salt and white pepper

2 Tbsp tomato paste

Zest of 1 orange

1 tsp ground cinnamon

1 tsp ground turmeric

1 tsp ground ginger

1 tsp ground cumin

1 tsp ground coriander

1 tsp saffron threads, ground down with the back of a spoon in a small dish

¾ tsp harissa powder

½ tsp smoked sweet paprika (see Note)

1 (28 oz/796 ml) can whole tomatoes

Warm the oil in a large stockpot over medium-low heat. Add the carrots, celery, onions, and garlic and season with ½ teaspoon of salt and ¼ teaspoon of pepper. Cook, stirring, until the onions are translucent, 8 minutes. Add the tomato paste, orange zest, cinnamon, turmeric, ginger, cumin, coriander, saffron, harissa, and paprika. Cook, stirring, for another 3 minutes.

Add the whole tomatoes and their juices to the pot. Using your hands or the edge of a wooden spoon, break up the tomatoes into small pieces. Add the stock and lentils, season with ½ teaspoon each of salt and pepper, and bring to a boil. Cover, drop the heat to medium-low, and simmer until the lentils are tender, about 30 to 45 minutes. Add the chickpeas and let them warm through, about 5 minutes. Add the noodles and spinach and continue to cook, uncovered, until the noodles and spinach are softened, about 5 minutes.

Chop half of the cilantro and parsley leaves. Add the chopped cilantro and parsley to the soup, along with half of the scallions. Season with salt and pepper, if desired.

6 cups low-sodium chicken or vegetable stock

¾ cup French green lentils, rinsed

1 (14 oz/398 ml) can chickpeas, drained and rinsed

2 oz (50 g) thin egg noodles or vermicelli

2 cups baby spinach

⅓ cup cilantro leaves, divided

⅓ cup parsley leaves, divided

3 scallions, thinly sliced, divided

4 Tbsp grated Parmesan, for serving (optional)

Lemon wedges, for serving (optional)

Yogurt Flatbread (page 274) or warmed pita bread, for serving (optional)

To serve, divide the soup among the bowls and top with the whole cilantro and parsley leaves and the remaining scallions. Serve with a sprinkling of Parmesan and with lemon wedges and flatbread on the side, if desired.

NOTES

Look for "Pimentón de la Vera" on the smoked sweet paprika label. If you can't find it, use any smoked paprika as long as it isn't hot (Hungarian paprika is just too hot!).

To reheat leftovers, warm the soup in a pot over medium-low heat. Thin it out with a bit of water, about 1 tablespoon at a time, if it thickened in the fridge.

**NOTES**
You'll have more Russian dressing than you need, so just make half a batch if desired—or use leftovers as a dip for fries, onion rings (page 203), or even chips (page 94)!

# bathurst street sheet pan reubens

SERVES 4
MAKES 1¼ cups dressing
PREP TIME 30 minutes
COOK TIME 25 minutes

A Reuben in Manhattan often means a sandwich packed with enough meat to feed a family of four. Even in Toronto, all the great Bathurst Street delis give generous servings. A Reuben is a layered delight of sauerkraut, pastrami, and Swiss cheese. Some suggest cooking it grilled cheese–style, but the flip can get messy. Enter the sheet pan! Once it's baked, I take the cheese-only bread and smoosh it over the one with the meat, sauerkraut, and cheese. Tada! All the taste and none of the mess. Plus, everything warms through evenly—even when the sandwich is fully loaded. Russian dressing is the classic Reuben spread, but Jim usually just wants mustard. It's up to you. Just don't leave out the pickles—they are mandatory!

## Russian Dressing

1 cup mayonnaise

¼ cup chili sauce or ketchup

1 Tbsp horseradish, squeezed to remove extra liquid

1 tsp Worcestershire sauce, or 2 tsp coconut aminos

1 tsp hot sauce

Salt and pepper

## Reuben Sammies

12¼ oz (350 g) rinsed and drained sauerkraut

2 Tbsp chicken stock, water, or dry white wine

Salt and pepper

8 slices rye bread

1¼–1½ lb (560–680 g) shaved or sliced corned beef, pastrami, or Montreal smoked meat

8 slices Swiss or Jarlsberg cheese

Pickles, for serving

French fries or onion rings, for serving (optional)

Preheat the oven to 400°F.

### For the Russian Dressing

In a small bowl, mix together the mayonnaise, chili sauce, horseradish, Worcestershire sauce, hot sauce, and salt and pepper. Taste and adjust the seasoning as desired. Cover and chill in the fridge until needed.

### For the Reuben Sammies

In a small pot over medium-low heat, stir together the sauerkraut and stock. Season with ½ teaspoon each of salt and pepper. Simmer gently, until the sauerkraut is softened and warmed through, about 8 to 10 minutes. Set aside.

Place the bread on a baking sheet. Spread some Russian dressing over each slice. Divide the meat among 4 slices of the bread. Top the meat with the warmed sauerkraut. Place a slice of cheese on each slice of bread. Bake until the cheese starts to soften, about 8 to 10 minutes. Change the setting to broil and broil until the cheese has completely melted and started to bubble, about 5 to 8 minutes. If this is taking too long, move the oven rack to the upper part of the oven, but keep an eye on them!

### To Serve

Remove from the oven. Take the cheese-only slices and place them over their meat and sauerkraut counterparts. Serve with pickles, and french fries or onion rings, if desired.

# baby kale and romaine caesar salad

SERVES 4
PREP TIME 25 minutes
COOK TIME 10 minutes

Caesar salad is a touchy subject for me. When we go out, I rarely order it because so often the croutons are break-your-teeth hard, the bacon is missing, and the dressing is all watered down! The best Caesar salad I ever had was in a lovely inn in upstate New York. It was made table-side, like back in the day. The server made the dressing from scratch, mashing the garlic and anchovies into a rough paste in a large bowl. Then he added the bacon, the greens, and the croutons to the bowl and tossed them with the dressing. He plated the salad and served it with shaved Parmigiano-Reggiano over top. It was sublime. Here is my version. I like using romaine hearts and baby kale for a bit of color and texture. Fresh, hand-torn croutons ensure there are little nooks and crannies to soak up the dressing, and sautéing them in some of the bacon fat and herbs means that they make a statement. The anchovies add the perfect umami presence, but don't worry, you won't even know they are there. *Recipe pictured on page 282*

## Caesar Salad

4 handfuls romaine hearts, torn into bite-size pieces

2 handfuls baby kale

2 thick slices sourdough or any soft rustic bread

5 slices (about 4½ oz/125 g total) bacon, cut into ½- to ¾-inch pieces

1 tsp olive oil

1 tsp dried thyme leaves

1 tsp dried basil leaves

1 tsp dried oregano leaves

Salt and pepper

### For the Caesar Salad

Place the romaine and kale in a bowl, cover with a damp paper towel, and place in the fridge to keep crisp until needed. Cut the bread into 1-inch lengths, then tear each one into large bite-size cubes. Tearing the bread allows it to soak up all the lovely flavors more.

In a skillet over medium heat, sauté the bacon until cooked through and just crisp enough, about 6 minutes. Don't dry it out! Transfer to a paper towel–lined plate. Reserve 1 tablespoon of the bacon fat in the pan and discard the rest. Add the oil. Stir in the dried herbs and ½ teaspoon each of salt and pepper. Add the torn bread and toss to coat. Sauté until the bread is crispy on the outside but still soft on the inside, about 4 minutes. Transfer to a plate.

## Caesar Dressing

4 cloves garlic, finely minced (see Note)

6 anchovy fillets

Juice of 1 large lemon

3 Tbsp red wine vinegar

1½ Tbsp Dijon mustard

2 egg yolks or coddled egg yolks

2 good dashes Worcestershire sauce

½ cup extra virgin olive oil

Salt and pepper

2 oz (50 g) grated or shaved Parmigiano-Reggiano, to garnish

## For the Caesar Dressing

To make the dressing ahead, using a tall glass jar and an immersion blender, blend all the salad dressing ingredients. Place the lid on the jar and store in the fridge until needed. Bring back to room temperature 30 minutes before using.

To make the dressing and assemble the salad in front of your guests, place the garlic and anchovies in a large wooden bowl and mash them together with a fork. Add the lemon juice, vinegar, Dijon, egg yolks, and Worcestershire sauce and whisk to completely combine. Whisking constantly, slowly drizzle in the oil. Continue to whisk until emulsified. Season with ½ teaspoon each of salt and pepper. Taste and adjust the seasoning as desired.

## To Assemble

Add the crisp greens, half of the bacon, and half of the croutons to the wooden bowl. Pour in the dressing if you made it ahead. Toss to coat. Garnish with the remaining bacon, the remaining croutons, and the Parmigiano-Reggiano.

**NOTE**

If your garlic cloves are on the larger side, use three.

# winter slaw with orange yogurt dressing

SERVES 4
MAKES ¾ cup dressing
PREP TIME 20 minutes +
chilling

Returning to my theory that salad doesn't need a recipe (see page 17), this is a celebration of the lightness of a wintertime coleslaw, with citrus to spread sunshine when the skies are gray. This salad makes up for the inevitable winter carb loading, and it's a great side to a pork roast (page 189), a Reuben sandwich (page 183), mac 'n' cheese, or even sloppy joes! Slice or shred the slaw base ingredients of your choice (mine change depending on what is available) as part of your weekly food prep, using in whatever amounts you feel like; for 4 people, use about 6 cups of cut vegetables.

## Slaw Base

1 red or green cabbage, shredded

Broccoli, thinly sliced

Carrots, shredded or thinly sliced

Celery, thinly sliced on an angle

Fennel, thinly sliced

Sugar snap peas, thinly sliced

## Orange Yogurt Dressing

½ cup Greek yogurt

1 Tbsp honey

1 Tbsp red wine vinegar

1–2 Tbsp orange juice

Salt and pepper

1 tsp pink peppercorns, crushed

## Optional Slaw Toppings

1 scallion, sliced

1 red onion, thinly sliced

1 fuyu persimmon, cubed

Citrus segments

Sesame seeds, sunflower seeds, or chopped nuts, for garnish

### For the Slaw Base

Store the prepped vegetables in individual sealed containers in the fridge for up to 1 week. The cut carrots, celery, and fennel can be covered with cold water before sealing the container to keep them crisp. When you feel like slaw, just pull out whichever veggies are calling your name.

### For the Orange Yogurt Dressing

In a bowl, whisk together the yogurt, honey, and vinegar. Add the orange juice, 1 tablespoon at a time, until your desired consistency is achieved (I use it all). Season with salt and pepper. Stir in the pink peppercorns. Store in an airtight jar in the fridge for up to 3 days.

### To Assemble

A good hour before you want to serve your slaw, place about 6 cups of your desired slaw ingredients in a large bowl and toss to combine. Let the dressing come to room temperature and give it a good shake. Pour your desired amount of dressing over the slaw and toss. Cover and let sit for 1 hour in the fridge to let the flavors meld.

To serve, add any optional toppings and gently toss. Garnish with seeds or nuts.

### NOTE

You can also use Miso-Ginger Dressing (page 266) for fabulous results! You can add any other slaw toppings you like!

# creamed chard, kale, and spinach greens

SERVES 6
PREP TIME 20 minutes
COOK TIME 20 minutes

I'll be honest. I didn't care for creamed spinach as a kid. Oh, who are we kidding, I detested it! I constantly tried to find new ways to hide, it to convince my mum I'd cleaned my plate. But I'm all grown up these days (almost!), and now I get it. In fact, I enjoy not only creamed spinach but also creamed Swiss chard and kale. So I thought, why not combine all three for the ultimate greens side dish! Use lacinato kale, as its softer leaves make for easier cooking. Use Swiss chard with the white ribs, as the red ribs and veins could bleed into the béchamel sauce and muddy it up. Infusing the milk with cloves and a bay leaf adds a special dimension to the béchamel. I often find a dish like this also likes a bit of heat, so a sprinkle of cayenne or chili flakes is perfectly acceptable. I don't hide the creamed greens anymore! *Recipe pictured on page 164*

2 cups milk

4 whole cloves

1 bay leaf

2 Tbsp butter

1 Tbsp olive oil

3 Tbsp flour

1 tsp salt

½ tsp pepper

¼ tsp ground nutmeg

3 oz (85 g) lacinato kale, center rib removed, leaves roughly chopped

3 oz (85 g) Swiss chard, tough ribs removed, leaves roughly chopped

3 oz (85 g) baby spinach

Pinch of cayenne pepper or chili flakes (optional)

¼ cup Crème Fraîche (page 272) or sour cream, at room temperature

Juice of ½ lemon (optional)

Place the milk, cloves, and bay leaf in a small saucepan and bring to a gentle boil over medium heat, watching to ensure the milk doesn't boil over. Drop the heat to low and simmer for 15 minutes to meld the flavors. Strain the milk into a bowl, discard the cloves and bay leaf, and cover the bowl to keep the milk warm. Set aside.

In a large skillet over medium heat, melt the butter and warm the oil. Add the flour and whisk to combine. Cook, scraping up any browned bits from the bottom of the pan, for 1 minute. Whisk in the warm milk, ¼ cup at a time, stirring constantly until the sauce is thickened and getting bubbly. Stir in the salt, pepper, and nutmeg. Add the kale and Swiss chard, and cook until tender, about 3 minutes. Add the spinach and cook until softened, about 1 minute. Season to taste. Add the cayenne, if desired. Remove from the heat and stir in the crème fraîche. If you find it a little rich, add a splash of lemon juice. Serve.

# seville orange marmalade–glazed pork rib roast with kumquats

SERVES 6
PREP TIME 15 minutes
COOK TIME 1 hour,
40 minutes

Pork loin on the bone always makes for a juicy, flavorful meal and is equally perfect for company or a Sunday family dinner. Anytime we keep the meat on the bone, frenched to show off the rib bones, it looks super-impressive. My Spiced Seville Orange Marmalade (page 269) makes for the best glaze. I love the tang and texture the kumquats add, but if you can't find them, just use clementine or tangerine segments. Add a side of mash and creamed greens (page 188) for the best meal when it's chilly outside.

5–6 bone-in pork loin roast, frenched (see Note, page 190)

1 Tbsp chopped rosemary

1 Tbsp salt

2 tsp fennel seeds

2 tsp cracked black pepper

1 tsp sumac

2 cloves garlic, minced

8 oz (225 g) kumquats

⅓ cup + 2 Tbsp Spiced Seville Orange Marmalade (page 269) or store-bought marmalade

¾ cup chicken stock, or 1½ tsp Faux Chicken Bouillon Powder (page 265) dissolved in ¾ cup boiling water

1 tsp arrowroot starch or cornstarch, mixed with 1 tsp water

Place the rib roast in a 10-inch cast-iron skillet.

Using a mortar and pestle, crush together the rosemary, salt, fennel seeds, pepper, sumac, and garlic, making sure the fennel seeds get broken down. Rub this seasoning all over the roast, including its underside. Position the roast fat side up and let sit at room temperature while the oven is preheating.

Preheat the oven to 425°F.

Loosely cover the roast with foil and bake for 30 minutes. Drop the heat to 375°F. Remove the foil and roast for 30 minutes. Meanwhile, cut the kumquats in half crosswise and remove any obvious seeds. Thin the ⅓ cup of marmalade with 1 to 2 teaspoons of water.

After the 30 minutes are up, place the kumquats around the roast. Spoon the pan juices over the kumquats and baste the roast with the thinned marmalade. Take the internal temperature at the thickest part of the meat, near but not touching the bone, to get a sense of how it's cooking. Continue roasting, basting occasionally, until the internal temperature at the thickest part is 145°F, about 35 to 40 minutes. If the meat still needs to roast longer, remove the kumquats and set them aside. When the meat is done, transfer it to a cutting board and tent it with foil.

*recipe continues*

Meanwhile, preheat a skillet over medium-high heat. Add the remaining marmalade and whisk to soften. Add the stock and increase the heat to medium-high. Cook for 1 minute. Add the arrowroot mixture and stir. Stir until nicely thickened, about 1 minute. Season with salt and pepper.

Slice the pork between the bones, garnish with the kumquats, and serve with the basting sauce.

**NOTES**

Have your butcher french a loin roast for you. If needed, use butcher twine to tie the meat off firmly between each bone.

# koshari stuffed peppers

SERVES 6
PREP TIME 1 hour +
resting
COOK TIME 2 hours

Here's a really great mashup. Koshari is classic Egyptian street food, a combo of rice, lentils, and pasta, served with a spicy tomato sauce and fried onions on top. It's kind of a cross between North American chili and mujadara, a Levantine rice pilaf dish that contains lentils. I thought this most flavorful dish would make a fantastic stuffing for peppers. And it does! I never gravitated to the stuffed peppers my mum made me as a kid, but I realized it wasn't her recipe, it was me! I prefer the slightly sweet red, yellow, and orange bell peppers cooked this way over the more bitter green peppers—especially with this slightly spicy vegetarian filling. The frizzled onion topping is a breeze to make. Its crunch adds a great texture and harks back to the traditional way of serving koshari. You can have the onions ready to go before the peppers are done, and then, for serving, just sprinkle some on top of each pepper. Serve with a side salad, like the Levantine-Inspired Salad (page 232). *Recipe pictured on page 164*

## Rice

2 Tbsp olive oil

¾ cup basmati rice, rinsed

1 tsp ground cumin

1 cup + 2 Tbsp vegetable stock or
  water

¼ tsp salt

## Lentils and Pasta

¾ cup dried green or brown
  lentils, rinsed and picked
  over

1 bay leaf

1 clove garlic, smashed

2½ cups vegetable stock or
  water (see Note, page 193)

¾ cup macaroni, or whole-grain
  or gluten-free small pasta

Olive oil

Salt and pepper

½ tsp ras el hanout

### For the Rice

Heat the oil in a saucepan over medium-high heat. Add the rice and cumin, and stir to coat. Add the stock and salt. When the rice starts to bubble and foam, drop the heat to medium-low, cover the pot, and cook for 12 minutes. Remove from the heat and let rest, covered, for 10 minutes. Fluff the rice with a rubber spatula, transfer to a large bowl and set aside.

### For the Lentils and Pasta

In a large saucepan, combine the lentils, bay leaf, garlic, and stock, and bring to a boil over medium-high heat. Drop the heat to low and simmer, covered, until the lentils are tender but still hold their shape, about 15 to 20 minutes. Start checking on them at the 12-minute point.

Meanwhile, bring a pot of salted water to a boil. Add the macaroni and cook according to the package instructions until al dente. Drain and toss with a little oil. Transfer to the bowl of rice.

When the lentils are ready, drain off any excess liquid and season with salt and pepper. Transfer to the bowl of rice. Add the ras el hanout and toss to combine. Set aside.

## Tomato Sauce

2 Tbsp olive oil

1 yellow onion, diced

2 cloves garlic, minced

1 (14 oz/398 ml) can crushed
    tomatoes

2–3 tsp baharat spice blend

1 tsp chili flakes

1 Tbsp red wine vinegar

Salt and pepper

## To Assemble

6 red, yellow, or orange bell
    peppers

Salt and pepper

1 cup shredded fontina

## Frizzled Onions

1 large yellow onion, finely
    sliced lengthwise

¼ cup flour

Neutral oil, for frying

2 tsp baharat spice blend

1 tsp chili flakes (optional)

### NOTES

If using water to cook the lentils, why not add 2 tablespoons of Faux Chicken Bouillon Powder (page 265) for added flavor? The filling can be made a day ahead. Chill in an airtight container in the fridge and bring to room temperature before assembling. The peppers can be stuffed and refrigerated up to 1 day ahead of baking. Add about 10 minutes to the baking time.

### For the Tomato Sauce

Heat the oil in a saucepan over medium-high heat. Add the onions and sauté until golden, about 5 minutes. Add the garlic and sauté for 1 minute. Add the tomatoes and their juices, 2 teaspoons of the baharat, the chili flakes, and vinegar. Drop the heat to medium-low and simmer, uncovered and stirring occasionally, until the sauce thickens slightly, about 20 minutes. Season with salt and pepper, taste. Add more seasonings if needed.

### To Assemble

Preheat the oven to 375°F.

Using a sharp knife, remove the stem and top ½ inch or so of each pepper to create a wide opening. You can bake the "lids" alongside the stuffed peppers. If not, just snack on them! Remove the core, seeds, and membranes. Generously sprinkle the insides with salt and pepper. Place the peppers cut side up in a baking dish that will hold them tightly so that they won't tip over.

Stir the tomato sauce into the rice and lentil mixture. Season to taste. Spoon the filling into the peppers, packing it in until it reaches the top. Carefully pour 1 cup of water between the peppers. Sprinkle the cheese over the peppers. Spray one side of a large piece of foil with cooking spray and place it sprayed side down over top, sealing tightly around the dish. Bake until the peppers are softened but not mushy, about 1 hour. Check the side of a pepper with a sharp knife. If needed, bake for another 10 minutes or so.

### For the Frizzled Onions

Meanwhile, in a bowl, toss the onions with just enough flour to coat. Fill a saucepan with about ¾ inch of oil and warm over medium-high heat. Once the oil is shimmering, add 1 onion slice. As soon as it starts frying up, the oil is hot enough. Once the oil is heated through, working with small handfuls of onions at a time, shake off any excess flour off the onions, and use a spider to gently submerge them into the oil. Fry, turning occasionally, until golden, about 2 to 3 minutes. Transfer to a paper towel–lined plate and sprinkle with some baharat spice and chili flakes, if using. Continue until all the onions are done. To serve, scatter the onions on top of the peppers.

# spiced savoy cabbage rolls

SERVES 6
MAKES about 12 rolls
PREP TIME 1 hour
COOK TIME 2 hours

If there is one dish that I most vividly remember my mum making, it's cabbage rolls. I can see clear as crystal her slender fingers wrapping the tender cabbage leaves around the filling of meat, rice, and seasonings. She folded them in the most elegant manner, if making cabbage rolls can ever be elegant! After adding those little bundles to the casserole, she prepared her tomato broth (usually consisting of a large can of tomato juice!) and let it all simmer for a few hours. And while the cabbage rolls were in the oven, she made the mashed potatoes. Then we ate. However, I didn't come to love cabbage rolls until I was older. Then I married Jim. If I made him cabbage rolls each month, his smile would be permanent. I always turn to savoy cabbage (the "winter cabbage") for its ruffly, lacy leaves, so full of flavor and easy to fold. To keep things flavorful, I spice up the filling with coriander, Aleppo pepper, paprika, nutmeg, and white pepper. *Recipe pictured on page 164*

1 head savoy cabbage

### Filling

¾ cup long-grain white rice, rinsed

1 Tbsp olive oil

1 large yellow onion, chopped

4 cloves garlic, minced

1 lb (450 g) lean ground beef

½ lb (225 g) ground pork

½ cup parsley leaves, chopped

¼ cup dill leaves, chopped

1 tsp salt

¾ tsp black pepper

½ tsp white pepper

½ tsp paprika

½ tsp cracked coriander seeds (see Note)

½ tsp Aleppo pepper

¼ tsp ground nutmeg

2 eggs

Bring a large pot of salted water (I use about 3 tablespoons of fine sea salt) to a boil. Use your hands to gently pull the outer leaves off the cabbage. As you get closer to the core, where the leaves are tougher, use a sharp knife to cut right along the core to release them.

Working in batches if need be, gently slide the leaves into the water and cook until they are tender and pliable, about 3 to 4 minutes (depending how thick the rib is in the middle). Transfer the leaves to a tea towel. Repeat. Reserve 3 cups of the cooking water and set aside.

### For the Filling

Add the rice and 1½ cups of water to a saucepan and bring to a boil over medium-high heat. Drop the heat to low and simmer, covered, until the water is absorbed and the rice is tender, about 18 to 20 minutes. Remove from the heat and let sit for 10 minutes. Gently fluff the rice. Transfer to a large bowl and let cool.

In a skillet over medium heat, warm the oil and sauté the onions and garlic until just softened, about 4 to 5 minutes. Transfer the onions and garlic to the bowl of rice.

## Sauce

1 (28 oz/796 ml) jar or can whole or crushed tomatoes, or passata

1 Tbsp tomato paste

1 tsp salt

¾ tsp pepper

¾ tsp paprika

½ tsp garlic powder

½ tsp Aleppo pepper

3 bay leaves

Sour cream, mashed potatoes, or sauerkraut, for serving

### NOTES

To crack coriander seeds, crush them with a mortar and pestle or the back of a butcher knife. The filling can be made the day before and stored in an airtight container in the fridge. Just bring it back to room temperature before assembling the cabbage.

Double the recipe if you want plenty for the freezer. Just divide the sauce in freezer-proof containers, arrange the cabbage rolls in the sauce, and freeze for up to 1 month. Then, when the craving hits, thaw one container in the fridge overnight and bake the next day as directed above.

Add the beef, pork, parsley, parsley, dill, salt, black and white peppers, paprika, coriander seeds, Aleppo pepper, and nutmeg to the bowl of rice and mix to combine.

In a small bowl, whisk the eggs. Add the eggs to the meat mixture and use your hands to gently mix the filling until well blended. Take a piece of filling about the size and thickness of a quarter and sauté in the same skillet until just cooked through. Let cool slightly, then taste, and adjust the seasonings in the bowl if needed.

### For the Sauce

In a food processor fitted with the steel blade or a blender, combine 2 cups of the reserved cabbage water, the tomatoes and their juices, and the tomato paste. Season with the salt, pepper, paprika, garlic powder, and Aleppo pepper.

### To Assemble

Preheat the oven to 350°F.

Using a sharp knife, cut out the large rib (about 2½ inches of the bottom, depending on the size) from each cabbage leaf. If the rib is very thick, shave away some of the outer rib so that it will bend more easily.

Sprinkle the leaf with a pinch of salt and pepper. Shape about ½ cup of the filling to form a little log and place it on the lower center of the leaf. Fold the leaf's side edges and then the bottom edge over the center, to enclose like an envelope. Roll until the top end is tucked under. Repeat until all the filling is used up. The smaller the leaves, the less filling you will need.

Use the remaining small leaves to cover the bottom of a casserole, braising dish, or 9- × 13-inch baking dish. Arrange all the cabbage rolls snugly in the dish. Pour the sauce gently around all the cabbage rolls so that they are almost covered. If the sauce only goes up halfway, add a bit more of the cabbage water. Nestle the bay leaves into the sauce.

Cover with an ovenproof lid or foil and bake on the center rack of the oven until tender, about 1 to 1½ hours.

Serve with sour cream, mashed potatoes, or even sauerkraut!

# cocoa and red wine–braised short ribs with herbed polenta

SERVES 6
PREP TIME 40 minutes + overnight resting
COOK TIME 3 hours, 20 minutes

After savoring the braised short ribs at Balthazar—the great French bistro in Manhattan—I set out to master the recipe. This is one of the first French dishes I perfected after Jim and I were married. I've since made it my own, and it's now a winter staple. I add raw cocoa powder, which gives depth to the braising sauce and intensifies the goodness of the meat's flavor. Don't worry, it won't taste like chocolate. This dish works wonderfully with a side of herbed polenta to soak up the liquids. Bonus: this tastes even better the next day. So cook it a day ahead, and warm it up for a perfect dinner! Soaking the cornmeal on the counter the night before, a trick from the *Serious Eats* blog, reduces the cooking time by half, so, you can finish the polenta while the short ribs are warming.

## Short Ribs

2 Tbsp olive oil

5 lb (2¼ kg) short ribs, cut crosswise (see Note, page 198)

1 large yellow onion, diced

6 cloves garlic, minced

2 large carrots, diced small

2 stalks celery, diced small

Salt and pepper

2 Tbsp chopped rosemary

1 Tbsp chopped thyme

1 bay leaf

½ cup oil-packed sun-dried tomatoes, chopped

2 cups dry red wine

2 cups beef broth (see Note on page 98)

3 Tbsp butter, softened

2 Tbsp flour

2 Tbsp raw cocoa powder

## For the Short Ribs

The day before serving, in a braiser or a large, wide pan over medium-high heat, warm the oil. Add the short ribs in a single layer, working in batches if necessary, and sear on all sides until well browned, about 3 minutes per side. Transfer to a plate.

Drop the heat to medium and add the onions and garlic. Stir to coat them in fat and cook for about 1 minute. Add the carrots, celery, and 1 teaspoon each of salt and pepper. Stir and cook until just starting to soften, about 4 to 5 minutes.

Nestle the meat into the vegetables, so that everything fits in one layer. Sprinkle the rosemary and thyme over top and then add the bay leaf and sun-dried tomatoes. Pour in the wine and stock, and bring to a boil over medium-high heat. Drop the heat to low, cover the pot, and bring to a low simmer. Cook until the meat is very tender, almost falling off the bone, about 2½ hours, depending on the thickness of the ribs. Transfer the meat to a plate, keeping the sauce in the braiser.

*recipe continues*

### Herbed Polenta

3 cups water

2 cups milk

1 cup medium- or coarse-
   ground cornmeal (not
   instant polenta)

### To Serve

Salt and pepper

2 Tbsp butter

2 Tbsp chopped parsley

#### NOTES

You can replace the short ribs with osso buco, veal shanks, oxtails, or lamb shanks, which all also taste great the next day. The cooking time will vary, from 2 hours upward, but you can easily continue to cook until the meat is ready to fall of the bone. You really can't dry them out, as you are cooking over low temperature and they are surrounded by great liquids.

In place of the herbed polenta, you can use mashed potatoes, any short pasta, like penne or rigatoni, or even gnocchi.

To store leftovers, let the meat and sauce cool, place them in an airtight container, and store in the fridge for up to 4 days. To reheat an individual serving of short ribs and sauce, cook them in a saucepan set over medium-low heat until warmed through.

In a small bowl, use a fork to mash the butter into the flour and cocoa powder until a paste forms. Add the paste to the braiser, stir to combine, and bring to a boil over medium heat. Cook until the sauce starts to thicken nicely, about 5 to 6 minutes. Season with salt and pepper. Discard the bay leaf. Return the meat to the braiser and turn to coat it on all sides.

For best results, let cool at room temperature. Transfer the meat and sauce to an airtight container and let rest in the fridge overnight.

### For the Herbed Polenta

The night before serving, or the morning of, combine the water, milk, and cornmeal in a large saucepan, cover, and let stand at room temperature until ready to cook.

### To Serve

Preheat the oven to 325°F.

Place the meat in a baking dish just large enough to hold it comfortably and add the sauce. Cover with foil and heat in the oven until warmed through, about 20 to 25 minutes.

About 20 minutes before serving, bring the saucepan with the cornmeal to a boil over medium-high heat. Stir frequently until it has thickened and is starting to split, about 5 minutes. Immediately drop the heat to a simmer and use a silicone spatula or wooden spoon to stir it frequently, scraping along the bottom to ensure nothing starts to scorch. Continue to simmer until the mixture is perfectly thick and pulls away from the sides of the pot, about 30 minutes. Season with salt and pepper and stir in the butter to create a creamy, smooth, and glossy texture. If it is too firm, you can thin it out with a bit more water or milk, whisking it in about 1 tablespoon at a time until the polenta is smooth. Stir in the parsley.

Immediately divide the polenta among shallow bowls (pasta bowls work great). Place the short ribs on top.

# québécois tourtière 2.0

SERVES 8
MAKES one 9- or 10-inch
double-crust pie
PREP TIME 40 minutes
COOK TIME 1½ hours

Tourtière is a French-Canadian savory pie that contains pork and spices (and sometimes wild game) and is usually served in the winter. The meat, spices, and potatoes are cooked down in a pot until thickened, then spooned into a pie crust and baked. I've had some bland versions with a soggy crust in the past, so I went on a mission to perfect a tourtière where each bite will result in a party in your mouth—as it should! Cinnamon, cloves, allspice, and nutmeg are prominent, as are garlic, thyme, sage, pepper, and even cayenne pepper for a warm kick at the end. Unlike the most traditional versions, I added carrots and celery to the onions. I apologize to the die-hard tourtière traditionalists, but I find that they add texture and flavor (and fiber and nutrients!) to the pie without detracting from it. I serve it with store-bought Branston Pickle, a spicy, tangy chutney of sorts, because this is what I had in Cornwall with my first meat-filled Cornish pasty. It's the perfect contrast to this rich meat pie. Again, to the traditionalists, I guess I should apologize, but I also encourage you to at least try my variation!

2 Yukon gold or yellow-flesh potatoes, peeled

Salt and pepper

1 lb (450 g) lean ground pork

½ lb (225 g) lean ground beef

1 yellow onion, finely diced

½ carrot, finely diced

½ stalk celery, finely diced

3 cloves garlic, minced

½ tsp dried sage leaves

½ tsp dried thyme leaves

½ tsp ground white pepper

½ tsp ground cinnamon

¼ tsp ground cloves

¼ tsp ground allspice

¼–½ tsp cayenne pepper

Place one oven rack in the bottom third of the oven and one in the middle. Preheat the oven to 425°F.

Cut the potatoes into eighths and transfer to a pot. Cover with water and add a heaping tablespoon of salt. Bring the water to a boil over medium-high heat, then drop the heat to medium and cook the potatoes until just tender, about 12 minutes. Reserve ½ cup of the potato water, then drain the potatoes. Immediately pass the potatoes through a potato ricer to turn them into a fluffy mound of feathery potatoes. Alternatively, use a masher, but this will give you chunkier mash. Set aside.

In a large pot, mix together the pork, beef, onions, carrots, celery, garlic, dried herbs and spices, and reserved potato water. Bring to a boil over medium heat, stirring to ensure that nothing sticks to the bottom of the pot. Continue to cook, breaking up the meat, until the meat is in uniformly small bite-size pieces, the vegetables are just tender, and about 2 tablespoons of liquid remains, about 20 minutes. Remove from the heat.

*recipe continues*

¼ cup chopped parsley

1 recipe No-Fail Pie Pastry, savory variation (page 279), divided into 2 disks and chilled

1 egg, whisked with a bit of water

¼ tsp flakey finishing salt

Add the potatoes and parsley to the pot and stir. The potatoes should soak up any remaining liquid. If the mixture is still watery, continue to cook for a few more minutes. Season with salt and pepper. The potato water will have salt, so you may not need too much salt. (If you're making this a day ahead, let the mixture cool, transfer it to an airtight container and pop it in the fridge. Just bring to room temperature before moving on to the next step.)

Roll out one disk of pastry and transfer it to fit a 9- or 10-inch pie plate (see page 277). Remove excess pastry and crimp the bottom shell as you desire (see page 277). Spoon the meat mixture into the pie shell, smoothing it out so it has an even top. Firmly press the mixture down to remove any air pockets.

Roll out the other pastry disk to form a top crust or lattice crust and/or cookie cutouts (see pages 278 to 279). Cover the pie with the top pastry, ensuring the meat is covered, and crimp or finish the edges as desired (see page 277). Brush with a little egg wash and sprinkle with the flakey finishing salt.

Place the pie plate on a baking sheet and bake the pie in the bottom third of the oven for 30 minutes. Drop the heat to 400°F. Carefully move the pie to the middle rack and continue baking until golden brown, about 25 minutes. If parts of the crust are starting to turn brown before the pie is ready, cover with foil or a pie crust protector. Let cool for at least 15 minutes before serving.

**NOTES**

If you have leftover filling, place it in a small ramekin or baking dish, cover with scrap pastry, and bake until the crust is golden brown, about 45 minutes. Serve this with a hearty salad or coleslaw, or roasted broccoli or asparagus.

If you want to pull out all the stops, you could serve with a port and demi-glace reduction sauce. Cook 1 cup of beef gravy with ¼ cup dry port and 1 tablespoon of demi-glace in a heavy saucepan over medium-high heat. Cook until the liquid reduces to 1 cup, then stir in ⅓ cup dry port and season with salt and pepper. Before serving, whisk in 1 tablespoon of butter.

This recipe calls for a potato ricer, which creates the perfect mound of fluffy snow.

# german meat patties with stout gravy and onion rings

SERVES 6

MAKES 12 patties

PREP TIME 30 minutes + chilling time

COOK TIME 1 hour, 10 minutes

Meat patties, or Frikadellen—a hamburger without the bun—were eaten regularly at my house with a side of potatoes. When I started making these for Jim, I added a bit of gravy just so that the Frikadellen didn't look naked. This gravy is a nod to my mum, thanks to Maggi (see the Note on page 95). Yes, you could add mushrooms to the gravy, but hey, Jim feels a certain way about 'shrooms. The choice of side these days is beer-battered onion rings, the perfect accompaniment!

## Frikadellen

2 slices day-old sourdough or white bread, thick crusts removed

2 Tbsp olive oil, divided

1 onion, finely diced

2 cloves garlic, minced

1 lb (450 g) ground beef

8 oz (225 g) ground pork

3 Tbsp chopped parsley

1 tsp dried marjoram

1 tsp salt

½ tsp white pepper

½ tsp paprika

½ tsp caraway seeds, crushed

1 Tbsp German or spicy mustard (see Note, page 204)

1 tsp Worcestershire sauce or Maggi

1 egg, beaten

¼ cup milk

1 Tbsp oil, for frying

1 Tbsp butter, for frying

### For the Frikadellen

Place the bread in a food processor fitted with the steel blade and pulse until rough breadcrumbs form, about 1 to 2 minutes. Add the breadcrumbs to a large bowl.

In a large skillet over medium heat, warm the olive oil and sauté the onions and garlic until softened and just turning golden. Set aside to cool.

Add the beef, pork, parsley, marjoram, salt, pepper, paprika, caraway seeds, mustard, and Worcestershire to the breadcrumbs. Add the cooled onions and beaten egg and give everything a gentle mix. Add the milk. Using your fingers, gently mix together. The mixture should be moist and hold together when you press it together. If it's too dry, add more milk, 1 teaspoon at a time, until it holds together.

Lightly oil the same skillet and place it over medium heat. Break off a small piece of the mixture and form it into a small patty (about the size of a quarter). Sauté until cooked through, about 2½ minutes on each side. Taste, and adjust the seasonings in the bowl as desired. This way your meatballs will taste the way you want them to.

Line a sheet or plate with wax paper. Pat down the mixture in the bowl and divide it into four equal parts. Using lightly oiled or wet hands, shape each into three patties. Place them on the prepared sheet (if stacking the patties, use wax paper between layers) and chill in the refrigerate for 30 minutes.

## Gravy

1 Tbsp butter

1 onion, minced

2 cloves garlic, minced

2 tsp brown sugar

2 cups beef broth

½ cup stout

1 tsp Worcestershire sauce

1 Tbsp arrowroot starch

Pepper

## Onion Rings

2 large sweet onions, sliced into
    ½-inch rings and chilled for
    1 hour

2 cups flour, divided

5 Tbsp cornstarch, divided

3 tsp salt, divided

Neutral oil, for frying

½ tsp baking powder

¼ tsp baking soda

½ tsp white pepper

12 oz can regular or blonde
    lager, ice cold

Flakey finishing salt

In the same skillet over medium-high heat, warm the neutral oil and butter. Working in batches, sear the patties on one side until browned, about 4 to 5 minutes. Drop the heat to medium, turn them over, and fry until cooked through, about 4 to 5 minutes. Turn once more and cook until crispy on both sides and a thermometer inserted horizontally into the center of a patty reads 145°F. Transfer the patties to a baking dish and tent with foil. Reserve the skillet, discarding any excess fat and blackened bits.

### For the Gravy

Preheat the oven to 250°F.

Return the skillet to medium heat and warm the butter. Sauté the onions, garlic, and sugar until softened. Add the beef broth and stout, and bring to a boil over medium-high heat. Drop the heat to medium-low and cook, uncovered, for 10 minutes. Stir in the Worcestershire. In a small glass, combine the arrowroot starch with 1 tablespoon of water. Stir in the arrowroot mixture. Simmer, uncovered, until the gravy is thickened, about 6 to 8 minutes. Season with pepper. Pour the gravy over the patties. Keep them warm in the oven while making the onion rings.

### For the Onion Rings

Remove the thin inner membranes from the chilled rings. In a large freezer bag, combine 1 cup of flour, 1 tablespoon of cornstarch, and 2 teaspoons of salt. Place the onions in the bag and give everything a good shake to coat thoroughly and evenly.

Half fill a Dutch oven or wok with oil. Set it over medium-high heat and heat the oil to 375°F. Make sure any long handles are pointed away from you. Line a cooling rack with paper towels and place on a baking sheet.

In a bowl, combine the remaining flour, cornstarch, and salt with the baking powder, baking soda, and pepper. Whisk in one-third of the beer, being careful not to overmix. Keep adding the beer, 1 tablespoon at a time, until a very thick pancake batter with small clumps of flour forms. To test, dip an onion ring into the batter and raise it over the bowl. The batter should cling to the onion ring without dropping back into the bowl when raised.

*recipe continues*

**To Serve**

Spicy or German Mustard

Dill pickles

Sliced radishes

Sliced cucumbers

Working with one onion at a time, dip the onion into the batter and shake off any excess. Repeat with the other onions.

When you're ready to fry, working in batches, use a spider to lower the onions into the oil. Fry until they turn a golden brown, about 2 minutes on each side. Monitor the oil and keep it around 350°F while the onions are frying to ensure they don't brown too quickly. You may need to give it a few minutes to come back to temperature between batches. Drain on the prepared cooling rack and sprinkle with finishing salt. Keep warm in the oven until ready to serve.

**To Serve**

Serve the meat patties on a platter with extra gravy on the side, and the onion rings in a bowl. Pickles and mustard on the table! Or serve two patties with gravy on each plate, onion rings on the side.

**NOTES**

Form all the Frikadellen, even you are only going to eat half. To freeze the rest, place the uncooked patties on a tray in the freezer. Once they are frozen, transfer them to a large freezer bag for up to 2 months. Just take out as many as you need and cook as directed.

German mustards are often spiced or hot, but some can also be sweet. They often come in a tube, and can be found at any respectable European deli!

# chocolate pecan date cake with butterscotch sauce

MAKES one 8-inch cake
PREP TIME 30 minutes +
resting
COOK TIME 45 minutes

When we were in Scotland, Jim ordered sticky toffee pudding cake every time he could. With its rich moist cake, the sweetness from the dates, and all that lovely thick caramel-like sauce, what's not to love?! This recipe, which has a similar flavor and texture to the cake from that trip, is a variation of a handwritten recipe that Jim's mom gave me when Jim and I were first married. She was giving me a head start on making Jim's belly happy! I've added a slightly salty butterscotch sauce to complete this dessert for a cozy winter's eve. A couple of fingers of single malt on the side would complete it perfectly. Make this early in the day and let it cool. *Recipe pictured on page 164*

## Cake

4 Tbsp (55 g) butter

½ cup packed (80 g) finely chopped dates (see Note, page 207)

½ tsp baking soda

1 Tbsp instant coffee powder or espresso powder

¾ cup boiling water

1 egg

½ cup (115 g) sugar

¾ cup (110 g) flour

½ tsp baking powder

½ tsp salt

½ cup (80 g) finely chopped dark chocolate

¼ cup (30 g) finely chopped pecans

## For the Cake

Preheat the oven to 350°F. Grease an 8-inch round springform cake pan and line the bottom and sides with parchment paper.

In a small saucepan over medium-low heat, melt the butter. Set aside to cool.

Place the dates and baking soda in a large bowl. Add the coffee powder to a measuring cup. Pour the boiling water over top and stir to blend. Pour the coffee over the dates. Stir well to combine. Set aside.

Beat the egg in a medium bowl. Add the melted butter and sugar, and use a handheld mixer to blend them well with the egg.

In a small bowl, whisk together the flour, baking powder, and salt. Sift the dry ingredients over the wet mixture. Mix with a wooden spoon until just blended. Do not overmix.

Fold the batter into the date mixture. Fold in the chocolate and pecans. Pour the batter (it will be rather loose) into the prepared pan.

Place the pan on a baking sheet and bake until a skewer inserted in the center of the cake comes out clean, about 40 to 45 minutes. While the cake is baking, prepare the sauce.

## Butterscotch Sauce

1¼ cups (200 g) packed muscovado or dark brown sugar

¼ tsp salt

1½ cups heavy cream

½ tsp bourbon vanilla paste or extract

¼ cup + 1 Tbsp (70 g) butter, cubed

Cinnamon Sugar No-Churn Ice Cream (page 254) or vanilla ice cream, for serving (optional)

## For the Butterscotch Sauce

Place the sugar, salt, cream, and vanilla in a saucepan. Whisk to blend well. Add the butter and cook over medium heat until the butter has melted, stirring regularly. Drop the heat to medium-low and simmer for 3 minutes, stirring to blend until quite smooth. Remove the pan from the heat.

When the cake comes out of the oven, place the baking pan on a cooling rack and use a wooden skewer to poke a good number of holes into the surface of the cake. Using a spoon, slowly spread about ⅓ cup of the sauce over the surface of the cake, letting it settle into the holes. Let the cake cool for 30 minutes. Remove the sides of the pan.

Serve at room temperature or warmed up slightly (in a toaster oven or oven at 300°F for a few minutes), along with more sauce and a scoop of ice cream, if desired.

**NOTES**

I store pitted dates in the freezer. Then I partially thaw them for easier chopping.

If you don't have a springform cake pan, you can use an 8-inch square cake pan lined with parchment paper hanging over the edges.

If you store extra butterscotch sauce in the fridge, warm it on low heat for about 3 to 5 minutes before using.

# mincemeat tart with citrus crème anglaise

MAKES one 9-inch tart
PREP TIME 1 hour +
chilling
COOK TIME 1 hour,
20 minutes

I think I was born in the wrong era. I just love all the old-time recipes— you know, the ones that use treacle, suet, and other not-so-fashionable ingredients. Yes, I like fruit cake, and I adore mincemeat pie. I could eat it year-round (I'm looking at you, Eccles cakes). Mincemeat pie was originally a way of preserving meat without salting or smoking it in the Middle Ages. It used a Middle Eastern mixture of cloves, cinnamon, and nutmeg, along with dried fruit. The preserved meat was stored and relied on by farmers' wives to feed the workers throughout the cold winter months. While "meat" is still part of the name, the meat got dropped about a hundred years back. Today, I'm happy to skip mutton or venison in this recipe (although I do want to come up with a savory lamb recipe using these spices). For this recipe, I combine all the classic ingredients of a lovely mincemeat with the bright contrast of a citrus crème anglaise.

## Mincemeat Filling

2 Granny Smith apples

1 large or 2 medium Bosc pears

1 cup (60 g) walnuts or pecans

2 Tbsp candied ginger

1 cup (140 g) dried currants

½ cup (80 g) sultanas

1 cup sugar

4 Tbsp butter

Zest and juice of ½ lemon

Zest of ½ navel orange

1 tsp salt

1 tsp ground cinnamon

¼ tsp ground nutmeg

¼ tsp ground allspice

¼ tsp ground cloves

¼ cup apple cider

¼ cup brandy, cognac, or rum

1 Tbsp apple cider vinegar

### For the Mincemeat Filling

Peel the apples and pears, and cut them into ¼-inch cubes. Finely chop the walnuts, and finely dice the candied ginger.

Combine all the ingredients in a large, heavy-bottomed pot. Place over medium-high heat, bring to a boil, and then drop the heat to a simmer. Cook, stirring regularly with a wooden spoon while scraping any bits off the bottom, until the liquid has reduced to a good 2 tablespoons and the thick syrup has coated all the ingredients, about 25 minutes. Let cool. The remaining liquid will solidify as it cools, so you want some syrup there or you'll have a stiff, dry filling. Store in a glass jar in the fridge until it is chilled or for up to 1 month. Bring back to room temperature before using.

*recipe continues*

## Tart

1 recipe No-Fail Pie Pastry (page 277), divided into 2 disks and chilled

1 egg, whisked with a bit of water

Turbinado sugar, for sprinkling

1 recipe Crème Anglaise, Citrus Variation (page 272), for serving

## For the Tart

Place one disk of pastry between two sheets of parchment paper. Roll out the pastry to about 12 inches in diameter and ⅛ inch thick. Use the bottom layer of paper to transfer and flip the pastry into a 9-inch tart pan with a removable bottom. Let the pastry naturally settle into the pan, filling the corners without stretching up the sides. Using a rolling pin or knife, smooth the dough against the edges. Prick the base of the tart shell with a fork. Chill in the fridge for 20 to 30 minutes.

Meanwhile, place a rack in the bottom third of the oven. Preheat the oven to 400°F.

Roll out the remaining disk of pastry as you did the first and use your favorite cookie cutters to make shapes to decorate the top (see page 279). You want enough shapes to cover most of the exposed mincemeat or it will dry out as it bakes. Reroll the scraps of dough and make more cutouts as needed. Place these on a parchment paper–lined baking sheet and store in the fridge until needed.

Place the chilled tart shell on a baking sheet. Line the tart with foil or parchment paper and top with pie weights or beans. Blind-bake the pie in the bottom third of the oven for 15 minutes. Remove the parchment and weights and use a tea towel to push down any air holes that have appeared. Return the tart shell to the oven until just baked through and starting to turn golden, about 10 minutes. Remove the tart shell from the oven and drop the heat to 375°F.

Spoon the mincemeat filling into the tart shell, pushing it down gently to fill every corner. Continue to fill until the mixture reaches the top of the shell. Cover with the pastry cutouts. Brush the tart shell edges and cutouts with the egg wash, and sprinkle with turbinado sugar. Bake until the pastry cutouts and edges are nice and golden, about 20 to 30 minutes. Serve with citrus crème anglaise.

# nuremburg lebkuchen

MAKES 32 to 36 cookies
PREP TIME 20 minutes
COOK TIME 22 minutes
per batch

If you cut me open, you'll probably find that I am made of Lebkuchen! Lebkuchen (or honey cake) is a German cousin of North American gingerbread. In addition to being sweetened by honey—instead of molasses—it contains a few different spices than gingerbread, most strikingly, white pepper and anise seed. Both help to create a unique but warm spice blend. Some of you may have reservations about its licorice leanings, but I promise, this is a good thing. Each area of Germany seems to have its own special version, but one of the most beloved is the Nuremburg Lebkuchen, also known as Elisenlebkuchen. Unlike most German baking, this is flour-free, relying totally on nuts, candied peel, and eggs. There is something so special about the soft and chewy texture, the spices, and the interaction of the bittersweet chocolate with the sweet cookies. The aromas are downright heady when you open the container . . . even 3 weeks after you make them!

**Lebkuchen Spice Blend**

2¼ tsp ground cinnamon

1¼ tsp ground ginger

½ tsp ground cardamom

½ tsp ground cloves

½ tsp ground allspice

½ tsp ground nutmeg

¼ tsp ground white pepper

¼ tsp ground anise seed
    (see Note, page 212)

Preheat the oven to 300°F.

**For the Lebkuchen Spice Blend**

In a small bowl, whisk together the cinnamon, ginger, cardamom, cloves, allspice, nutmeg, white pepper, and anise. Set aside.

**For the Cookies**

In a stand mixer fitted with the whisk attachment, or using a handheld mixer and a large bowl, whisk together the eggs and sugar. Using the large side of a box grater, grate the marzipan into the bowl. Whisk again until well blended and slightly frothy. Add the Lebkuchen spice blend, the salt, lemon zest, candied peels, ground hazelnuts, almond meal, and almonds. Switch to the paddle attachment or use a wooden spoon to blend well.

Measure a sheet of parchment paper that will fit your baking sheet. Using a marker or pencil, trace circles, 2½ inches in diameter (a round biscuit cutter will guide you) and about ¾ inch apart. You should be able to draw about eight circles. Turn the parchment upside down and check that the markings are still visible. Spoon 1½ tablespoons or so of cookie batter onto each circle. Using a small offset spatula or your finger dampened with water, spread the batter to just fill the circle, leaving a bit more mounded in the center.

## Cookies

3 eggs

1 cup + 1 Tbsp (235 g) sugar

4½ oz (125 g) marzipan

¼ tsp salt

Zest of 1 lemon

½ cup packed (85 g) candied
  orange or lemon peel

½ cup packed (85 g) mixed
  candied peel (I like citrus)

1¼ cups (120 g) ground
  hazelnuts (see Note)

1¼ cups (120 g) almond meal

½ cup (80 g) finely chopped
  blanched almonds

7 oz (200 g) dark or bittersweet
  chocolate

Sliced almonds, for decoration
  (optional)

Bake on the center rack of the oven until golden brown and slightly puffed, about 20 to 22 minutes. Transfer the baking sheet to a cooling rack and let the cookies completely cool on the sheet before removing. An offset spatula may help loosen them.

Repeat the measuring and baking steps as many times as needed with the remaining cookie batter, using a new sheet of parchment for each batch.

Once all the batches are completely cooled, coarsely chop the chocolate, place it in a metal bowl over a pot of simmering water, and melt, stirring, until smooth and glossy. Let it cool for 1 minute. Use a silicone brush to spread the chocolate over the tops of the cookies. Make sure to get into every nook and cranny. If desired, decorate the cookies with the sliced almonds, lightly pressing them into the chocolate on top. Let cool completely.

NOTES

If you can't find ground anise seed, simply crush whole anise seeds using a mortar and pestle, and use ¼ teaspoon as directed.

If you can't find ground hazelnuts, toast 1 cup plus 2 tablespoons of whole hazelnuts in a dry skillet over medium heat, stirring occasionally, until fragrant and lightly browned, about 6 to 8 minutes. Transfer them to a tea towel, wrap well, and rub them vigorously to remove their skins. Grind the cleaned nuts to a medium-fine meal in a food processor fitted with the steel blade. Stop as soon as this texture has been achieved, as going further will release the oils and you'll find yourself with hazelnut butter!

The cookies can be stored in a sealed container at room temperature for up to 3 weeks or in the freezer for up to 4 months.

## Breakfast
Rösti with Bacon Scrambled Eggs
Bloor West Village Ham and Cheese "Croissants"
Savory Crepes Bretonnes

## Appetizers
Black Peppercorn and Bourbon Chicken Pâté
Manchego and Black Pepper Gougères
Tarte Flambée Flatbread

## Salads and Sides
Levantine-Inspired Salad
Miso-Ginger-Honey Three-Bean Salad
Broccolini Amandine
Miso and Thyme Roasted Mushroom Toasts

## Mains
Brothy Cacio Pepe Heirloom Beans and Kale
Detroit-Style Skillet Pizza
Italian Friend–Approved Meatballs
Manly Beach Chicken Satay

## Desserts
Brown Butter Maple Bacon Butter Tarts
Pistachio, Apricot, and Dark Chocolate Forgotten Meringues
Banana Split with Cinnamon Sugar No-Churn Ice Cream
Chocolate Cream Pie with Tia Maria Whipped Cream
Lemon Blueberry Basil Yogurt Pound Loaf

YEAR-ROUND

While each season has its own flavors, colors, and aromas, each to be savored, there are certain things that are truly timeless. I don't remember the season I ate my first butter tart, but I do remember knowing that I'd eaten something special. I don't remember the month I first tried poutine in Montreal, but I do remember having my first plateful sitting at a restaurant table with newfound friends.

There are also recipes that don't necessarily rely on a season's best harvest of a specific item. Would we really want to leave a good lemon blueberry loaf only to August, when blueberries happen to be in season? Not these days, when we can get great blueberries year-round. Greenhouses, especially local ones, are such a great source of quality produce for when the fields aren't bursting with tomatoes and strawberries.

This is why I wanted to include a chapter of go-to recipes that can be made no matter the month, the weather, or what is in season. Keep this chapter in mind when you are trying to figure out how to finish a menu and want to think outside the seasonal box.

Think breakfast "croissants" (page 221) that pay tribute to France and its people's love of all things ham and cheese. The scrambled eggs (page 219) that my mum made us (and that I must make weekly for Jim). The perfect salad (page 232) to accompany a winter soup or your favorite sandwich, or as a filling salad on its own, no matter the weather. My favorite vegetable side dish that goes with just about any main: Broccolini Amandine (page 236)! Enjoy an epic crusty pizza (page 241). Or how about a retro classic like Black Peppercorn and Bourbon Chicken Pâté (page 227)—a fab addition to a charcuterie board. If ever there were a dish that knows no season, it would surely be spaghetti and meatballs (page 243). I know you'll make it often, just as I do. In fact, if there is one meal prep that I find more soothing than any other (except maybe for making stock), it's making meatballs with some great music playing in the background. On the sweeter side, the most moreish butter tarts (page 249) imaginable can be enjoyed anytime. Everyone needs an ice cream or pie that knows no season, so try the Chocolate Cream Pie with Tia Maria Whipped Cream (page 257), inspired by Waverly Tavern in San Francisco (which we enjoy no matter what season we visit, because chocolate is needed year-round!).

Too many of our cooking conventions are arbitrarily set by custom, but if these dishes will make our bellies smile, I think we should make them with joyful abandon, whatever the date, whenever the craving strikes.

◄ Clockwise from top left: Black Peppercorn and Bourbon
Chicken Pâté (page 227), Broccolini Amandine (page 236),
Banana Split with Cinnamon Sugar No-Churn Ice Cream (page 254),
Miso and Thyme Roasted Mushroom Toasts (page 237)

# rösti with bacon scrambled eggs

SERVES 2
PREP TIME 25 minutes
COOK TIME 35 minutes

This is another dish that pays tribute to my mum. Every Saturday morning, we would have scrambled eggs studded with bacon. It had to be creamy and soft (the eggs, not the bacon) to meet our expectations. I'll never forget one time when I was visiting my mum. She was making this, and we got to chatting and the next thing we know, the eggs had overcooked. She served it up, we took a couple of hesitant bites, looked at each other, and laughed. "This will not do. Let's make another batch," she said. Anyone who knows my waste-nothing mother knows that for her to suggest this meant that a line had been crossed! I'm serving them here with another mum favorite: rösti, a crispy outside, creamy inside potato pancake. She likely learned how to make these when she was a governess in Switzerland. I'm so glad she did.

### Rösti

4 Yukon gold or yellow-flesh potatoes

¾ tsp Seasoning Salt (page 264)

¼ tsp white pepper

Good pinch ground nutmeg

3 Tbsp butter, divided

2 Tbsp olive oil, divided

**For the Rösti**

Peel the potatoes and then, using the large side of a box grater, grate them into a large tea towel. Wrap the potatoes in the towel and squeeze over the sink to remove as much excess liquid as possible. Transfer the potatoes to a bowl and sprinkle them with the seasoning salt, pepper, and nutmeg. In a 10-inch nonstick sauté pan over medium-low heat, melt 1 tablespoon of the butter, add the potatoes, and stir the butter evenly through them. Transfer the potatoes to a clean bowl.

In the same pan over medium-low heat, heat 1 tablespoon each of the butter and oil. When the butter is bubbling, stir in the potato mixture until evenly coated. Gently press down on the potatoes to smooth out the surface and clean up the edges. Cook on one side until golden brown, about 10 to 12 minutes, using a rubber spatula to check the underside. If by the 10-minute mark the potato has not started to turn golden or is browning too quickly, adjust the heat accordingly. When it's golden brown, using an offset spatula, loosen the potato circle all around, especially in the middle, and slide it onto a plate. Cover with a second plate and flip so the cooked side is face up.

*recipe continues*

**Scrambled Eggs**

3 slices bacon

5 eggs

Salt and pepper

1 Tbsp butter

Sour cream, for serving

Add the remaining 1 tablespoon each of butter and oil to the pan and swirl to evenly coat it. Slide the pancake back into the pan and cook until the second side is golden brown, about 8 to 10 minutes. Adjust the heat as noted above if it's cooking too slowly or quickly. Using your offset spatula again, loosen the potato, slide it onto a plate, and sprinkle with more salt and pepper. Using a sharp knife, slice the rösti into four to six wedges.

**For the Scrambled Eggs**

Slice the bacon into ½-inch pieces. Wipe your sauté pan clean and place it over medium heat. Sauté until the bacon is cooked but not overly dry and shatteringly crispy, about 6 to 8 minutes. While it's cooking, whisk together the eggs and 2 teaspoons of water in a bowl. Add about ½ teaspoon each of salt and pepper. Set aside. Keeping the bacon bits in the pan, remove most of the bacon fat. Add the butter to the pan, spreading the cooked bacon evenly throughout the bottom of the pan.

Pour the egg mixture over the bacon and let it set for about 10 seconds. Using a wooden spoon, slowly stir the eggs and bacon, pushing from the outer edge to the center and swirling the uncooked portion to the outside. For creamy eggs, remove the pan from the heat when everything is just starting to cook into creamy curds, about 45 seconds to 1 minute. The eggs will continue to cook when off the heat. For a firmer scramble, keep swirling for another 20 seconds or so. But don't cook for much longer, or you might end up with the dreaded rubbery eggs!

Divide the eggs and rösti between two plates. Season with more salt and pepper (don't forget the bacon will have some salt already). Serve with a side of sour cream.

**NOTES**

This recipe is easy to halve or double up as you see fit. Just work in batches as needed. If you end up cooking in a larger skillet, feel free to make smaller rösti, say 4 inches in diameter, in which case you might be able to fit two per batch.

Leftover rösti can be stored in an airtight container in the fridge for 1 day. Just reheat in a skillet with a touch of melted butter, or in a 375°F oven for 8 minutes. For a brilliant herbed egg dish, add 2 to 3 tablespoons of finely chopped fresh herbs (such as chives, tarragon, parsley, dill, or thyme) before cooking, and cook as directed.

# bloor west village ham and cheese "croissants"

MAKES 9 pastries
PREP TIME 45 minutes +
chilling and resting
COOK TIME 35 minutes

One of my favorite memories after first moving to Toronto is a breakfast of ham and cheese croissants in Bloor West Village with my friend Leslie. Their flakey pastry, gooey cheese, smoky ham … Years later, I wondered if rough puff pastry might work for croissants—without pounding the butter brick and all the precise folding. Filled and baked, they got two thumbs up from Jim. My trick: Dijon mustard, two types of cheese, and fresh ham. For best results, prep the dough the night before.

---

1 (2¼ tsp/7 g) package active dry yeast

½ cup lukewarm water (110°F–115°F)

1¾ cups (250 g) bread flour

1¼ tsp salt

6¾ oz (190 g) cold salted butter, divided

¼ cup cold water (from the tap)

2–2½ tsp Dijon mustard

9 slices prosciutto cotto or Black Forest ham

5 oz (140 g) Gruyère, cut into short matchsticks

1 oz (25 g) Cheddar, shredded

1 egg, whisked with a bit of water

1 oz (25 g) Gruyère, grated on the fine side of your grater

In a bowl, dissolve the yeast in the lukewarm water. Let sit until the liquid starts to bubble, about 5 minutes. Place the flour in a food processor fitted with the steel blade. Add the salt and pulse once or twice to combine. Cut 2 ounces (60 g) of the butter into ½-inch chunks, add to the food processor, and pulse until the butter is chopped into pebble-sized pieces and evenly mixed throughout. Cut the remaining butter into ½-inch chunks and add them. Pulse twice to combine (there will be big fat chunks of butter in the bowl).

Add the cold water to the warm yeast and mix. Pour the yeast mixture into the food processor and pulse three times. You'll see a shaggy dough mixture with large chunks of butter form.

Dust your work surface with flour. Empty the dough onto your surface and, using your hands, gather the dough and form it into a ball, firmly pressing it together. Gently push it down and shape it into a rough rectangle. Sprinkle more flour under the dough and flour your rolling pin.

Roll the dough into a 12- × 15-inch rectangle. Position the long side to face you. Try to make the rectangle edges and corners as even and square as possible, using your fingers to gently pull on them if necessary. If the streaks of butter get warm and sticky, dust the dough with a bit of flour, then use a pastry brush to brush it off. The more flour that remains on the dough, the harder it is for the dough to puff up (or laminate).

*recipe continues*

Use a bench scraper to fold the upper third of the dough down into the center (so your rectangle is now 8 inches wide). Brush off any excess flour as you go. Fold the dough from the bottom side up and over your initial dough fold, as if folding a long skinny letter (so the dough is now 4 inches wide). Fold one short end into the middle, and fold the other end over it, making sure all the edges meet squarely. Place the flattened dough in a large resealable bag and let it rise for 30 minutes at room temperature. Place your hand on the bag and squish the dough down (it may not rise much, but it will feel a little squishy). Chill in the fridge for at least 1 hour or overnight.

Remove the dough from the bag, place it on a floured surface, and let it rest for 1 minute. Roll the dough out into a 14- × 18-inch rectangle and position it with the long side facing you. Try to make the rectangle edges and corners as square as possible. Fold one third of the dough from the right side to the center. Fold the left side over the first fold, so you have a 6- × 14-inch rectangle. Ensure that the edges and corners are square, again using your fingers to adjust the dough as necessary. Turn the dough so that the long side is facing you. Roll it out again to a 14- × 18-inch rectangle, keeping the corners and edges square. Fold it in thirds one last time, flouring the surface as needed. Turn the dough so that the long side is facing you. Roll the dough out to a 9- × 24-inch rectangle. Try to keep the thickness even throughout (sometimes the ends get thinner, which is not ideal). Use a sharp knife to trim ½ inch from the edges. This will expose the layers inside.

Using a metal ruler, if you have one, or just eyeballing it if you don't, measure about 4½-inch intervals along one long side of the dough, making small notches with a sharp knife as you go. On the other long side, starting 2¼ inches from the end, measure 4½-inch intervals again. The notches on each side will be staggered. Starting with the first notch you

made, use a pizza cutter to cut across to the closest notch on the opposite side, cutting evenly in one smooth motion. You can use a ruler to help guide you. Then cut back across to the next notch on the opposite side. Continue zigzagging between the notches until you have nine triangles with 4½-inch wide bases. There will be a bit of excess dough.

Spread about ¼ teaspoon of Dijon over two-thirds of each triangle, leaving the points clear. Place a slice of ham over two-thirds of the wider part of each pastry, again leaving the points clear. Divide the Gruyère matchsticks, followed by the Cheddar, among all the croissants, leaving the points clear again.

Line two smaller baking sheets with parchment paper. Using your hand to hold the wide end of each triangle, pull on the point a little to stretch it. Starting at the wide end, roll up the croissant tightly, pressing down as you go, and then lightly press the point onto the rest of the dough (it will stick). Place the croissants on the prepared baking sheets, point side down and spaced 2 to 3 inches apart. Cover loosely with plastic wrap and let rise at room temperature until puffy and slightly risen, 1½ hours.

Place a rack in the bottom third and one in the upper third of the oven and preheat the oven to 375°F. Brush the exposed surface with the egg wash, being careful not to brush the inner layers exposed on the sides (or they won't rise properly). Bake on the bottom rack for 15 minutes. Quickly sprinkle the grated Gruyère over each croissant and bake on the upper rack until golden brown and crisp, about 15 to 20 minutes. Place the sheets on a cooling rack for about 5 minutes before serving warm.

**NOTES**
After the cheese oozing from the croissants melts and sizzles, it hardens into little puddles of crispy goodness called frico. Break these off and enjoy! The croissants can be stored in an airtight container at room temperature for up to 3 days or wrapped individually and stored in a freezer bag in the freezer for up to 3 months. Just warm in a 350°F oven until crisp, about 5 to 8 minutes.

# savory crepes bretonnes

SERVES 4
PREP TIME 30 minutes + resting
COOK TIME 25 minutes

This recipe originated in Brittany, France, and celebrates my love of everything ever-so-slightly *français*—crepes, eggs, Gruyère, ham, oh my! What makes this brunch (or even dinner) a particular treat is the buckwheat flour in the crepes. Buckwheat is not shy and may be somewhat of an acquired taste, but its earthy, almost mineral influence gives it a rustic appeal. True buckwheat crepes, called galettes, are made solely with buckwheat flour, which can be challenging to work with as it doesn't have any gluten. Adding some all-purpose flour gives the batter a little elasticity and stability and is NOT a cop-out for those of us who don't have years of making these under our belts. Wrapping a finished crepe around grated cheese and tender shaved or thinly sliced ham and a sunny-side-up egg on top makes for a perfect meal. And adding some sautéed mushrooms takes them to the next level! But you can totally omit the mushrooms if you are like Jim.

## Crepes

⅓ cup buckwheat flour (see Note, page 226)

2½ Tbsp all-purpose flour

½ tsp salt

1 egg

¾ cup milk

3 Tbsp melted butter, divided

2 Tbsp olive oil

### For the Crepes

In a bowl, whisk together both flours and the salt. In a separate bowl, whisk together the egg and milk. Add the wet ingredients to the dry ingredients and whisk until completely smooth. Whisk in 1 tablespoon of the butter. Let sit for 20 minutes at room temperature. If the batter thickens to the point of not pouring like a traditional crepe batter, stir in 1 teaspoon of cold water.

Preheat the oven to 200°F.

Heat a 10-inch nonstick pan over medium heat. In a small bowl, use a fork to combine the butter and oil and swirl. Brush the pan with some of the butter and oil mixture to coat. Remove the pan from the heat and pour in about ¼ cup of the crepe batter, swirling so that it evenly fills the bottom of the pan. Return to the heat and cook until the top is dried, the edges are just turning golden, and the underneath is golden brown, about 1 minute. Using an offset spatula, loosen the crepe and flip it. Cook until golden underneath, about 30 seconds. Place on a plate and keep warm in the oven. Repeat with the remaining ingredients. You should have 5 crepes in total. The first one is the tester. Munch on it while you make the rest!

*recipe continues*

## Galettes Bretonnes

3 Tbsp butter, divided

1 Tbsp olive oil

Handful of cremini or button mushrooms, thinly sliced (optional)

4 eggs, at room temperature

Salt and pepper

4 thin slices fresh ham

1¼ cups grated Gruyère

1 Tbsp chopped chives or thyme for serving

## For the Galettes Brettones

If you're using the mushrooms, in a skillet over medium-high heat, heat 1 tablespoon of the butter and the oil. Add the mushrooms and sauté until they are softened and browned, about 5 to 8 minutes. Set aside. These can be made in advance and kept warm in a small pot.

You can use the same pan or a larger one to fry up the eggs. Set the pan over medium heat. Add the remaining 2 tablespoons of butter and heat until just starting to foam. Swirl it around the pan. Carefully crack the eggs into the pan and season with salt. Cook until the whites are just set on top and the yolks are still runny, about 3 minutes. Season with pepper. Set aside in the pan.

Meanwhile, place one crepe in a 10-inch nonstick pan set over medium-low heat. Place a ham slice in the center of the crepe. Sprinkle with 2 heaping tablespoons of the Gruyère. Place one sunny-side-up egg on top. Add one-quarter of the sautéed mushrooms, if using, along with another heaping tablespoon of cheese. Using a silicone spatula, fold one side of the crepe over to the middle, pushing down gently so that the cheese helps adhere it to the egg. Fold the other side over top, pressing it down gently. Cover with a lid and let the heat warm through the cheese and egg. Transfer to a plate. Repeat with the remaining crepes. Serve sprinkled with chopped chives.

### NOTES

I like using dark buckwheat flour rather than light, but use whatever you can find.

You can let the batter rest overnight in the fridge (and then bring it to room temperature before frying) instead of resting for 20 minutes. The crepes will taste great either way. You can also easily double the crepe recipe and make more to freeze (see page 276 for freezing steps). Thaw and cook as directed.

To make sweeter buckwheat crepes, add 1 tablespoon of sugar to the batter, cook as directed, and drizzle with 2 to 3 teaspoons each of molasses and maple syrup mixed together.

# black peppercorn and bourbon chicken pâté

MAKES 1½ cups
PREP TIME 30 minutes + chilling
COOK TIME 5 minutes

This is pure 80s retro goodness! When we were grown up enough to have our own cocktail or dinner parties, pâté was always part of the appetizer spread. To this day, I have a soft spot for this creamy, flavorful whipped chicken and cream cheese spread. It's like a fancier version of liverwurst. I definitely don't like a bland pâté, and I bring it into the new millennium by using bourbon instead of brandy to give it a good kick. Serve with toast, radishes, and cornichons to cut through all the creamy richness, and watch the pâté disappear. *Recipe pictured on page 216*

½ lb (225 g) chicken livers

½ small yellow onion, chopped

1 tsp dried thyme leaves

1 bay leaf

2 hard-boiled eggs, roughly chopped

3½ oz (100 g) farmer's-style or plain cream cheese, softened

1 Tbsp finely minced parsley

¾ tsp salt

⅛ tsp white pepper

1 Tbsp bourbon

½ Tbsp black peppercorns

Crostini, radishes, and cornichons, for serving

Place the chicken livers, onions, thyme, and bay leaf in a skillet. Add ½ cup water. Bring to a boil over medium-high heat, drop the heat to medium-low, and simmer, uncovered, until the livers are just tender but cooked through, about 3 to 4 minutes, depending on the thickness. Don't cook any longer than needed or they'll become tough. Drain, and then discard the bay leaf. Once the livers are cool to the touch, roughly chop them.

Add the liver and onion mixture and the eggs to a food processor fitted with the steel blade. Pulse until everything is evenly distributed but not ground down completely.

In a small bowl, use a wooden spoon to break up the cream cheese and loosen it up a bit. Add the cream cheese to the food processer, along with the parsley, salt, white pepper, and bourbon. Blend until smooth and creamy. Crack the peppercorns with a mortar and pestle or spice grinder. You don't want the pieces too small. Fold the peppercorns into the pâté. Transfer the pâté to a serving bowl, cover with plastic wrap, and chill for several hours or overnight. Bring to room temperature about 10 minutes before serving. Serve with crostini, radishes, and cornichons.

NOTE
You can also serve this with some sliced baguette, chips, and lots of briny vegetables like pickles and olives. Yum!

# manchego and black pepper gougères

MAKES 20 to 24 gougères
PREP TIME 30 minutes +
resting
COOK TIME 30 minutes

My mum was trained in French cooking, and it influenced her savory dishes, but she wasn't a big baker. It wasn't until I was on my own that I discovered gougères. These little puffy, cheesy morsels are the perfect nibble for drinks with friends before dinner or as part of a charcuterie or cheese board. You can play with the cheese flavors, but stick to dry cheeses or you run the risk of the dough not drying out properly in the oven.

1 cup water

½ cup butter, cut into large cubes

½ tsp salt

1 cup (150 g) flour

4 eggs, lightly beaten

6 oz (170 g) grated Manchego cheese + ¼ cup for sprinkling

1 tsp freshly cracked black pepper

½ tsp cayenne pepper

Preheat the oven to 450°F. Line two baking sheets with parchment paper.

Place the water, butter, and salt in a medium saucepan and bring to a rolling boil over medium-high heat, stirring constantly to melt the butter. Remove from the heat and add the flour all at once. Stir vigorously with a wooden spoon until the mixture comes together. It should look like mashed potatoes. Place the pot over medium-low heat, and stir the mixture for 3 to 5 minutes. You want the dough to dry out completely, come away from the sides, and leave a film on the bottom of the pot. You'll know it's ready when it smells nutty, has a lovely sheen, and is thick enough for a spoon to stand upright in it.

Remove the pot from the heat and, switching to a silicone spatula, continue to stir for 1 minute, letting the mixture cool down. Using the silicone spatula, beat in three-quarters of the eggs in three additions (one-quarter at a time), waiting for each addition to be absorbed and for the dough to smooth out, and scraping down the sides of the pot if needed, before adding the next. The batter should be smooth, but firm and creamy. If you scoop some batter out with a spatula, it should stick to the spatula as it slides slowly off it and back into the pot. If it's too thick to achieve this, add the remaining egg portion. Fold in the 6 ounces (170 g) of cheese, pepper, and cayenne. If the batter is still not quite thick enough, add a bit more cheese.

*recipe continues*

Scoop rounded tablespoons of dough onto the prepared baking sheets, spacing them about 1 inch apart. Sprinkle some more cheese over each one.

Bake the gougères for 5 minutes. Drop the heat to 350°F and continue baking, rotating the sheets halfway through, until the gougères are puffed, deep golden brown, and dry to the touch (the cheese on top may still be bubbling a bit), about 20 to 25 minutes. They will feel light and hollow when picked up. Take a sharp knife and pierce a small hole in the lower side of each gougère to allow steam to escape. Turn off the heat and let them rest in the oven for 15 minutes. Transfer the baking sheets to a cooling rack. Let cool slightly. Serve warm or at room temperature.

**NOTES**

Many gougères deflate while baking. For best results, ensure the flour is completely dried out before adding the eggs in batches. Give the gougères room to breathe as they bake, and let the steam escape as they rest. And if they deflate after all that, don't worry. Even David Lebovitz says he has seen great French cooks serve deflated ones!

If you want to freeze these before baking, place the rounded table-spoons of dough on a wax paper–lined baking sheet, as close together as possible without touching, lightly cover with plastic wrap, and freeze on the sheet until solid. Transfer to an airtight container or a freezer-safe resealable bag and freeze for up to 2 months.

Leftovers can be stored in an airtight container in the fridge for up to 3 days or frozen for up to 3 months. To reheat and keep them crispy, sprinkle each with a few drops of water, then warm in a 325°F oven for about 7 minutes.

# tarte flambée flatbread

SERVES 4 as a main, or
8 as an appetizer
PREP TIME 15 minutes
COOK TIME 30 minutes

**G**rowing up, we had a family friend, a chef from Alsace Lorraine. He taught me about this region of France tucked close to Germany, enjoying the best of both cuisines. This tarte, also known as Flammkuchen (or "flamed cake"), is Alsace's take on a flatbread pizza. The base's creamy layer of cheese, nutmeg, and egg yolk is topped with sautéed onions and bacon (is there a better flavor combo?!), and is baked until bubbling and browned. After a long, busy Friday, I often cheat with store-bought flatbreads or naan I keep in the freezer. Nothing like keeping things easy breezy! Enjoy with prosecco, a good rosé, or even a crisp Belgian beer, to introduce another country to the mix! *Recipe pictured on page vi*

---

½ lb (225 g) double-smoked bacon, cut into ½-inch pieces or lardons

2 large yellow onions, thinly sliced lengthwise (about 2 cups)

Salt and pepper

1 cup farmer's-style cream cheese, fromage blanc, or quark (see Note)

1 cup Crème Fraîche (page 272)

1 large egg yolk, whisked

1 tsp ground nutmeg

4 flatbreads or naan

2 scallions, thinly sliced, for garnish

Flakey finishing salt

Finishing olive oil

Preheat the oven to 400°F.

Set a large skillet over medium-high heat. Once hot, add the bacon. Cook, stirring occasionally, until the fat has rendered, about 3 minutes. Add the onions, drop the heat to medium, and cook, stirring occasionally, until the onions are a light golden brown and the bacon is lightly crisped, about 10 minutes. Drain and season lightly with salt and pepper. Chill in the fridge for up to overnight. Bring it to room temperature before using.

In a bowl, whisk together the cream cheese and crème fraîche. Add the egg yolk and nutmeg, season with ¼ teaspoon each of salt and pepper, and mix to combine. Place the flatbreads on one or two baking sheets. Spread the cheese mixture over the flatbreads. Sprinkle the bacon mixture over the cheese.

Bake until the crust is browned, the onions are fragrant and burnished, and the cheese sauce is bubbling, about 10 to 15 minutes. Sprinkle with the scallions and finishing salt. Drizzle with oil, slice, and serve warm or at room temperature.

**NOTE**
Farmer's-style cream cheese is a tangy, smooth, and creamy fresh pressed cheese. French Neufchatel or Petit Suisse are in the same vein. Fromage blanc has the consistency of sour cream, is a little less tart. Quark is a German version. Any of these can easily be sourced at your local cheesemonger.

# levantine-inspired salad

SERVES 4 to 6
PREP TIME 20 minutes

This is the ultimate mashup of salads, if I do say so myself. This is my take on horiatiki, fattoush, and tabbouleh, all in one bowl. To make it fridge- and picnic-worthy, I've used chickpeas rather than pita and bulgur. Hey, I never said it was authentic, just an homage to the salads that feel like summer year-round. Forget a side salad, this is totally meal-worthy all on its own.

## Vinaigrette

⅔ cup extra virgin olive oil

3 Tbsp lemon juice

3 Tbsp white or red wine
vinegar

1 Tbsp runny honey

1 Tbsp Dijon mustard

2 cloves garlic, minced

1 tsp dried oregano leaves

1 tsp dried basil leaves

Salt and pepper

## Levantine-Inspired Salad

1 cup halved cherry tomatoes

2 Persian cucumbers, cut into
bite-size half moons

½ green bell pepper, cut into
bite-size slices

½ red bell pepper, cut into bite-
size slices

½ red onion, thinly sliced

1 (15 oz/425 g) can chickpeas,
drained and rinsed

3 scallions, thinly sliced

1 cup baby kale, torn

½ cup chopped mint, divided

½ cup chopped parsley, divided

½ cup kalamata olives, pitted

### For the Vinaigrette

Place the oil, lemon juice, vinegar, honey, Dijon, garlic, oregano, basil, and ½ teaspoon each of salt and pepper in a jar with a lid. Seal and shake to combine. Season with more salt and pepper, if desired.

### For the Levantine-Inspired Salad

In a bowl, gently toss together the tomatoes, cucumbers, bell peppers, onions, chickpeas, and scallions. Drizzle with a little dressing and gently toss to coat. Season with a little salt and pepper, if desired.

Place the baby kale, three-quarters of the mint, and three-quarters of the parsley in a serving bowl. Drizzle with a little dressing and gently toss. Season to taste. Spoon the tomato mixture over the greens and give it a final toss. Garnish with the remaining mint and parsley and the olives.

### NOTES

Don't feel you need to use all the dressing. The leftovers will keep for up to 1 week in the fridge. Just bring it to room temperature and loosen with about 1 teaspoon of olive oil before serving.

If you can't find Persian cucumbers, you can use ½ English cucumber instead.

# miso-ginger-honey three-bean salad

SERVES 4
MAKES about 5 cups
PREP TIME 20 minutes + chilling

When I was growing up, every backyard potluck, picnic, barbecue, and lunch always seemed to include a bean salad of some sort. Back then, I wasn't really a fan. But through the years the concept has grown on me. I became a full-fledged proponent when I came up with this easy-peasy salad! It takes the sweet, spicy, umami, and garlicky goodness of my Miso-Ginger Dressing (page 266) and kicks it up with extra honey and sriracha. Tossing the fresh, crunchy green beans, mild and poppy edamame beans, and smooth, earthy black beans makes for a superb dish to serve any time of year. Making this in January is just as easy as it is in July.

## Dressing

4 Tbsp Miso-Ginger Dressing (page 266)

3 Tbsp runny honey

1 Tbsp sriracha

1 tsp chili flakes

Salt and pepper

## Three-Bean Salad

8 oz (225 g) fresh green beans

8 oz (225 g) frozen shelled edamame beans

1 (14 oz/398 ml) can black beans, drained and rinsed

3 scallions, chopped into small rounds

Pepper

2 tsp sesame seeds, for garnish (optional)

### For the Dressing

Place the miso-ginger dressing, honey, sriracha, chili flakes, and ½ teaspoon each of salt and pepper in a small jar with a lid. Seal and shake to combine. Season with more salt and pepper, if desired. Set aside at room temperature.

### For the Three-Bean Salad

Trim the green beans into 1-inch pieces and transfer to a steamer basket. Fill a pot with 1 inch of water and set the steamer basket inside. Add the edamame. Bring the water to a boil over high heat and steam the beans until just tender, about 10 to 20 seconds. (If you don't have a steamer basket, place the beans in a large skillet with a lid. Add ¼ cup water and bring to a boil over high heat. As soon as the water begins to boil, cook, covered, for 2 minutes. Remove the lid and cook until the water evaporates and/or the beans are tender-crisp.) There should still be some crunch!

Transfer the green beans and edamame to a bowl. Add the black beans and scallions. Drizzle with three-quarters of the dressing and toss to coat. Chill in the fridge, uncovered, for a good hour or more to let the flavors meld. To serve, add the remaining dressing, toss well, and sprinkle with pepper and the sesame seeds, if using.

### NOTE

This salad keeps well in an airtight container in the fridge for up to 3 days. Leftovers the next day are not to be underestimated!

# broccolini amandine

SERVES 6
PREP TIME 10 minutes
COOK TIME 15 minutes

Every good meat and potato dish needs a veggie side. Or how about: every good vegetable dish needs a side of meat and potatoes? This is one of those veggie dishes that goes with everything, and in a pinch will stand as an entire meal for me. Broccolini is pretty well available year-round, so it's the ideal vegetable when you are trying to come up with the perfect dinner party or weekday meal menu. Making it amandine-style means taking the classic French application of sliced almonds and garlic and creating a sauce with plenty of butter. So whether you're serving it with a pork roast (page 189), roast turkey (page 141), tourtière (page 199), or short ribs (page 197), this quick-to-prepare side will always be perfect.

*Recipe pictured on page 216*

2 bunches broccolini (about 12 oz/340 g)

¼ cup butter

¼ cup sliced almonds

3 cloves garlic, minced

Juice of ½ lemon

½ tsp salt

½ tsp black pepper

¼ tsp white pepper

Bring a large pot of salted water (use around 2 teaspoons of salt) to a rolling boil. Prepare a large bowl of ice water. Trim off the bottom ½ inch or so of the broccolini stems, then add the broccolini spears to the boiling water, and boil for 2 minutes. Immediately submerge the broccolini in the ice water to stop the cooking and retain the color. Drain and set aside.

In a large skillet over medium-low heat, melt the butter. Add the almonds and sauté until just turning golden, about 4 minutes. Using a slotted spoon, transfer the almonds to a small plate or bowl. Set aside.

Add the broccolini and garlic to the pan and cook, stirring, until the broccolini is warmed through and the garlic is softened and aromatic, about 5 to 7 minutes. Add three-quarters of the almonds and gently mix them in. Remove the skillet from the heat, drizzle the broccolini with the lemon juice, season with the salt and both peppers, and garnish with the remaining almond slices. Serve.

# miso and thyme roasted mushroom toasts

SERVES 4
PREP TIME 15 minutes
COOK TIME 25 minutes

**D**on't tell Jim that this recipe is in this book! I've never seen someone so averse to fungi. When we were dating, he willingly ate every meatloaf, Bolognese, and lasagna I put in front of him. One day, he mentioned that he was deathly allergic to mushrooms. *Really?!* When I told him he had been eating them for months and seemed very much alive, he made me swear to never add them again. To this day, he will ask, "There aren't mushrooms in this, right?" *Paranoid much?!* I'm sharing this as a tribute to my mum, though. It's a modern take on her mushroom à la king, serving the earthy 'shrooms and sauce over toast. I can still picture the pair of us enjoying this meal. Serve these with a seasonal green salad for a great dinner. *Recipe pictured on page 216*

5 Tbsp butter, at room temperature

3 Tbsp white miso

1½ lb (680 g) mixed mushrooms (see Note)

4 Tbsp olive oil, divided

1½ Tbsp chopped thyme + more for garnish

Salt and pepper

4 thick slices crusty sourdough bread

Flakey finishing salt, for garnish

Chili flakes, for garnish

**NOTES**
So many mushrooms work: hen of the woods, chanterelle, shiitake, cremini, oyster, etc. You can prepare the miso butter ahead of time. Store it in an airtight container in the fridge overnight and bring it to room temperature before using.

In a small bowl, use a fork to combine the butter and miso.

Preheat the oven to 425°F.

Brush away any dirt or grit from the mushrooms. Place them in a large cast-iron skillet or rimmed baking sheet. Drizzle with 2½ tablespoons of the oil and season with the thyme, and 1 teaspoon each of salt and pepper. Gently toss to coat, then arrange in a single layer. Scatter 4 tablespoons of the miso butter, 1 tablespoon at a time, randomly over the mushrooms. Set the remaining butter aside at room temperature. Roast the mushrooms, basting occasionally with the buttery juices at the bottom of the pan, until they are tender and just starting to crisp, about 20 to 25 minutes.

While the mushrooms are roasting, lay out the bread on a baking sheet. Drizzle it with the remaining olive oil, using a brush to evenly cover the bread's surface. Place in the oven about 5 minutes before you think the mushrooms are done, and cook until the bread is golden brown. Meanwhile, in a small saucepan over low heat, warm the remaining miso butter.

Divide the toasts among four plates and top each with roasted mushrooms. Drizzle with the warmed miso butter. Sprinkle with more thyme, finishing salt, and chili flakes.

# brothy cacio pepe heirloom beans and kale

SERVES 4
PREP TIME 15 minutes
COOK TIME 1 hour,
20 minutes

A lot of my dishes have an Italian bent. Italian cuisine (actually all Mediterranean cuisines) is just so bright and fresh—Jim and I crave this way of eating. I also grew up in a town that was 65% Italian. My eyes lit up when a neighboring Italian family served our family spaghetti and sugo. Little did we know that this was just the FIRST course. The Italian influence has been with me almost daily throughout my life. Prego! For this dish, I decided cranberry and green flageolet heirloom beans deserve the classic pecorino cheese and black pepper treatment.

---

1 Tbsp olive oil

1 small yellow onion, chopped

2 cloves garlic, minced

1 cup mixed dried heirloom beans, rinsed and soaked for at least 6 hours in 1 Tbsp salt per 4 cups water, then drained

4 cups + ⅔ cup chicken stock

1 sprig rosemary

1 sprig thyme

Salt and pepper

3¾ oz (105 g) pecorino romano cheese, finely grated, divided

1 Tbsp butter, melted

½ tsp chili flakes

3 oz (85 g) lacinato kale, roughly chopped (about 3 cups packed)

Thyme leaves, for garnish

Crusty bread, for serving

In a pot over medium heat, warm the oil. Add the onions and garlic, and cook, stirring, until just softened. Add the beans, followed by 4 cups of the stock, the rosemary, and thyme.

Turn up the heat to high and bring to a rolling boil. Drop the heat to low and gently simmer, partially covered, until the beans are tender. This should take between 45 minutes and 1 hour. Discard the rosemary and thyme sprigs. Season with salt and pepper, starting with ½ teaspoon of each and adjusting to taste. To check for doneness, taste five beans, one at a time, to give you an accurate idea of whether the beans are cooked through. Remove from the heat and let the beans sit to soak up some of the stock while you work on the next step. This can be done the day ahead; if they thicken overnight, add more stock to thin them out when reheating.

Heat the remaining ⅔ cup of stock in a small pot over medium-high heat. Meanwhile, place 1 cup (60 g) of the cheese in a small bowl. Add the warm stock and whisk to smooth out the cheese. Stir in the butter until blended. Add 2 teaspoons of pepper and the chili flakes.

Return the beans to a simmer over medium heat and add the kale. Let it simmer until the kale has softened, about 5 minutes. Add the cheese sauce and stir through. Season with more chili flakes, salt, and pepper if desired. Garnish with thyme leaves, more pepper, and the remaining cheese. Serve with crusty bread to soak up the sauce.

# detroit-style skillet pizza

MAKES one 12-inch skillet pizza, or two 6- to 8-inch pizzas
PREP TIME 30 minutes + rising + resting
COOK TIME 20 minutes

Even though I grew up just across the river from Detroit, my family never ate pizza there (we had great pizza in Windsor—I'm looking at you, Capri Pizza!). I eventually discovered what I'd been missing out on! When Jim came home one night with a Detroit-style pizza from Toronto's Descendant Pizza. We were stunned by every mouthful. It was crunchy, cheesy, and doughy in the best way possible. But it isn't for the faint of heart. The crust is a meal unto itself. But that's what leftovers are for! Detroit-style pizza also uses a more flavorful cheese than mozzarella. What really makes a classic Detroit-style topping, though, is starting with the cheese to create a barrier to stop the crust from going soggy, then adding the pepperoni, and then the sauce. Sure, you can add more toppings, but go lightly, as too many will weigh it down and it won't rise correctly.

2 cups + 2 Tbsp (300 g) bread flour

1 Tbsp salt

1 tsp instant yeast

1 cup less 1½ tsp water

Olive oil, as needed

12 oz (340 g) natural-casing pepperoni (I like Hungarian csabai), cut into ⅛-inch slices

12 oz (340 g) fontina, Monterey Jack, and/or mozzarella, cut into ½-inch cubes

1 recipe Marinara Sauce, Pizza Sauce Variation (page 267)

In the bowl of a stand mixer, use a fork to combine the flour, salt, and yeast. Add the water. Fit the mixer with the dough hook attachment and mix on the lowest speed until the dough comes together into a rough ball, about 10 minutes. Let the dough rest for 10 minutes. Mix on medium-low speed until the dough turns into a silky ball, about another 10 minutes. It will stick to the bottom of the bowl as it kneads. Remove the dough from the dough hook, transfer to the counter, and form it into a tight ball. Grease the mixer bowl with a bit of oil. Place the dough ball back in the bowl, cover the bowl tightly with plastic wrap, and set aside at room temperature until the dough has roughly doubled in size, about 2 hours, depending on the temperature of the room.

Pour a couple of tablespoons of oil into a 12-inch cast-iron skillet (or heavy metal cake pan) or two 8- to 10- inch skillets. Transfer the dough to the skillet(s) and turn to evenly coat. Press the dough into the edges of the pan, dimpling it with your fingertips as you go. If it starts to resist and shrink back, just cover the skillets with plastic and let it rest for about 15 minutes, then repeat the dimpling and pressing. If the dough still isn't pliable, let it rest, covered, for another 15 minutes. Stretch it just beyond the edges of the pan, so it will relax back down into the pan. Cover with a damp towel and set aside for 30 minutes.

*recipe continues*

Meanwhile, set one oven rack to the lowest position, and another about 6 inches from the top and preheat the oven to 500°F (or 450°F if this is what your oven can manage).

If any large air bubbles have formed in the dough, gently press down with your fingertips to remove them. Evenly scatter half of the pepperoni over the dough. Top with cheese, spreading it evenly all the way to the very edges of the pan, then add the remaining pepperoni. In three concentric circles, spoon the sauce over the surface. You may only need about half the sauce—save the rest for dipping, or for a future pizza. (If you're making two smaller pizzas, just divide all the topping layers between each one.)

Bake the pizza on the lowest rack until the edges of the crust are a rich golden brown (you can use a spatula to check) and the cheese is crusty and bubbling, about 15 to 20 minutes (12 to 15 minutes if you're making two smaller pizzas). If the cheese is bubbling but the bottom is not browned, cook for another 2 to 4 minutes. However, if the bottom is brown but the top isn't ready, transfer the pizza to the top rack and bake for another 2 to 4 minutes. Transfer the skillet to a cooling rack. As soon as it's cool enough to touch, run a thin metal spatula around the edges of the skillet to loosen the pizza. Carefully lift it out and slide it onto a cutting board. If you leave it in the skillet too long, it will go soggy. Cut the pizza and serve.

NOTES
If you want a vegetarian option, swap out the pepperoni with 2 cups of cremini mushrooms, cut into ⅛-inch slices.

Leftovers will keep in an airtight container in the fridge for a few days. To reheat, place in a cast-iron pan set over medium-low heat and cook, covered, until warmed through, about 8 minutes. You can also reheat it in a 325°F toaster oven or oven, directly on the rack (as long as there is a baking sheet below to catch any drips) until warmed through and bubbly.

# italian friend–approved meatballs

MAKES 22 to 24 meatballs
PREP TIME 30 minutes
COOK TIME 50 minutes

This may sound like a bold statement, but when my Italian-born-and-bred friends told me that they now use this recipe for their polpette (or meatballs), it felt like the highest honor and achievement of my cooking life. I was honestly humbled. Once I knew this meatball recipe could hold its own against the homemade polpette that my friends' mums and nonnas make, I was ready to share it with the world. The key is fresh bread soaked in milk and plenty of cheese, and don't spare the spices. Also, don't use meat that is too lean—you need the fat from the pork. The ultimate meatball test is that a fork should be able to slide down through them effortlessly. Meatball-making day is one of my favorite times in the kitchen, rivaled only by pie-making days. Make a full batch, even if there are just two of you, as these freeze perfectly. Having a bag ready to go in the freezer means that dinner with friends is just moments away. You can roll them large or small—I lean toward large.

1 lb (450 g) spicy Italian sausage, casings removed

1 lb (450 g) extra-lean ground beef

1 cup grated Parmesan or grana padano

3 Tbsp chopped parsley

2 cloves garlic, minced

Salt and pepper

½ tsp cayenne pepper

2 eggs, beaten

2 cups fresh breadcrumbs (see Note, page 244)

1¼–2 cups milk, divided

Olive oil

1 recipe Marinara Sauce (page 267)

Pasta, for serving

Combine the sausage meat and beef in a large bowl. Using your fingers (remove any rings!), gently break up and mix the sausage meat into the beef until combined. Add the cheese, parsley, and garlic. Season with about 2 teaspoons each of salt and pepper and the cayenne. Better to add less and adjust later as you don't know how seasoned the sausages are. Add the beaten eggs and then the breadcrumbs. Using your fingertips, mix until everything is just blended. Add 1 cup of the milk, and mix again using your fingertips. Let sit for a minute to soak up the milk. Continue adding the milk, ¼ cup at a time, until the mixture is very moist and sticky. The amount of milk you will need will depend on how dry the breadcrumbs are.

Lightly oil a small sauté pan and place it over medium heat. Break off a small piece of the mixture and form it into a small patty (about the size of a quarter). Sauté until cooked through, about 3 minutes on each side. Taste, and adjust your seasonings in the bowl as desired. This way your meatballs will taste the way you want them to.

*recipe continues*

Line a baking sheet with wax paper. Pat down the mixture in the bowl and gently use the side of your hand to divide it in half. Using lightly oiled or wet hands, shape the first half of the mixture into 10 to 12 balls, 2 to 2½ inches in diameter. Place them on the prepared baking sheet. You can either bake this batch per the next step, bake what you need and freeze the rest (see Note), or freeze them all and then bake as directed when the mood strikes.

When you're ready to bake, preheat the oven to 450°F. Bake the meatballs, uncovered, until they're crisping up on the outside but aren't done on the inside, about 15 minutes. Remove the meatballs from the oven.

In a saucepan over medium-low heat, heat the marinara sauce until warmed through, about 15 minutes. Add the meatballs and let them simmer in the sauce until cooked through to an internal temperature of 160°F, about 20–25 minutes. Remove from the heat and cover to keep warm while you prepare the pasta.

Cook the pasta according to the package instructions. Serve the meatballs and sauce over the pasta. Enjoy with a side salad and garlic bread!

**NOTES**

Never use old dried breadcrumbs! It's better to tear fresh bread into small pieces instead.

If you roll the meatballs smaller, bake for 10 minutes (until just browned), then cook in the sauce for 15 to 20 minutes.

To freeze unbaked meatballs, place the tray with the formed meatballs in the freezer. Once they are frozen, transfer them from the baking sheet to a large freezer bag for up to 2 months. Just take out as many as you need and thaw them in the fridge overnight before baking as above.

SYDNEY
AUSTRALIA

# manly beach chicken satay

SERVES 4 to 5
PREP TIME 15 minutes +
marinating
COOK TIME 40 minutes

When I lived in Australia, I was introduced to so many new dishes and foods. Because Australia is located in the Indian Ocean, Asian cuisine has influenced the Australian food scene for generations. One day, my roommate and I were hanging out with friends at Manly Beach and popped into a local Thai restaurant for lunch. I let them order, since I'd never experienced Thai food before—this was the late 80s, and Thai cuisine had yet to find Amherstburg, Ontario! Next thing I knew, I was eating these amazing skewers of beef and chicken covered in the most intriguing sauce. It was sweet, hot, curried, spicy, and peanutty!! Whoa, baby! But back home, everyone was skeptical of a curry sauce with peanut butter in it, and there was no internet to help me out. A year or so later, I finally learned how to make satay, which also has Indonesian roots, from the owner of a great little hole-in-the-wall Thai restaurant in Brooklyn! I have refined my recipe over the years, and I enjoy those memories of Manly Beach every time I make it.

## Chicken

2 lb (900 g) boneless, skinless chicken thighs

## Marinade

¼ cup water

2 large shallots, roughly chopped

3 cloves garlic, chopped

½ cup natural smooth peanut butter

3 Tbsp runny honey or coconut palm sugar

2 Tbsp curry powder

1 Tbsp sambal oelek

1 tsp salt

1 tsp pepper

### For the Chicken

Slice the chicken into 1-inch-wide strips and place them in a shallow baking dish, just big enough to hold them all without crowding. (You'll need about 40 pieces of chicken.)

### For the Marinade

In a food processor fitted with the steel blade, combine the water, shallots, garlic, peanut butter, honey, curry powder, sambal oelek, salt, and pepper. Blend until smooth. Pour this marinade over the chicken, massaging it into all the nooks and crannies. Cover with a lid or plastic wrap and chill in the fridge for at least 2 hours or overnight.

*recipe continues*

## Peanut Sauce

1 Tbsp olive oil

2 large shallots, minced

3 cloves garlic, minced

½ cup natural smooth peanut butter

4 Tbsp runny honey

2 Tbsp curry powder

½–1 Tbsp sambal oelek

½ cup canned coconut milk

20 medium bamboo skewers, soaked in water for at least ½ hour, or metal skewers

Chopped cilantro, for garnish

### NOTES

This can make about 20 skewers for an appetizer tray.

There will most likely be sauce left over. Serve crudités on the side to dip into any extra. This sauce will also work wonderfully on pork chops, shrimp, chicken wings, and noodles. Great for game night. Sometimes when I make it, I divide the dipping sauce in half and store one half in an airtight container in the fridge for up to 1 week or the freezer for up to 2 months.

### For the Peanut Sauce

In a saucepan over medium heat, heat the oil. Add the shallots and garlic, and cook until softened, about 5 to 10 minutes. Add the peanut butter, honey, curry powder, and ½ tablespoon of sambal oelek, stirring to combine. Cook for about 1 minute, then add the coconut milk and stir well. Remove from the heat. Using a blender or an immersion blender, blend until smooth. Adjust to taste, adding a smidge more sambal oelek for a touch more heat. Chill in the fridge, covered, until needed, or up to overnight. If the sauce thickens up in the fridge, just thin it with about 1 teaspoon of coconut milk or even water. Bring it to room temperature for 30 minutes before using.

### To Serve

Preheat an outdoor grill to medium heat or set the oven to a low broil (if your oven has a low broil option, use the upper rack; if it only has one broil setting, use the middle rack). Spray the grill with nonstick cooking spray. Or line a baking sheet (or more if necessary) with foil—if you have an oblong cooling rack, you can set this over the foil—and spray with nonstick cooking spray.

Push each skewer through the center of two pieces of chicken so that the tip of the skewer is trapped inside the meat. Remove any excess marinade to avoid scorching.

Grill, turning the skewers regularly, until the chicken is evenly cooked through and pleasantly charred, about 15 minutes.

Or broil the skewers, turning them every 8 to 10 minutes to avoid scorching, until they are cooked through, 24 to 30 minutes. If you used the low broil setting and they are cooked but not browned enough for your taste, adjust the setting to high and broil until brown, keeping a careful eye on them. Or—third option!—move the rack to the top third of the oven and broil until browned.

Serve the skewers on a platter with the peanut sauce on the side. Garnish the skewers with cilantro.

# brown butter maple bacon butter tarts

MAKES 12 butter tarts
PREP TIME 1½ hours + chilling
COOK TIME 22 minutes

Ask any Canadian whether this classic sweet treat should have raisins or not, and you will start a very vocal debate, whether you're in a coffee shop or on the street corner. Suddenly our collective reputation of being polite and diplomatic goes out the window. Everyone has an opinion. Mine? No raisins. Ever. But bacon? Yes! Between the bacon, maple syrup, molasses, and whole wheat crust, these tarts bring an earthy, cozy vibe with all the wonder of brown butter.

## Pastry

1 cup + 1 Tbsp (165 g) flour

1 cup (105 g) whole wheat flour

¼ tsp salt

4 oz (115 g) frozen or chilled butter

1 egg

4 Tbsp cold water

1 Tbsp lemon juice

## Filling

3–4 slices bacon (see Note on page 250)

¼ cup butter, at room temperature

2 eggs

½ cup packed dark brown sugar

¼–½ tsp salt (depending on the saltiness of your bacon)

½ cup pure maple syrup (see Note on page 250)

1 Tbsp fancy molasses (see Note on page 250)

1 tsp apple cider vinegar

Flakey finishing salt

### For the Pastry

Whisk together the flours and salt in a bowl. Quickly grate the butter into the bowl to keep it cold. Toss to coat the butter in flour and distribute it evenly throughout. In a small bowl, whisk together the egg, water, and lemon juice. Drizzle this mixture over the flour-butter mixture and toss to evenly distribute the liquid. Using your hands, fold the mixture together until a rough ball forms. If it isn't coming together, add 1 more tablespoon of cold water (I often have to do this on a dry winter day).

Transfer the dough to a floured surface and continue to quickly bring the dough together. Pat it down and shape it into a disk, wrap in plastic, and chill in the fridge for at least 1 hour or overnight. When ready to use, bring it to room temperature.

Spray or grease a 12-cup muffin tin and set aside. Dust your work surface and rolling pin with flour and roll the disk out to ⅛ inch. Using a 4-inch cookie cutter, create 7 to 8 rounds. Set the scraps aside. Using your rolling pin, starting at the edges, gently roll each round out to a 5-inch circle about ⅛ inch thick, but keeping it a little thicker in the middle. Don't roll it any thinner. The pastry needs to hold the weight of the filling once baked, and the thicker middle will help create stability.

*recipe continues*

Avoid thick-cut or high-sodium bacon. The bacon can be cooked in advance and stored in the fridge. Do not use any substitutes for the maple syrup—pure maple syrup is key!

Avoid blackstrap molasses—it will be bitter.

Leftovers can be stored in an airtight container at room temperature for up to 4 days. You can also wrap them individually in plastic wrap and freeze in a freezer bag for up to 2 months. Thaw and enjoy.

Take each round and gently create folds or pleats as you place them into the cups of the muffin tin. Let them sink into the cups, ensuring the sides are as high as or slightly higher than the muffin tin. Pleat the edges, they shouldn't look perfect—their imperfection is part of their charm. Collect the scraps of dough, roll them out, and then let it rest 5 to 10 minutes before cutting the rest and proceeding as above. Chill the muffin tin in the fridge while you work on the filling.

### For the Filling

Preheat the oven to 375°F.

Meanwhile, in a sauté pan over medium heat, fry the bacon until cooked through. Transfer to a bowl and pat dry. Once cool to the touch, crumble into small pieces. You will need ½ cup of crumbled bacon for this recipe. Store the rest in a sealed container in the fridge for up to 3 days (can be used in scrambled eggs—see page 219!).

Place the butter in a small pot over medium heat, stirring regularly. The butter will start to foam and become light tan. Continue to cook until the butter is toasty brown with solid bits on the bottom of the pan and has a fragrant nutty aroma, about 5 to 8 minutes. Immediately remove from the heat. Transfer the browned butter to a clean bowl and let cool at room temperature.

In a bowl and using a handheld mixer or a whisk, whisk together the eggs, sugar, and salt until very smooth. Add the cooled brown butter, the maple syrup, molasses, and vinegar. Beat or whisk vigorously for 2 minutes to combine. Gently stir in the crumbled bacon. Fill the pastry shells two-thirds full with this mixture.

Bake the butter tarts until the filling is bubbling and the crusts are golden, about 20 to 22 minutes. Transfer the muffin tin to a cooling rack and sprinkle each tart with finishing salt. Cool in the muffin tin for at least 20 minutes. Remove from the tin to finish cooling, ideally using a small offset spatula to gently loosen and lift them out.

# pistachio, apricot, and dark chocolate forgotten meringues

MAKES 30 meringues
PREP TIME 15 minutes
COOK TIME 8 hours

The best part about these is that you whip up the meringue, fold in the nuts and chocolate, spoon little mounds, put them in the warm oven, turn off the oven, and go to bed! In the morning, these fluffy nuts and chocolate–filled clouds will be waiting for you. These come together so easily (but not on a humid day!), you may even forget they're in the oven. But don't forget! Surprisingly elegant and deceptively easy to whip up, these cookies are great for all seasons. Just switch up the accents. White chocolate and dried cherries, almonds and dried figs, cranberries and candied orange peel are all great seasonal options. The sky is the limit.

¾ cup (90 g) chopped slivered pistachios (see Note)

5¼ oz (150 g) dark or bittersweet chocolate, chopped

⅓ cup (50 g) soft chopped dried apricots

¼ tsp ground cardamom

2 egg whites

Good pinch salt

Good pinch cream of tartar

½ cup + 1 Tbsp (120 g) sugar

1 tsp vanilla extract

Preheat the oven to 350°F and keep it on for 30 minutes. It must be thoroughly heated through when you add the meringues, not just at temperature. Line two baking sheets with parchment paper.

In a bowl, toss together the pistachios, chocolate, apricots, and cardamom. If desired, reserve 3 tablespoons. Set aside.

In a stand mixer fitted with the whisk attachment, or using a handheld mixer with a bowl, whisk together the egg whites, salt, and cream of tartar until stiff and dry with a foamy texture, about 5 minutes. Whisking constantly, gradually add the sugar, until you have a thick, glossy meringue that maintains a peak when you lift the whisk. Gently fold in the pistachio and chocolate mixture and the vanilla.

Drop 30 heaping teaspoonfuls (but no larger) onto the parchment, spaced 1 inch apart. Top the cookies with the reserved pistachio and chocolate mixture, if desired. Put the baking sheets in the oven and immediately turn off the oven. Let sit in the oven overnight (do not open the door!). In the morning, they should easily come off the parchment paper.

Taste one. If the inside is still sticky, they aren't completely cooked through. Remove the cookies from the oven. Preheat the oven to 350°F. Put the cookies back in and turn off the oven. Let sit for 4 hours. Enjoy.

**NOTES**
If you can't find slivered pistachios, measure the required weight of whole pistachios, remove the skins, and chop finely. For the Summer Berry and Lemon Trifle (page 102), use mixed white chocolate, dried blueberries, and chopped hazelnuts.

# banana split with cinnamon sugar no-churn ice cream

MAKES about 6 cups ice cream, 1 banana split
PREP TIME 30 minutes + chilling
COOK TIME 6 minutes

As far as Jim is concerned, dessert isn't dessert unless there is a scoop of ice cream on the side. And he is very particular about the ice cream to dessert ratio. "There should be enough ice cream that each bite of pie gets a decent amount of ice cream," he says. If I fail to be generous, he says, "Is there a sudden ice cream shortage that I am not aware of?" This ice cream is not only great on its own but also provides the perfect accent for apple pie, Chocolate Pecan Date Cake with Butterscotch Sauce (page 206), and the Mincemeat Tart (page 209, but skip the crème anglaise!), to name only a few, thanks to its cinnamon-sugar flavor. Halva, a lovely nougat-like treat made with sesame paste, has a long history that some say dates back as early as 3000 B.C.E. It has since become a delicious treat among Middle Eastern, Mediterranean, and Central Asian cuisines. Here, it adds a lovely flavor and texture. Once you try halva, you'll catch yourself nibbling it with cheeseboards, with fruit, or even with a glass of bourbon. *Recipe pictured on page 216*

### Ice Cream

2 Tbsp brown sugar

1 Tbsp ground cinnamon

½ tsp sea salt

1¼ cups sweetened condensed milk

2 tsp vanilla extract

4 oz (115 g) mascarpone cheese

2 cups heavy cream

1 cup roughly chopped halva (see Note)

### For the Ice Cream

Chill a loaf pan or insulated ice cream container in the freezer.

In a large bowl, combine the sugar, cinnamon, salt, condensed milk, and vanilla.

In a stand mixer fitted with the whisk attachment, or using a bowl and a handheld mixer, beat the mascarpone cheese on medium speed until completely softened. Pour in the cream and, starting at medium speed, whisk until foamy. Increase the speed to high and continue to whisk until stiff peaks form. Stop before the peaks get too stiff and the liquid starts to separate and you find yourself with butter!

Using a silicone spatula, gently fold one-third of the whipped cream mixture into the sweetened condensed mixture until combined. Gently fold in the remaining whipped cream until no streaks remain. You don't want the air you whipped into the cream to deflate.

## Banana Split, for One

1 banana

1 Tbsp sugar

2–3 scoops Cinnamon Sugar No-Churn Ice Cream

¼–⅓ cup whipped cream

Drizzle of Salted Bourbon Caramel Sauce (page 270)

### Optional Toppings (mix and match)

1 Tbsp sprinkles

1 Tbsp semisweet chocolate chips or chunks

1 Tbsp chopped nuts, such as almonds or hazelnuts

2 tsp sesame seeds

4–5 bourbon-soaked cherries

Mint, for garnish

Spoon one-third of the mixture into the chilled loaf pan. Sprinkle one-third of the halva chunks on top and swirl a couple of times into the ice cream. Repeat twice with the remaining ingredients. Cover with a lid (if you are using an insulated ice cream container) or press a piece of plastic directly onto the ice cream, and then seal with one tight layer each of plastic and foil. Freeze for 8 hours, or overnight for best results. Allow the ice cream to rest at room temperature for about 15 minutes before scooping.

### For the Banana Split (optional)

If you're craving a banana split, carefully split the banana lengthwise and sprinkle the cut side with the sugar. Place under the broiler for about 6 minutes or use a torch to brûlée the sugar. Let the banana slices cool slightly so the ice cream doesn't melt immediately when placed on top. Place the banana slices on a plate or bowl and add the ice cream. Top with whipped cream (as much as you like!) and desired toppings. Drizzle with some caramel sauce.

### NOTE

Halva can be any flavor, from pistachio to chocolate, or plain. These days you can find it in any Middle Eastern grocery store or market that specializes in global ingredients.

# chocolate cream pie with tia maria whipped cream

MAKES one 9-inch pie
PREP TIME 15 minutes + chilling + setting
COOK TIME 50 minutes

Chocolate cream pie is the quintessential diner pie, in my humble opinion. Those pies under glass, topped with mounds of whipped cream or meringue, are just begging to be ordered. Also, pudding. Full stop. Chocolate pudding was always a treat when I was growing up, and putting it into a pie crust just makes the baker in me very happy. Here in Toronto, these are the kind of pies we can find at the Senator, a classic diner dating back to the 1920s. Every time we visit, the first thing I study is the dessert cupboard, with all the cakes and pies under glass, wondering which one I'll need to leave room for! My chocolate cream pie is for all the diners and all the cooks who keep retro classic meals alive for all of us to be comforted by. The coffee in the pudding brings out the chocolate flavor even better—but don't worry, it doesn't overpower the chocolate. And yes, you can omit the Tia Maria in the whipped cream, if you must!

## Pie Shell

No-Fail Pie Pastry, single crust (page 277), chilled

## Filling

1¼ cups (280 g) sugar

6 Tbsp (20 g) cocoa powder, sifted

⅓ cup (45 g) cornstarch

1 Tbsp instant coffee

¼ tsp salt

4 egg yolks

2½ cups milk

2 Tbsp butter, at room temperature and cubed

1 tsp vanilla extract

### For the Pie Shell

Roll out the pastry to a circle 12 inches in diameter. Transfer the pastry to a 9-inch pie plate plate (see page 277). Trim the pastry, leaving ½ inch hanging over the edges. Fold the pastry underneath to create a finished edge. Pinch, crimp, or even use a fork to create a pattern around the edge. Chill in the fridge for 30 minutes.

Meanwhile, place an oven rack in the bottom third of the oven and preheat the oven to 350°F.

Line the pastry shell with foil or parchment paper, pushing it up against the edges, and fill the shell with pie weights or dried beans.

Bake until the edges are set and just starting to turn golden, about 15 to 20 minutes. Remove the lining and weights, rotate the plate, move to the center rack, and continue baking until completely set and golden brown, another 15 to 20 minutes. If you notice the crust sliding down at all, just use a tea towel to push the sides up. If it is puffing up, you can use a small sharp knife to pierce the bubble and then push down gently with the tea towel. Transfer the pie shell to a cooling rack and let cool completely, about 30 minutes.

*recipe continues*

Whipped Cream Topping

1 Tbsp icing sugar

½ cup heavy cream

2 tsp Tia Maria

Chocolate shavings, chocolate curls, or mini chocolate chips, for garnish

## For the Filling

In a pot, whisk together the sugar, cocoa powder, cornstarch, coffee, salt, and egg yolks. Place the pot over medium heat and, whisking constantly, slowly pour in the milk. Switch to a wooden spoon or silicone spatula and cook, stirring to avoid getting clumps at the bottom of the pot, until bubbling and thickened, about 10 to 12 minutes.

Remove from the heat and stir in the butter and vanilla until melted and combined. Wait 1 minute and then gently pour the filling into the cooled pie shell. If need be, smooth out the top with an offset spatula. If there is extra filling, simply add to a ramekin and hide it for a midnight snack! Chill in the fridge, uncovered, until set, about 3 hours.

## For the Whipped Cream Topping

When you're ready to serve, whisk the icing sugar in a small bowl to remove any lumps. Using a stand mixer fitted with a whisk attachment, or a bowl and handheld mixer, whip the cream, starting on low speed and slowly increasing to medium, until soft peaks start forming. Add the sugar and the Tia Maria. Increase the speed to high, and whip until stiff peaks form.

Mound the whipped cream over the surface of the chocolate cream pie, letting some pie filling peek through. Scatter shaved chocolate, chocolate curls, or even mini chocolate chips over everything, because there can never be too much chocolate.

**NOTE**
You can use Kahlúa instead of Tia Maria.

# lemon blueberry basil yogurt pound loaf

MAKES one 5- × 9-inch loaf
PREP TIME 15 minutes + chilling
COOK TIME 1 hour, 5 minutes

As the title of my blog indicates, I have a real soft spot for lemons! And I really think that they shine in this cake. At its heart it is just a tender, moist pound cake, thanks to both the olive oil and the yogurt. But I've really tried to make sure that the lemon isn't an afterthought. A strong lemon presence in both the batter and the optional glaze (see Note, page 260) takes care of that. And what goes better with lemon than blueberries! Thankfully we can get blueberries, or "bloobs," all year round these days, so yes, go ahead and make this in January. It will make you think it's July.

¾ cup (170 g) sugar

Zest of 3–4 lemons

1¼ cups (180 g) + 1 Tbsp flour, divided

2 tsp baking powder

¾ tsp salt

2 Tbsp packed chopped basil

1 cup Greek yogurt

⅓ cup (70 g) light brown sugar

3 large eggs

½ cup extra virgin olive oil

1 cup blueberries, divided

Preheat the oven to 350°F. Grease a 5- × 9-inch loaf pan and line it with parchment paper so that it hangs over the long sides by at least 1 inch (for handles!). Place a cooling rack over a wax paper– or parchment paper–lined baking sheet.

In a small bowl, combine the sugar and lemon zest, rubbing the zest into the sugar to release its oils. Set aside. You can make this a day ahead and store it in an airtight container in the fridge (it will smell amazing!).

In a bowl, whisk together the 1¼ cups (180 g) flour, baking powder, and salt. Add the basil and toss to evenly coat. In another bowl, whisk together the lemon-sugar mixture, yogurt, brown sugar, and eggs until smooth. Slowly whisk the dry ingredients into the wet ingredients. Using a rubber spatula, fold in the oil until incorporated.

In a small bowl, toss the blueberries with the 1 tablespoon flour to coat. Fold ¾ cup of the blueberries into the batter. Pour the batter into the prepared pan and give it a gentle tap to get rid of any air bubbles. Dot the top with the remaining blueberries, pushing them in gently.

*recipe continues*

Bake until a cake tester inserted into the center of the loaf comes out clean, about 50 to 65 minutes. Place the pan on a cooling rack and let cool for 30 minutes. Remove the cake from the pan by running a knife along the short ends and then lifting it up with the parchment paper. Place the cake on the cooling rack and let cool at room temperature for another hour.

**NOTE**

To glaze the cake, sift ¾ cup (100 g) icing sugar into a bowl. Whisk in 1 tablespoon each of lemon juice and milk until smooth. If it's too thick, add 1 teaspoon lemon juice or milk at a time. Slowly pour the glaze over the cooled cake. Chill in the fridge for 1 hour to set.

## Blends and Mixes
Chai Spice Blend

Seasoning Salt

Berbere Spice Blend

Faux Chicken Bouillon Powder

## Savory Condiments
Champagne Mustard Vinaigrette

Miso-Ginger Dressing

Labneh Tzatziki

Marinara Sauce

## Sweet Condiments and Toppings
Lemony Lemon Curd

Spiced Seville Orange Marmalade

Salted Bourbon Caramel Sauce

Spiced Coffee and Chocolate Granola

## Dairy
Crème Anglaise

Crème Fraîche

Simple Fresh Ricotta

## Breads and Pastries
Yogurt Flatbread

Basic Buttermilk Waffles

Basic Crepes

No-Fail Pie Pastry

STAPLES

# chai spice blend

MAKES about ¾ cup | PREP TIME about 5 minutes

¼ cup ground cinnamon

¼ cup ground ginger

2 Tbsp ground cardamom

4 tsp ground cloves

2 tsp ground coriander

2 tsp ground nutmeg

2 tsp ground allspice

1 tsp white pepper

In a bowl, whisk together all the ingredients. Store in a labeled airtight glass jar at room temperature for up to 6 months.

# seasoning salt

MAKES about ¾ cup | PREP TIME about 5 minutes

½ cup flakey finishing salt

2 Tbsp medium-grind pepper

2 Tbsp garlic powder

2 tsp smoked paprika

In a bowl, whisk together all the ingredients. Store in a labeled airtight glass jar at room temperature for up to 6 months.

# berbere spice blend

MAKES about ¾ cup | PREP TIME about 5 minutes

4 Tbsp smoked paprika

4 tsp ground coriander

4 tsp garlic powder

4 tsp onion powder

4 tsp cayenne pepper

3 tsp salt

2 tsp crushed fenugreek seeds (can crush with a mortar and pestle)

2 tsp ground black pepper

1 tsp ground cardamom

1 tsp ground cinnamon

1 tsp ground ginger

1 tsp ground nutmeg

½ tsp ground allspice

½ tsp ground cloves

In a bowl, whisk together all the ingredients. Store in a labeled airtight glass jar at room temperature for up to 6 months.

# faux chicken bouillon powder

MAKES about 2½ cups  |  PREP TIME 5 minutes

3 cups nutritional yeast

5 Tbsp salt

3 Tbsp dried onion flakes or powder (not onion salt!)

3 Tbsp dried parsley leaves

2½ tsp dried sage leaves

2½ tsp celery seed (not celery salt!)

2½ tsp garlic powder (not garlic salt!)

2½ tsp dried thyme leaves

2½ tsp dried marjoram leaves

2½ tsp dried rosemary leaves

2½ tsp paprika

2 tsp dried basil leaves

Place all the ingredients in a food processor and blend into a fine, smooth powder. Store in a labeled airtight glass jar in the fridge for up to 6 months.

When ready to use, add 1 tablespoon per 1 cup of boiling water.

NOTE
I use this every time a little bit of chicken stock is needed in a recipe, or sometimes just to flavor the water if I'm cooking veggies, potatoes, or rice.

# champagne mustard vinaigrette

MAKES about 1 cup  |  PREP TIME 10 minutes

2 large shallots, finely minced

1 clove garlic, finely grated or minced

2 tsp finely chopped thyme

¼ cup champagne vinegar

¾ cup olive oil

1 tsp Dijon mustard

1 tsp grainy mustard

1 Tbsp sugar

1 Tbsp water

½ tsp salt

¼ tsp freshly cracked black pepper

Place all the ingredients in a bowl and whisk to combine. Alternatively, place them in a mason jar, seal, and then shake vigorously until combined. Adjust the salt and pepper to taste.

Store in a labeled airtight glass jar in the fridge for up to 2 weeks. Because of the olive oil, it will solidify in the fridge. Bring to room temperature and shake well before using.

# miso-ginger dressing

MAKES about 2 cups | PREP TIME 10 minutes

2 cloves garlic, finely minced

1 Tbsp finely chopped or grated ginger

2 tsp finely chopped shallots

4 tsp light miso

2 Tbsp white sesame seeds

2 Tbsp fresh poppy seeds

5 Tbsp runny honey

4 tsp tamari

2 tsp sriracha

2 tsp toasted sesame oil

½ tsp Dijon mustard

¾ cup extra virgin olive oil

⅓ cup rice wine vinegar

1 tsp sea salt

¾ tsp finely ground black pepper

Place the garlic, ginger, shallots, and miso in a bowl. Mix well with a fork to break up the miso. Add the sesame and poppy seeds, honey, tamari, sriracha, sesame oil, and Dijon, and whisk to combine. Add the oil, vinegar, salt, and pepper. Season with more salt and pepper, if needed. If desired, run the dressing through a small blender. Store in an airtight glass jar in the fridge for up to 3 weeks. Because of the olive oil, it will solidify in the fridge. Bring to room temperature and shake well before using.

**NOTE**

If you buy poppy seeds from bulk stores, check the packaged or best before date and store them in the freezer to keep them fresh.

# labneh tzatziki

MAKES 1¼ cup | PREP TIME 15 minutes + chilling

1 cup labneh or skyr

1 Persian or small cucumber

4–5 cloves garlic

1 Tbsp lemon juice

Salt and pepper

Place the labneh in a medium bowl. Grate the cucumber on the small side of a box grater into a cheesecloth or tea towel. It's perfectly all right if some of the skin makes its way in. Give the cucumber a good squeeze over the sink to remove any excess liquid. Add the cucumber to the bowl.

Finely mince or grate the garlic cloves. Add to the bowl. Give the mixture a good stir. Add the lemon juice, 1 teaspoon at a time, until you are happy with the consistency. Add 1 teaspoon of salt and ½ teaspoon of pepper. Stir and then season to taste. Cover and chill for 1 hour before using for best results.

# marinara sauce

MAKES 4 cups | PREP TIME 15 minutes | COOK TIME 35 minutes

1 Tbsp olive oil

1 large yellow onion, chopped

2 large cloves garlic, minced

1 tsp dried thyme leaves

1 tsp Italian seasoning

1 tsp dried basil

1½ tsp salt

1 tsp pepper

1 tsp sweet paprika

½ tsp crushed red peppers or chili powder

3 Tbsp tomato paste

1 (28 oz/796 ml) can crushed or whole tomatoes

1 bay leaf

2 Tbsp butter

1–1½ tsp sugar (optional)

Heat a stockpot over medium-high heat and add the oil. Add the onions and cook until just starting to soften, about 5 minutes. Add the garlic and cook for another minute. Add the thyme, Italian seasoning, basil, salt, and pepper. Stir to combine. Add the paprika, crushed red peppers, and tomato paste, and stir to evenly coat the onions and garlic.

Add the tomatoes. (If you're using whole tomatoes, add their juices and break up the tomatoes with a cooking spoon.) Add the bay leaf and butter. Stir well. Drop the heat to medium-low and simmer, partially covered, for 30 minutes, stirring occasionally.

Transfer to a blender. Remove the bay leaf (I learned this one the hard way!) and blend until smooth. Return the sauce to the pot. Taste and season with salt and pepper as needed. If the flavor is slightly acidic, stir in about 1 teaspoon of sugar to create more of a balanced sauce, adding more if you desire sweeter. Let the sauce cool completely.

### Harissa Marinara Variation

Replace the basil with 1 tsp dried oregano. Replace the sweet paprika and crushed red peppers with 1½ tsp harissa paste (or 2 tsp harissa powder). Taste to see if you are satisfied with the heat. Cook as directed.

### Pizza Sauce Variation

Cook the sauce for 45 minutes, until it's a little bit thicker than a typical pasta sauce. Add ¼ cup grated Parmesan in the last 5 minutes of simmering. You will have more than enough sauce for 2 or 3 medium to large pizzas.

### NOTE

The sauce, and its variations, will keep in an airtight container in the fridge for up to 3 days, or in a freezer-safe container in the freezer for up to 3 months. Thaw in the fridge overnight before using.

# lemony lemon curd

MAKES 2 cups | PREP TIME 10 minutes + chilling | COOK TIME 15 minutes

6 Tbsp unsalted butter, at room temperature

1 cup sugar

2 eggs

2 egg yolks

⅔ cup lemon juice (about 2 to 3 large lemons)

Zest of 1 large lemon

5–6 dashes lemon bitters

Using a stand mixer fitted with a paddle attachment, or a large bowl and a handheld mixer, beat the butter and sugar until well incorporated and fluffy, 2 minutes. Add the eggs and yolks, and beat for another minute. Add the lemon juice and mix until incorporated. It will look curdled, but don't worry, it's supposed to.

Pour the mixture into a saucepan and cook over low heat, stirring regularly with a wooden spoon, until the butter melts and the mixture is smooth. Increase the heat to medium-low and cook, stirring constantly in a figure-eight motion, until the mixture thickens and an instant-read thermometer shows 170°F, about 10 to 15 minutes. If you pull out the spoon that you are using to stir and run your finger down the back through the curd, it should leave a good path that doesn't disappear. Don't let it boil.

Remove from the heat and stir in the lemon zest and bitters. Let cool in the pot for about 10 minutes. Transfer to an airtight container, but don't put on the lid of the container. Press plastic wrap over the surface of the curd to keep a skin from forming as it cools. Chill in the fridge for at least 1 hour, or up to 3 hours. It will continue to thicken there. Once cooled, remove the plastic wrap and top the container with its lid. This will keep in the fridge for 2 to 3 months.

# spiced seville orange marmalade

MAKES 1½ cups | PREP TIME 25 minutes | COOK TIME 45 minutes

3 lb (1¼ kg) Seville oranges, scrubbed

1½ lemons

2 star anise pods

5 whole cloves

3 cardamom pods

1 vanilla pod, sliced lengthwise

2⅓ cups water

2½ cups (530 g) super-fine sugar

If you don't have a thermometer, place a small plate in the freezer for later. Using a bar zester, zest the oranges, and zest and juice the lemons. (Alternatively, use a sharp paring knife to remove the outer peel—avoid the white pith—and slice the peels into thin strips.) Add the zests and juice to a large, heavy-bottomed pot. Using a manual or crank-style juicer (or your preferred method), juice all the oranges. Strain out any seeds and add the juice to the pot.

Using a sharp spoon (I like a grapefruit spoon with a serrated edge), remove all the pulp and membranes from the orange skins and place on a double-layer piece of cheesecloth. Add the star anise, cloves, cardamom, and vanilla. Gather the cheesecloth and tie it tightly with kitchen twine.

Add the water to the pot with the juice and stir to combine. Place the cheesecloth bundle in the liquid. Bring the mixture to a boil over medium-high heat, drop the heat to medium, and simmer, partially covered, until the zest becomes soft and pliable and the liquids have reduced by one-third, about 25 minutes.

Add the sugar and cook, stirring, until the sugar has melted. Turn up the heat to high and bring to a rolling boil. Let it boil for 2 minutes, then drop the heat to medium-low and bring back to a simmer. Using tongs, remove the cheesecloth bundle and squeeze it to release as much of the flavors and syrup as possible. Continue to cook until the liquids thicken and are reduced by another one-quarter, and an instant-read thermometer shows 220°F, about 20 minutes. Remove from heat. If you don't have a thermometer, place a small amount of marmalade on the chilled plate. The plate should cool the marmalade immediately. After 2 to 3 minutes, test it by pushing the dollop gently with your finger. If it wrinkles, it is done. If not, keep cooking and retest after 5 minutes.

You can follow a traditional canning method (but who has the time?!) or you can let the marmalade cool at room temperature for 20 minutes before transferring it to clean jars. Then, simply place as is in airtight jars in the fridge for up to 4 months or the freezer for up to 6 months.

# salted bourbon caramel sauce

MAKES 1 cup  |  PREP TIME 5 minutes  |  COOK TIME 30 minutes

½ cup heavy cream, at room temperature

1 cup sugar

¼ cup water

4 Tbsp butter, cubed, at room temperature

1 Tbsp bourbon

1 tsp kosher or sea salt

Add the cream to a measuring cup or pourable container and place it by the stove.

Place the sugar and water in a pot over medium-low heat. Stir once. Let it cook slowly, until it foams, about 15 to 20 minutes. If a slight crust of hard sugar forms on top and the sauce is already a caramel color underneath, break up the crust with a spoon and stir it back into the caramel underneath. It will melt back into the sauce.

Using a wooden spoon, stir to help reduce the foam and then remove the pot from the heat. Standing as far back as possible from the pot, carefully add the cream. (The cream will spit.) Stir regularly until the mixture is smooth and the most beautiful copper color, about 1 to 2 minutes. Immediately add the butter and bourbon. Stir until the butter is melted and the mixture is smooth. Add the salt and stir a bit more. Let cool and serve.

Store in a glass jar in the fridge for up to 3 months. Bring it to room temperature or reheat in a small pot over low heat before using.

# spiced coffee and chocolate granola

MAKES about 5 cups | PREP TIME 20 minutes | COOK TIME 1 hour, 10 minutes

1¼ cups (190 g) hazelnuts

3 Tbsp coconut oil, melted and still warm

2 Tbsp dark maple syrup

2 Tbsp runny honey

1½ Tbsp very strongly brewed coffee, slightly cooled

½ tsp vanilla paste or extract

1½ Tbsp freshly ground coffee beans

1 Tbsp sugar

½ tsp ground cinnamon

½ tsp ground cloves

½ tsp ground cardamom

¼ tsp salt

2 cups (180 g) old-fashioned rolled oats

½ cup (75 g) dried cranberries

7 oz (200 g) chopped dark (70% cocoa) chocolate

Preheat the oven to 350°F. Line a baking sheet with parchment paper.

Lay the hazelnuts on the prepared baking sheet and toast until they are light golden and the skins are starting to release, about 10 minutes. Transfer to a big tea towel. Bundle the hazelnuts up, then rub them to remove the skins. Let them cool slightly. Roughly chop half of the hazelnuts. Set both the chopped and whole hazelnuts aside.

Drop the oven heat to 325°F. Line a large baking sheet, or two smaller sheets, with parchment paper. In a bowl, combine the coconut oil, maple syrup, honey, brewed coffee, vanilla, ground coffee, sugar, cinnamon, cloves, cardamom, and salt. In a large bowl, combine all of the hazelnuts with the oats and cranberries. Pour the coffee mixture over top and toss to coat. Evenly spread the granola mixture out in one layer on the prepared baking sheet(s). Bake until it's golden brown and feels dry to the touch, about 50 minutes to 1 hour, stirring once, and then checking toward the end.

Let cool completely on the baking sheet, then use your hands to break it into clusters. Add the chopped chocolate.

Store in an airtight container at room temperature for up to 2 weeks or in the freezer for up to 1 month.

# crème anglaise

MAKES 2 cups | PREP TIME 15 minutes | COOK TIME 10 minutes

6 egg yolks

½ cup sugar

1 cup milk

1 cup heavy cream

2 tsp vanilla paste or extract

**NOTE**
Store leftovers in an airtight glass jar in the fridge for up to 1 month. It will thicken once chilled. Just warm it over low heat for a minute or two to loosen it up before using.

In a bowl, whisk together the egg yolks and sugar until slightly thickened. Place the bowl on a damp tea towel. In a heavy-bottomed saucepan over medium heat, cook the milk and cream until bubbles start to appear along the edges of the pan, about 8 to 10 minutes. Turn off the heat.

Whisking continuously, add ½ cup of the warm milk-cream mixture to the egg and sugar mixture. Add another ½ cup, all while whisking.

Return the milk and egg mixture to the pan. Place over medium-low heat. Using a silicone spatula or wooden spoon to gently stir, scraping the bottom and corners of the pan, cook until the sauce has thickened, an instant-read thermometer shows 170°F, and you can scrape the back of the spatula through the sauce and leave a path that doesn't disappear. This will only take about 5 minutes.

Remove from the heat. Pour the sauce through a small sieve set over a small pot to catch any bits of egg that may have cooked. Add the vanilla and stir to evenly distribute. You can serve this warm or chill in the fridge for a few hours and serve cold.

**Citrus Variation**

Add ½ ounce (15 ml) of Grand Marnier or other citrus liqueur and 1 tablespoon of finely grated orange zest with the vanilla.

# crème fraîche

MAKES 1 cup | PREP TIME 5 minutes + overnight resting

1 cup heavy cream

2–3 Tbsp buttermilk

In a small jar, stir together the cream and 2 tablespoons of the buttermilk. Cover and let sit at room temperature for 24 hours. If it hasn't thickened completely (the cooler the environment, the longer it may take), add another tablespoon of buttermilk and let rest at room temperature for up to 12 hours.

Store in an airtight container in the fridge for up to 10 days.

# simple fresh ricotta

MAKES about 2 cups | PREP TIME 5 minutes + resting + draining | COOK TIME 15 minutes

8 cups milk

⅓ cup lemon juice (about 1 to 2 large lemons) or white vinegar

1 tsp salt (see Note)

In a saucepan over medium heat, warm the milk to 200°F, checking the temperature with an instant-read thermometer. The milk will start to steam and foam up. This will only take about 10 to 12 minutes. Remove from the heat before the foam reaches the top of the pan. Immediately add the lemon juice and salt. Gently stir to combine.

Let the milk sit undisturbed at room temperature for about 10 minutes, then dip a slotted spoon into it. The milk should have separated into clumps of milky white curds and a thin, watery whey. If you still see a good amount of milk that hasn't curdled yet, add another tablespoon of lemon juice, stir once, and wait a few more minutes before testing again.

Line a strainer with two to three layers of cheesecloth and set it over a bowl wide enough to hold the whole strainer, but small enough that the strainer doesn't touch the bottom of the bowl. Let the ricotta drain for up to 1 hour, depending on how wet or dry you like it. Check every 15 minutes or so. If the ricotta becomes too dry, stir some of the whey back in before serving. Reserve the whey in a glass container (see Note).

Use the fresh ricotta right away or store it in an airtight container in the fridge for up to 1 week.

**NOTES**

I like some salt in my ricotta, even for a sweet dish. It ensures that the ricotta isn't bland. You can even add a little more if the ricotta will be used for savory dishes.

For a sweeter ricotta, you can add some honey.

If your ricotta dries out in the fridge and is firmer than you desire, add 1 tablespoon of the reserved whey at a time, stirring gently to combine.

The leftover whey will keep in an airtight container in the fridge for up to 4 days. It's high in protein and can be used in place of water in any baking recipe, or even added to smoothies.

# yogurt flatbread

MAKES 8 flatbreads | PREP TIME 15 minutes | COOK TIME 15 minutes

2 cups flour

1 Tbsp baking powder

1 tsp salt

½ tsp baking soda

1⅔ cups Greek yogurt

2 Tbsp melted butter

¾ tsp garlic powder

1 Tbsp sesame seeds or za'atar

In a large bowl, whisk together the flour, baking powder, salt, and baking soda. Add the yogurt. Using a spoon, start to mix everything together. Use your hands to form a sticky dough. No kneading, as this will make the breads tough.

Divide the dough into eight evenly sized balls. On a well-floured surface and with well-floured hands, pat down the dough and then use a well-floured rolling pin to roll each piece out into a circle about 8 inches in diameter. (The rolled-out dough should fit comfortably inside the skillet you are using. If your skillet is smaller than 10 inches, divide the dough into more than eight balls and roll them to fit.)

In a small bowl, mix together the melted butter and garlic powder.

Heat a large cast-iron skillet or griddle over medium heat for 10 minutes. Add one circle of dough to the dry skillet and cook until the bottom browns and bubbles appear, about 30 seconds. Flip the bread, use a silicone brush to coat the surface with a thin layer of the garlicky butter, sprinkle with some of the sesame seeds, and cook for an additional minute or so. Once the underside is browned, transfer to a plate. Repeat with the remaining balls of dough. Serve.

**NOTE**
You can store flatbreads in an airtight container or plastic bag at room temperature for several days. They can be easily reheated in a dry cast-iron pan for just a few seconds per side, or in a toaster oven set at 325°F.

# basic buttermilk waffles

MAKES 12 (6-inch) waffles | PREP TIME 15 minutes | COOK TIME 30 minutes

1¾ cups + 1 Tbsp flour

2 Tbsp sugar

1 Tbsp baking powder

½ tsp baking soda

½ tsp salt

3 eggs

1½ cups buttermilk

8 Tbsp butter, melted and cooled

In a bowl, whisk together the flour, sugar, baking powder, baking soda, and salt. Store this waffle mix in a sealed glass container until needed; it will last for a few months. (Tip: Write out what needs to be added to it and stick the note inside the jar!)

Place the waffle mix in a large bowl and create a well in the center. In another bowl, beat the eggs. Add the buttermilk and butter, and whisk to combine. Pour the wet ingredients into the well of the dry ingredients. Using a spoon, stir the flour into the center to catch some of the eggs. Keep mixing until incorporated. It should look pebbled, like muffin mix. If it's too thick, thin it out with a tea-spoon of buttermilk at a time.

Heat your waffle iron per the manufacturer's instructions. Pour in ½ cup of the batter and spread it out. Follow the manufacturer's instructions for cooking times. If the waffle iron does not release the waffle, it isn't done yet.

### Chai-Spiced Wild Blueberry Variation

Add 1½ Tbsp of Chai Spice Blend (page 264) and 1 Tbsp sugar to the dry ingredients. Fold in 1 cup of blueberries before pouring the batter into the waffle iron.

**NOTES**

You may get more or less waffles, depending on the size of your waffle maker.

You don't have to make all the waffle mix at once. Use half the amount of both dry and wet ingredients and cook as directed (whisk the full 3 eggs and store the unused half in the fridge for scrambled eggs the next day!).

To freeze cooked waffles, lay out the waffles on a baking sheet for 1 hour. Transfer the cooled waffles to a freezer-safe bag and freeze for up to 2 months. Pop them in the toaster when a craving strikes.

# basic crepes

MAKES 16 crepes | PREP TIME 15 minutes + resting | COOK TIME 20 minutes

1½ cups flour

¼ tsp salt

3 large eggs

1½ cups milk (approx.)

1 Tbsp vegetable oil or butter, melted and cooled

Neutral oil, for frying

**NOTES**

Letting the batter rest allows the flour to absorb all the liquid, the glutens to relax, and any lumps to smooth out.

The first crepe is ALWAYS lousy (snack on it while making the rest)! Don't worry, you'll get the hang of it. If you want another sweeter option, add a 2 teaspoons of cocoa and 1½ tablespoons of sugar!

Sometimes I replace ¾ cup of the all-purpose flour with chestnut or buckwheat flour, just to kick up the flavor a bit.

If you won't be using the crepes right away, use wax paper to separate each one, wrap first in plastic wrap and then in foil, and freeze for up to 6 months. You can remove them as needed. Simply thaw in the fridge and reheat in a covered pan over medium-low heat for a few minutes. Or wrap a few thawed crepes in foil and warm in a 300°F toaster oven for about 8 minutes.

Sift the flour and salt into a bowl and make a small well. In another bowl, beat the eggs lightly with a handheld whisk. Pour the eggs into the well. Using a wooden spoon, stir the flour into the center to catch some of the eggs. Keep mixing until incorporated. Slowly add one-third of the milk and incorporate. Add half of the remaining milk, and switch to a whisk to combine. Add the final portion of milk, whisking out all the lumps. Mix in the vegetable oil and cover. Let sit for at least 30 minutes at room temperature, or overnight in the fridge before using (see Note).

Pour the batter into a smallish pitcher. This is easier than using a spoon or measuring cup to add the batter to the pan. If you find that the batter has thickened too much and isn't pouring gracefully, add a tablespoon of milk at a time, to thin it out.

Preheat a crepe pan or sauté pan about 6 to 8 inches in diameter, with low sides, over medium heat. Pour the neutral oil into a small bowl and have it ready by the stove. Using a silicone brush, brush the pan with oil. Lift from the heat and pour in about 2 tablespoons of batter to cover the bottom, swirling the pan as you pour. Too much batter will result in a thick crepe that takes too long to cook; too little won't fill the bottom of the pan.

Return the pan to the heat. Cook until the crepe is set and the edges are drying, about 40 to 45 seconds. Slide a small offset spatula under the crepe to loosen it. Carefully lift the crepe and gently flip. The second side should start to turn golden brown in just a few seconds. Shake the pan to loosen the crepe. With the aid of the spatula, slide the crepe onto a plate. Repeat with the rest of the batter.

### Lemon Zest Variation

Add 1 tablespoon of lemon zest and 1½ tablespoons of sugar to the batter before frying.

### Savory Herb Variation

Add 1 tablespoon of chopped thyme and ½ teaspoon of cracked pepper (perfect for savory blintzes or dinner crepes) to the batter before frying.

# no-fail pie pastry

MAKES one 9-inch double-crust pie (or single-crust with leftovers) | PREP TIME 45 minutes + chilling

2 cups (300 g) flour

3 Tbsp sugar

½ tsp salt

½ cup/8 Tbsp (110 g) unsalted butter, fully chilled and cubed

3 Tbsp (45 g) shortening, fully chilled and cubed

1 egg

3–4 Tbsp ice water

1 Tbsp lemon juice

Egg wash (1 egg whisked with a splash of water, for double crust)

**To Prepare the Dough**

Using a food processor fitted with the steel blade, or a large bowl and a handheld whisk, combine the flour, sugar, and salt. Add the butter and shortening and pulse two or three times, or use a pastry blender or knife to cut the butter and shortening into the dry ingredients, until a rough, crumbly texture with some large marble-sized pieces of fat forms. Don't use your hands, as they will warm up the fat too much.

In a small bowl, whisk the egg with 3 tablespoons of ice water and the lemon juice. Add to the flour mixture and pulse, or use a fork to mix, until the dough just comes together into a rough ball, ideally with pieces of fat still visible. Don't worry about grabbing every little bit from the sides; you can add this to the ball when you shape the dough. If it isn't coming together, add another 1 tablespoon of ice water and pulse or mix to incorporate.

Place the dough on the counter, along with any bits of flour that didn't get combined, and bring it together by hand. Shape the ball into two disks—even for a single crust—wrap in plastic wrap, and chill in the fridge for at least 1 hour.

**To Roll Out the Dough**

Dust your work surface and rolling pin well with flour. Working with one disk at a time, begin to roll the dough out, reducing the pressure as you reach the edges. Keep rolling, spinning the pastry a quarter turn after each roll, until it's 3 inches larger in diameter than the pie plate. It should be about ⅛ inch thick. Dust with flour as needed.

**To Transfer the Dough to the Pie Plate**

Lightly flour the surface of the pastry. Roll it around the rolling pin and release it gently over the pie plate; or dust with flour, fold it loosely in half and then in half again, lay it across the pie plate, and then open it up. Allow the pastry to sink down along the sides of the pie plate, so that there are no gaps between the dough and the plate. This will ensure that the dough will not pull up from the base or shrink during baking. Trim the edges of the pie, leaving a good ¾ inch as overhang.

## For a Single Crust

Fold the overhang under, and use two fingers from one hand and the thumb or knuckle from your other hand to create a fluted pattern all the way around. Alternatively, use a fork to crimp the edges or create a cross-hatch pattern around the edges. Place the prepared pie shell in the fridge to chill for about 20 minutes. Fill the pie and bake as directed.

## For a Double Crust

Roll out the bottom crust and transfer it to the pie plate as described. Chill in the fridge while you prepare the top crust.

Repeat the rolling instructions for the top crust, but roll it out to about 2 inches larger than the pie plate (you won't have the sides of the plate to account for), allowing it to cover any raised filling. It should be about ⅛ inch thick.

Fill the pie as directed in your recipe. Using the rolling pin or folding the dough loosely, place the top crust over the filling. Wrap the edge of the top crust under the edge of the bottom crust. Seal the edges by fluting, crimping, or cross-hatching. Using a sharp knife, cut three or four ¾-inch-long vents in the top crust. Brush with the egg wash and bake as directed.

## For a Lattice Crust

Chill the bottom crust in the fridge while you prepare the top crust. Roll out the dough to a 13-inch circle, about ⅛ inch thick. Using a sharp knife and a ruler, cut out the lengths you want into even strips, and more than you need in case of breakage! For a 9-inch pie, I use ten strips and cut out two extra. Chill the strips on a parchment paper–lined baking sheet in the fridge for 30 minutes.

After filling the pie, lay one of the longest strips down the middle of the pie. Lay two more strips on each side, ensuring they are evenly spaced between the middle and the edge. Fold back every other strip, going past the middle point, and lay the other longest strip down the middle, perpendicular to the first strips. Bring the folded strips back over this new middle strip. Fold back the alternating strips and lay out the next one. Weave it back in and repeat with the final strip on this side. Repeat with the remaining two strips on the opposite side. Trim the edges to the same size as the pie crust edge.

Adhere the edges of the strips to the crust with a bit of water. Crimp as desired. Brush with egg wash and bake as directed.

### For Cookie Cutouts

Roll out the dough to about ⅛ inch thick. Using cookie cutters or a sharp knife, cut out as many decorations as desired. Get creative! Place the cutouts on a parchment paper–lined sheet and chill in the fridge for 15 minutes. Dab the top crust or lattice piece you are adhering the cutout to with some water, then securely place the cutouts on the pie as desired, brush with egg wash, and bake as directed.

### Savory Pie Crust Variation

Omit the sugar and increase the salt to 1¼ teaspoons. Add 1 heaping tablespoon finely chopped fresh herbs or 1 teaspoon dried herbs (but avoid woody ones like rosemary) when adding the salt.

**NOTES**

You can personalize your pastry for the filling you are using. If you are making a quiche or tomato tart, replace 2 tablespoons of the butter with ⅓ cup of your favorite shredded cheese.

Fresh herbs are also wonderful in sweet fruit-filled pies. Just add 1 heaping tablespoon chopped mint, thyme, basil, or even lavender when adding the sugar.

You can freeze unbaked dough in freezer-safe bags for up to 3 months. Just thaw the dough in the fridge the night before you plan to use it. Let the dough warm up a bit at room temperature before rolling.

# thank you

**WHILE MUCH OF THE TIME** writing a cookbook is spent alone, whether in the kitchen or at the computer, no cookbook is created without many helping hands. I am so appreciative for all the hands that helped me pull this off!

This book started off as a thank you card to my mom, my travels, and my city for all the inspiration they gave me and for fostering my love of food, cooking, and feeding others. So my heartfelt thanks go to all those I crossed paths with on the journey. Your willingness to open your kitchens and share your knowledge has had an immeasurable impact on me. I've learned how to can tomatoes, how to bake sourdough, and how to feed crowds—and these skills will stay with me forever.

Special thanks to Robert McCullough and Lindsay Paterson of Appetite for your support and confidence in me. I am truly grateful.

I have to thank Katherine Stopa and Whitney Millar for, first of all, getting me and my quirky ways! And for, all through this endeavor, giving me the needed constructive guidance to help hone my words and keep me focused.

Johann Headley, your skill as a photographer was such a support, especially when you were trying to figure me out and interpret my vision. Joanna Headley, thank you for being my coconspirator in creating the visual feel for the photos. I think we were sharing a brain at times! And doing it all through a pandemic, with restrictions as to when we were even allowed to shoot, we still did it!

Thank you so much to St. Lawrence Market and all its vendors. Writing a book during a pandemic might not seem like a big deal, but when it is a cookbook and you need ingredients, and with many grocers and shops depleted of yeast, flour, etc., you never let me down. I never once had to think about replacing or revising a recipe because I didn't have access to everything I wanted or needed. You were all rock stars!

Mairlyn Smith, thank you for pushing me to do this, for seeing a spark of a book in the crazy recipes I share with everyone on my blog.

To everyone who helped out with recipe testing, a big thanks.

To all the readers and supporters of *The Lemon Apron* blog, thank you!

And to Jim, for all the last-minute runs to the grocery store, for eating all the leftovers on photo shoot days, for your enthusiastic support of the dishes you felt should be in the book, for being the master taste tester, for eating takeout when I just couldn't cook another meal, and for just being you, *thank you.*

# index

◄ *Clockwise from top left: Sambal Oelek Roasted Shrimp Cocktail (page 173), Baby Kale and Romaine Caesar Salad (page 184), North African–Inspired Harira Soup (page 180), Cinnamon and Sumac Sautéed Brussels Sprouts (page 36)*